MW00635114

THE SHAAR PRESS

THE JUDAICA IMPRINT
FOR THOUGHTFUL PEOPLE

by
Carmela Raiz

**Translated from
the Hebrew**
Tinok She'nishbah **by**

Malky
Heimowitz

THE
SHAAR
PRESS

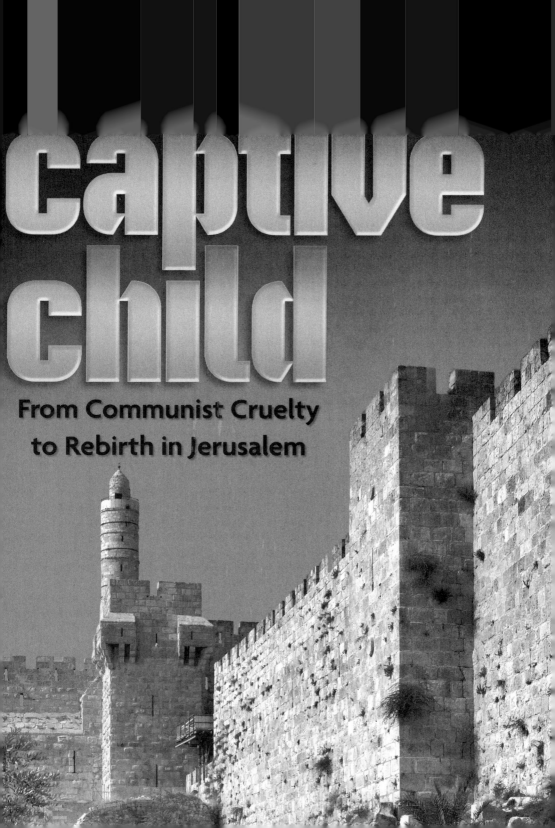

captive child

From Communist Cruelty
to Rebirth in Jerusalem

Published by **SHAAR PRESS**
Distributed by MESORAH PUBLICATIONS, LTD.
4401 Second Avenue / Brooklyn, N.Y 11232 / (718) 921-9000

Distributed in Israel by SIFRIATI / A. GITLER
6 Hayarkon Street / Bnei Brak 51127

Distributed in Europe by LEHMANNS
Unit E, Viking Business Park, Rolling Mill Road / Jarrow, Tyne and Wear, NE32 3DP/ England

Distributed in Australia and New Zealand by GOLDS WORLD OF JUDAICA
3-13 William Street / Balaclava, Melbourne 3183 / Victoria Australia

Distributed in South Africa by KOLLEL BOOKSHOP
Ivy Common / 105 William Road / Norwood 2192, Johannesburg, South Africa

ISBN 10: 1-4226-1173-6 / ISBN 13: 978-1-4226-1173-9

Printed in the United States of America
Custom bound by Sefercraft, Inc. / 4401 Second Avenue / Brooklyn N.Y. 11232

This book is dedicated
to the narrator's departed
parents and grandparents

Moshe, the son of Shepsel Wolf,
Zissel, the daughter of Hershel,
and
Zaide Shepsel Wolf and Bubbe Faiga

The English edition of the book
is dedicated to

Shepsel ben Moshe
the narrator, who passed away
on Hoshana Rabbah 5771.

Table of Contents

Preface   9

Author's Introduction   11

Acknowledgments   13

Prologue   17

Part I — Farewell to the Shtetl   21

Part II — From Whence Will Come My Help?   35

Part III — Coming Home   61

Part IV — Stranger   85

Part V — To Scale the Peak   141

Park VI — Yaakov's Ladder   203

Preface

"If pure angels were taken and lowered into this world in 1917, and were allowed to live through the Bolshevik revolution, going through those terrible events, I am sure nothing would be left of those angels.

But in Russia, in spite of everything, there were Jews who risked their lives for the sake of keeping mitzvahs ... who taught children Torah ...."

by R' Yitzchak Zilber

*C*aptive Child is the riveting — and sometimes jarring — story of Shepsel Gutman, a young child who was torn away from his family during the Holocaust. Adopted by a German family, Shepsel was eventually dispatched to a concentration camp, and later to a Soviet orphanage, experiencing the worst of both Nazi Germany and Soviet Russia. By a miracle, he was reunited with his family as an adolescent, but by that time he had been so thoroughly indoctrinated with Communist ideology that his family was forced to hide their Jewish observance from him for fear that he might accidentally reveal their secret. Only decades later, when Shepsel arrived in Israel after the Chernobyl disaster, did he return to his roots and become an observant Jew.

Captive Child is a complement to the author's previous work, *Blue Star Over Red Square*, which describes her extraordinary experiences as a refusenik and *baalas teshuvah* behind the Iron Curtain. In *Captive Child*, the author presents a different perspective of life under the Soviets, interspersing Shepsel's gripping story with historical information to help the reader understand the context of the events taking place in Shepsel's life.

This book portrays, at the same time, the devastation wrought upon Jewish life by the Communists, and the triumph of spirit of one particular Jewish family in the Ukraine. Perhaps more than anything, this is the story of how a Bubbe's heartfelt prayers accompanied a lost, errant child throughout his travails and eventually drew him back to the loving embrace of his people.

Author's Introduction

The story you are about to read began a number of years ago with an unusual phone call to our home in the holy city of Jerusalem.

I lifted the receiver and heard an unfamiliar voice at the other end of the line saying "Shalom."

"A short time ago, I read your book, *Blue Star Over Red Square*," he began, "and I noticed that in it were pictures of my father's first cousins, your husband's parents. That means that we are related."

We arranged to meet that evening.

A thin man with a graying beard and a black yarmulke walked swiftly across the threshold of our home. Without saying a word, he hurried to withdraw something from his pocket and place it on the table, as though he was showing us an entry visa of sorts.

At first I thought that what he was showing us was a document or a family picture, but then I saw that the item on the table was … an old-fashioned silver spoon.

The visitor was visibly excited. It appeared that this visit with his second cousins was especially meaningful to him. He gazed at my husband with a questioning look, but my husband was not fazed at all by this strange initial acquaintance. He went into the next room, and returned holding a silver spoon that had seen better days — identical to the spoon that the visitor had brought! My husband had received this spoon from his mother when he was on the verge of making *aliyah*. Now, he placed his spoon alongside that of the visitor, and we noticed then that both spoons were engraved with the same year of manufacture: 1882.

The owners of the spoons understood that they were indeed related, and they greeted each other warmly. Then, as conversation flowed smoothly between them, they began trying to figure out exactly how they were related.

"But what connection is there to the spoons?" I could not contain my curiosity.

It turned out that their grandparents had received the spoons from their grandfather. The grandfather, who lived in a small shtetl in the Ukraine named Vachanovka, gave each of his many descendants a single piece of his set of silver cutlery. One received a fork, another a spoon. In this way, the grandfather hoped to unify his descendants at least somewhat. And indeed, the turbulent times that followed proved that his assessment had been correct. Pogroms and wars dispersed the extended family, but those who survived guarded their family heirloom zealously. Even during difficult times, when they suffered from intense hunger, they refused to trade their precious piece of silverware for food.

Perhaps it was all for the sake of this meeting in Yerushalayim?

Our newfound relative knew every detail of the family history, including the names of his forebears and the villages in which they had lived. He spoke of his ancestors with such warmth and familiarity that it almost seemed as though he had known them personally.

He did not talk much about himself, however. It seemed to us that if we would ask him one question too many, he would disappear into the fog of the night the same mysterious way he had come.

Time passed, no less than a year, before we had the privilege of hearing the incredible story of our newfound relative's life. It is a story of a captive child brought up by evil people in such a manner that he felt estranged from those close to him and close to those foreign to him.

His Jewish name was Shepsel; he was named after his righteous grandfather Reb Shepsel Wolf *Hy"d*, who had been killed in the prime of his life while trying to save the Jews of his shtetl from a pogrom.

It is said that the soul of a righteous person influences the soul of his namesakes. That may, in fact, be the only way to explain Shepsel's miraculous escape from certain death, as well as his near-impossible return to his roots, from which he seemed to be hopelessly cut off.

This book is Shepsel's life story, as he tells it. The story was edited, with some changes made. By request of Shepsel, the narrator, many names in this story have been changed, including Shepsel's own last name.

Carmela Raiz

Acknowledgments

In memory of Binyamin (Bernard) Kaplan *z"l* who had the idea for this book.

The author wishes to thank the following people for their assistance in the preparation of this book:

Rabbi Benzion Zilber, *shlita,* for his valuable advice;

Rabbi Aryeh Leib Trachtman for his kind assistance;

And the wonderful people who contributed greatly to the editing of the book but prefer to remain anonymous.

A special thanks to my sister, Dalia Naor, and my cousin, Felix-Ezriel Kochoveivsky, for their assistance.

captive child

Prologue

Ukraine, 1942

My hiding place was in a village called Granitnoe. I don't know the name of the family I had been given to, but they did not keep me for very long. Instead, they put me into a German orphanage in the village of Starobeshevo.

The caregivers in the orphanage were of Greek extraction, but the director was a kindhearted German doctor named Karl Theodore Schultz. He was a large, good-natured redheaded man, who seemed to be covered with freckles; even his hands were freckled. Schultz would often bring treats for us children, and we were very fond of him. When we would see his black leather coat from afar, we would run to greet him.

I was a three-year old child with blue eyes and curly blond hair, and Schultz took a liking to me. It was impossible for him not to have known that I was a Jewish child, but not only did he keep me alive, he favored me over the other children, and even brought me a rocking horse for a gift.

Hardly able to believe my good fortune, I refused to let go of the horse day or night, for fear that the other children would take it from me.

One day, Schultz arrived with a package containing a sailor outfit, shoes, and other handsome clothing. He asked one of the caregivers in the orphanage, a broad Greek woman, to bathe me and change my clothing. When she brought me to him, freshly bathed and dressed in the new finery he had provided, he told me that he wished to take me with him to his home in Germany.

I refused to part with my rocking horse, however. I held on tightly to it, and Schultz had no choice but to take the horse along with us.

I recall that the train station in Kiev was partially destroyed. I also recall that we traveled in style, sitting on comfortable upholstered seats, drinking tea, and eating tasty crispy rolls. On the seat opposite me sat my rocking horse, and I was finally able to sleep soundly, without fear that someone would take it from me.

When we reached the large train station in Berlin, Schultz's wife Elsa met us. Elsa was large, like her husband, with short blond hair. Outside the train station, a big black car driven by a chauffeur awaited us.

The drive from the train station to the Schultzes' home took a long time, and the car's steady movement lulled me to sleep on the wide cushioned seat, as I hugged the leather sleeve of Schultz's coat. Toward evening, the car stopped before a beautiful two-story house surrounded by a lush garden.

I remember the house as if it were yesterday: tall windows with lace curtains, dark living room furniture with curved legs, lace doilies, pictures on the walls, parquet floors that shone like mirrors.

I clung to Schultz, refusing to let go of him. He and Elsa had no choice but to put me to sleep in their bedroom.

In the morning, they brought me to a pink room full of toys. There was a child-sized bed in the room, covered with a down quilt. I stood there in shock, not daring to believe that this was all for me.

This was my most beautiful childhood memory.

The Schultzes had no children, and when Schultz returned to the battlefront, he asked his wife to raise me as their son.

I had it good at the Schultzes. In the morning, Elsa would serve me warm milk and a fresh roll. Then, I would run to the garden behind the house, where I was allowed to play. A large watchdog guarded the house, and a goat roamed the garden. At first, I was afraid of the dog, but I quickly got used to him. I made friends with the goat immediately, and I would always run to the garden to share my treats with him. I loved the way the goat would carefully take the treats from my hand with her rough lips.

Once, I got new shoes, and I wanted to share them with the goat. But when I reached the garden, I burst into tears. How could I share my shoes with the goat, if she had four feet and I had only two shoes?

I must have forgotten everything that had happened to me prior to being adopted by the Schultzes. I called Elsa "Mama" and her husband "Papa."

When Schultz returned on leave from the front, he brought me another gift: a large car made from painted wood.

I lived with the Schultzes for two-and-a-half blissful years. Then, in December of 1944, the news arrived. Karl Schultz had been killed in the battle.

After a few days, Elsa stopped crying, and she told me that we were going somewhere. At first we rode, then we walked for a long time, until we reached a long, one-story stone building. Elsa spoke to the people there, withdrew some documents from her purse, and handed these documents to the people. Suddenly, she bent down toward me hurriedly, gave me a kiss, and handed me a new toy: a furry white bunny rabbit. Then, she prodded me gently in the direction of the people, and said, "Go to them!"

Thoroughly frightened, I pushed away the toy and tried to grab Elsa's hand. She released herself from my grip, however, and turned around and walked away without looking back.

With the cry of "Mama!" on my lips, I dashed after her, but strangers grabbed me roughly and brought me to a different room with a stone floor, where a sharp, unpleasant smell greeted my nostrils. They confiscated the rabbit and ruthlessly shaved my head, cutting me and hurting me.

I cried, not understanding what was going on, waiting all the while for "Mama" to return. But she never came.

I didn't know, then, that she had brought me to a roundup site, from where I was to be sent to a death camp.

"*In all of Jewish history, it would seem that there was never a period as difficult as that endured by the Jews of the Soviet Union. In the time of the Maccabees, the Greeks enacted decrees against observance of Torah and mitzvos, but in the span of three years the Jews rebelled and triumphed …*

in Russia, the persecution and decrees went on for over 70 years."

— From the book *L'hisha'er Yehudi*
(Toldos Publications, Jerusalem 2003)
by R' Yitzchak Zilber

Part I

Farewell to the Shtetl

The Shtetl

At the end of the eighteenth century, Russia conquered the areas to the west of its borders — namely, Poland and Lithuania, home to some three million Jews, who had been expelled from other countries many years earlier. Practically speaking, it was impossible to expel all of these Jews across the border, outside of Russian territory. Indeed, the societal standards of modern times did not permit the type of cruelty demonstrated by earlier tyrants such as Ivan the Terrible. [Ivan the Fourth (1530-1584), known as "Ivan the Terrible," was the first Russian ruler to adopt the title "czar." He commanded that all of the Jews of the city of Polotsk who refused to convert to Christianity be drowned.]

In its stead, for over 120 years the Jewish communities were confined to certain restricted areas, from which they were not allowed to leave. These areas were known as the "Pale of Jewish Settlement." The only Jews who were allowed to live outside the Pale of Settlement were prominent merchants and a limited number of lawyers, doctors, and craftsmen.

A Jewish shtetl at the end of the 19ᵗʰ century

Shepsel Wolf and faiga

My grandfather, Shepsel Wolf Gutman,[1] was a rebbe in the Jewish village of Vachanovka. He was not a wealthy man, but was noteworthy for his outstanding *middos*.

At the end of the nineteenth century, Shepsel Wolf married Faiga, the eldest daughter of a large, downtrodden family.

Bubbe Faiga enjoyed relating how, after their wedding, her husband brought her to the nearest town, Vinnitsa, where he bought her rubber galoshes. (Rubber was the newest invention of the time.)

This was the first time that Faiga had ever left the village, and she was very excited. They traveled for a long time along a dusty country road, and when at last the wheels of their carriage rolled onto the town's cobblestone streets, the provincial town appeared to young Faiga like an enchanted capital city!

Shepsel Wolf brought Faiga to a shoe store, and her head began to spin from the dizzying selection. Faiga spotted shiny black galoshes lined with red velvet — she had never in her life seen such beautiful shoes. Shepsel Wolf tried to persuade her to choose something a bit more elegant, but all she wanted were the gleaming galoshes.

When the couple returned home, the young wife placed the galoshes on top of the closet, so they should not be ruined. Hiding a smile, her husband mentioned that galoshes were meant to be worn in the mud.

"In the mud?" she remonstrated. "How can someone wear something so beautiful in the mud?"

Bubbe Faiga always laughed when she recalled this incident.

---

1. Bubbe Faiga told me that Jews would give their children the double name "Shepsel Wolf" (Yiddish for "Sheep Wolf") as an allusion to the verse, "The wolf will live with the sheep" (*Isaiah* 11:6) in the hope that Isaiah's prophecy about the days of Mashiach would be speedily fulfilled.

Despite their poverty, Shepsel Wolf and Faiga lived a happy life, and eleven children were born to them.

After the Russian Revolution in 1917, the Communists came to power, and they categorically forbade Jews from observing their religion. In oppressing observant Jews, the Communists completed the work of the czarist regimes that had preceded them.

In the wake of this oppression, Shepsel Wolf decided to immigrate to Eretz Yisrael — then known as Palestine — with his wife and children. (At the beginning of the Communist era, people were still allowed to leave Russia.) After an arduous journey, they arrived at the border between Turkey and Palestine,[2] but they were unable to cross. At that time, Eretz Yisrael was governed by the British Mandate, and the British actively opposed the return of Jews to the Holy Land.

And so the Gutman family, like many others, was forced to turn back on its heels and return to the Ukraine.

At that time, a civil war broke out in the Ukraine, with a number of gangs rioting in the region. These gangs fought against each other, as well as against their common enemy — the Jews, robbing and murdering them and carrying out pogroms at will.

One of these murderous bands was comprised of soldiers of the national army, known as the Red Army. Led by the notorious Boudyoni,[3] these soldiers were supposed to protect the civilian population.

I recall that years later, whenever Bubbe Faiga would happen to notice a portrait of the commander-hero Boudyoni and his men, she would scream, "Bandits!"

The people around her would try to silence her, saying, "Faiga,

2. In those years, the territory of the British Mandate in Palestine bordered the territory of the French Mandate, which included parts of what had previously been the Ottoman Empire.

3. Boudyoni's cavalry achieved fame in the Russian civil war (1918-1922). What was less famous was that of all of the Red Army soldiers, Boudyoni's men were known for their unrestrained anti-Semitism and exceptional cruelty toward Jews. They carried out pogroms in all of the Jewish villages they encountered.

you can't talk that way! They can put you in jail for that!"

But she persisted, nevertheless.

Once, a gang led by the cruel Marusia[4] (a female chieftain) reached Vachanovka and commanded that the Jews gather in the shul and bring all their valuables with them. R' Shepsel Wolf learned that their intention was not only to plunder Jewish property, but also to lock the Jews into the shul and burn them alive.

Terrified, he ran to the homes of the Jews to warn them not to come to the shul. The people were indeed saved, but there was a "*moser*," an informant, among them who betrayed Shepsel Wolf to the members of the gang, telling them that he had been the one who had foiled their plans. (Faiga knew the identity of the informant, but she never in her lifetime revealed it.)

The barbaric gang members were furious, for they no longer had enough time to carry out their plot, and they took out their anger on Shepsel Wolf. They caught him, tied him to a bench, and began beating him brutally with the iron rods that they used to clean their rifles. Carrying her baby in her arms, Faiga ran toward the murderous bandits, trying to save her husband. Instead, they grabbed the baby from her and killed him brutally, right in front of her eyes.

The members of the gang hurried to leave the plundered village, and in their haste they did not realize that Shepsel Wolf was still alive. He lived for a short while after the beating, but was left crippled.

Faiga did everything she could to help her husband recover, bringing him to the best doctors in Vinnitsa and Kiev, but nothing helped. Shepsel Wolf became blind, and he passed away shortly thereafter, leaving Faiga on her own with ten surviving children.

---

4. Marusia's band: "Threatening to slaughter everyone, Marusia demanded an exorbitant ransom from the residents of Berezovka. The length of time given to them to make a decision was one day." (From the newspaper *Odessky Vistnik*, 1918.)

Destitute

Dispossession and Persecution

The Soviet regime made thousands of people illegal. The official name of this action was "Taking protective measures through the revolution." This "taking measures" was accompanied by confiscation of property, revocation of civil rights, revocation of the right to education and the right to work; people were thrown into the streets and even arrested. "Dispossessed" people, whose rights were revoked, were considered a "category of citizens of less than full value [i.e., defective], of the lowest variety." The percentage of Jews among the dispossessed was relatively higher than that of any other nationality, completely out of proportion to their numbers.

"Taking measures" included persecuting the Jewish religion; precluding any connection with Israel, the ancient Jewish homeland; and a prohibition to learn or teach the Hebrew language — the"Zionist-reactionary" language. Likewise, rabbanim were persecuted, and yeshivos and chadarim were closed.

In order to implement these measures, the Yevsektsia, the Jewish section of the Soviet Communist party — whose ranks comprised Jewish communists — was founded. The purpose of this organization was to have observant Jews persecuted by their own brothers, the Jewish communists. The official objective of the Yevsektsia was to "resocialize" the Jews into Soviet culture.

— [From documents dating back to the 1920s and 30s, Moscow State University]

Since the late Shepsel Wolf had been a rebbe, and their home was owned by the community for use by the rebbe, his widow and orphans were "dispossessed." Their lives were extremely difficult, and their 18-year-old son Moshe (who later became my father) had no choice but to travel to Donbas (or, formally, Donets Basin), the largest mining region in the country. Moshe took with him his brother and a Polish friend named Nikolai Olchovski, who was also dispossessed. Nikolai's father had been arrested for the "crime" of owning a flour mill, and his mill had been seized and converted into "state property," while he and his family were dispossessed.

> *After the Communist Revolution, affluent people were required to hand over their property to the state. People who did not do so voluntarily had their property confiscated, and were typically punished for not cooperating.*

Donbas was a thriving center, with coal mines and rapid construction. The work in the coal mines and construction sites was arduous and extremely dangerous, and because the government was eager to import manpower from all over Russia, it did not matter to which categories of society the workers belonged. Moshe and his friend had an easier time blending in among these unfamiliar people and keeping their "dispossessed" status a secret. The two young friends found themselves work in the city of Yuzovka.[5]

A year later, in 1923, when Moshe had already found his bearings in his new location and even had a room to his name, he traveled to Vachanovka to bring his mother and younger brother to join him; they were literally starving in their shtetl.

On the way to their destination, they had to travel by train. Faiga had never been at a train station before, and when the noisy, smoky locomotive — which to her was a technological wonder — pulled

---

5. Yuzovka was named after John Hughes, a Welsh industrialist who built the first steel plants in the area. Residents of Yuzovka represented 37 different nationalities, among them Russians, Ukrainians, Poles, Greeks, and others. In 1924, the city's name was changed to Stalino (after Stalin), and in 1961 it was changed to Donetsk.

into the station, she was terrified and refused to board the train. It took a long time for Moshe to convince her.

Late at night, they reached Yuzovka, and the next morning, at sunrise, Moshe left to work. At 6:00 a.m., a radio went on in his room. The radio was another "technological wonder" that Faiga had never encountered. When she heard a male voice emanating from the black box, she said, "Who are you talking to? Moishy isn't home, and I don't understand Russian."

Just then, the sound of a choir singing began to boom from the radio. Faiga retreated to the far corner of the room, and remained there until Moshe returned from work. "Take me back to Vachanovka!" she pleaded with him the moment he arrived. "I don't want to be here even one more minute! Your room contains evil spirits and the powers of the Satan!"

Slowly, Faiga acclimated to life in her new home. Despite the challenges of the time, she ran the house strictly according to halachah, brooking no compromises.

In the meantime, her son Moshe became the manager of a government store. He had a knack for business management, and eventually he achieved a certain status and earned a good reputation.

But then a new trouble struck: Apparently, someone informed the authorities that Moshe, the outstanding worker, was nothing but a dispossessed person.

During this period, the authorities extorted from the Jews every last penny that they had saved up for difficult times. The authorities did not believe the honest protests of those unfortunate individuals who had no money put away, and their refusal to turn over their supposed hidden wealth cost them their lives.

Moshe was jailed for failing to hand over his fortune to the authorities. Faiga, who by all appearances seemed to be a timid woman, risked her life and moved mountains in order to save her son. She traveled to Vachanovka, found several Ukrainians whom she recognized and who remembered her, and inquired which officials could be bribed. In exchange for a bribe, she received a document stating that her family was poor and her husband had been blind, and there was therefore no possibility that they had any hidden wealth.

This document saved Moshe's life. He was released from jail and reinstated at his job. (Until this day, this document is in the possession of the family.)

A Match Made in Heaven

In 5698/1938, Moshe traveled for Kiev for work purposes. He arranged his visit to coincide with the wedding of a friend in Kiev, and at the wedding, he was introduced to a lovely girl named Zissel. Moshe took an immediate liking to her, and after a long conversation, he asked her to marry him. Zissel just laughed.

Moshe did not try to convince her. He merely told her that he had to leave the city the following morning, and with that they parted. But he actually had other plans: He went to the train station, exchanged his ticket for one with a later date, and met Zissel the next day after she finished work.

When Zissel saw Moshe, the suitor she had rejected, she could not contain her elation. Since the previous day, she had been plagued by the thought that she had been too hasty in turning down Moshe's proposal, and she deeply regretted her decision. How happy she was that he hadn't listened to her!

Moshe accompanied her to her house, and they stood and spoke near the gate. Their conversation continued for quite a while, until Hershel, Zissel's father, approached them.

Hershel, an impressive-looking man, looked penetratingly at the tall, good-looking Moshe — who radiated tranquility and inner strength — and invited him inside.

Zissel had grown up without a mother. When her mother had passed away, her father Hershel could not be consoled, and he refused to remarry, opting instead to raise his children alone.

Inside the house, they sat and talked, and Moshe asked for Zissel's hand in marriage. "I will visit your parents' home," Hershel replied guardedly, "and then we'll talk."

The chronicles of my mother Zissel's family are a story in their own right.

Zissel's parents were an unusual couple. Hershel was orphaned at the age of 13, and he was forced to fend for himself. He therefore did not have the privilege of attending yeshivah or becoming learned. Nevertheless, he was a smart person and possessed unusual physical strength. He became the stuff of legends: People said that he could crush a five-kopeck copper coin with his fingers, and he could even straighten a horseshoe!

Hershel was very successful in business, and he was awarded a contract to supply meat to the czar's army in Kiev.

One day, the wealthy Hershel — who was known as *"der katzav"* (the butcher) — arrived at the home of the rav and asked to marry the rav's daughter Yides. Although Hershel was not a *talmid chacham*, he was known as a supporter of Torah.

"I might not be a Torah scholar," Hershel told the rav, "but if you give me your daughter as a wife, I promise you that your yeshivos and shuls will lack nothing."

The rav's family, the illustrious Twerski family, convened in the village of Skver from the surrounding villages of Chernobyl, Vachanovka, and Tolna in order to discuss the proposed *shidduch*. Many esteemed *rabbanim* were in attendance.

"Why don't we ask the girl herself?" one of the *rabbanim* suggested.

They summoned Yides and asked her opinion.

"I will do what my father tells me," Yides answered modestly, "but I personally have no opposition to this *shidduch*."

And so, within a short time, Hershel and Yides were married.

Hershel took his wife to the village of Chodorkovo, which was situated not far from Skver. There, in a prominent location adjacent to the market square, stood his magnificent wooden two-story house.

Hershel respected his wife greatly, and was very careful not to cause her pain. Their eldest daughter, Rochel, would recall how, when she was a young girl, a carriage would pull up to the house noisily every evening. It was her father Hershel, returning from business meetings. As he would hurry up the steps and enter his house, an abrupt change would come over him. Hershel was a tall, broad man with a powerful voice — but when he entered his own house, he seemed much shorter and quieter.

Yides, for her part, was a small, thin woman, but she was the mainstay of the home, and she ran the household with her small yet strong hand. Yides bore six children: three sons and three daughters.

The chassidim living in the region claimed that Yides managed to turn Hershel into a "mentsch."

This may very well have been the case. But Hershel's blissful family life did not last long. The revolution and subsequent civil war devastated the lives of the Jews in the village, and Hershel's family was not spared.

In the summer of 5678/1918, when one of the many gangs roaming the area stormed the village and exchanged fire with their foes, the Jews did the only thing they could: They covered the windows with down pillows and lay on the floor. But the bullets penetrated the pillows, and within moments Hershel lost his wife and six-year-old son.

There was no time to mourn their deaths, however. Hershel had to do what he could to save the remaining children. He hastily buried his beloved wife and his son, and fled from Chodorkovo with his five surviving children.

He traveled to the village where his married sister lived, and left his children under her care. His eldest daughter, Rochel, was nine at the time; his youngest son, several months old; and Zissel, three.

Hershel himself headed for Kiev. In Kiev, there was some semblance of authority and some protection from pogroms. Hershel opened a business of tanning hides and was quite successful. In time, he purchased a house, and then brought his children to Kiev, where he raised them on his own. When his married sister was widowed, she joined the household and helped Hershel to raise the children.

Many distinguished women would have been happy to marry Hershel and help raise his family, but Hershel's heart remained with Yides until the end of his life.

Now, Hershel traveled to Stalino to meet the family of his prospective son-in-law Moshe. It appears that both families were pleased with their future *mechutanim*, because the wedding took place shortly thereafter. Despite the government prohibitions, Hershel held an authentic Jewish wedding in his house, complete with a *chuppah* and a *kesubah* (the *kesubah* has been preserved until this day).

> The Russians forbade all Jewish ceremonies, including chuppahs, bris milahs, etc., whether held in public or in private. The punishment for holding such a ceremony was a lengthy prison term or a sentence to a Siberian labor camp — and the crime was considered far more grave if there was evidence of such a ceremony (a kesubah, for instance).

After their wedding, Moshe and his wife traveled to Stalino, where they lived with his mother Faiga. I was born one year later, and at my *bris milah* I was given the name Shepsel, after my grandfather.

Before my birth, something happened that could have changed the lives of my family forever: My father Moshe obtained a green card, permitting him entry into the United States. He had applied for the green card many years earlier, and only now was it issued.

But his young wife Zissel did not want to leave her homeland and part with her many relatives.

Moshe did not want to waste the precious green card, so he gave it to his cousin, whose last name was also Gutman. The authorities did not notice that there had been any deception, and this lucky relative immigrated to America with his family. All his life, he felt a debt of gratitude to my father. (I found out about this after half a century, as I will explain later.)

This cousin prospered in America. Wishing to help the relatives left behind in Russia, he would send us letters and packages. But the situation in Russia continued to deteriorate: The authorities were on the lookout everywhere for spies and enemies of the people, and any connection to foreign countries — including correspondence with relatives abroad — was considered treasonous to the Motherland.

Moshe was therefore compelled to go to the central post office and formally announce that he refused to accept such packages, declaring that he had no relatives living abroad.

Part II

From Whence Will Come My Help?

שֶׁלֹּא אֶחָד בִּלְבָד עָמַד עָלֵינוּ לְכַלּוֹתֵנוּ
אֶלָּא שֶׁבְּכָל דּוֹר וָדוֹר עוֹמְדִים עָלֵינוּ לְכַלּוֹתֵנוּ,
וְהַקָּדוֹשׁ בָּרוּךְ הוּא מַצִּילֵנוּ מִיָּדָם.

(הגדה של פסח)

For not only one has risen against us to annihilate us,
but in every generation they rise against us to annihilate us.
But the Holy One, Blessed is He, rescues us from their hand.

(Haggadah Shel Pesach)

Child inmates of Auschwitz on the day of liberation

The One-Way Journey

When the Germans invaded the Soviet Union in 5701/1941, my father Moshe and his two brothers, Isaac and Velvel, were conscripted into the Red Army. Isaac had already fought on the Finnish front in 1939, and had returned home unharmed. But this time, when they went out to war, Moshe and Velvel maintained their equanimity, while Isaac cried and told his mother that he was not going to return. His heart was filled with foreboding, and his premonition turned out to be correct. He was killed in the war, and never did marry Dina, my mother's younger sister, as he had planned. At the end, Dina was brutally murdered at Babi Yar.

Bubbe Faiga often expressed her regrets that the marriage had never taken place, for had they married, it is possible that both of them would have survived.

Babi Yar

Babi Yar is a valley northwest of Kiev, Ukraine. It was where Kiev's Jews were murdered en masse during World War II. On September 29 and 30 of 1941, approximately 33,771 Jews were killed at Babi Yar. During the months that followed, thousands of additional Jews were caught, dragged to Babi Yar, and shot. Babi Yar also became the execution site of many non-Jews, including gypsies and Russian prisoners of war. The Extraordinary State Commission, established in 1942 to "ascertain and investigate crimes perpetrated by the German-Fascist invaders and their allies," estimated that approximately 100,000 people were killed there during the war.

Kiev was captured by the Nazis shortly after World War II broke out, and tens of thousands of Jews who had not managed to flee the city were murdered in Babi Yar, near Kiev. Unlike many others, Hershel and his young daughter Dina could have fled. Hershel's eldest daughter Rochel, who was already married at that time, received a permit to leave by train together with her family because she was the wife of a soldier fighting on the battlefield. She ran to her father and begged, "Get ready quickly and come with me!"

Hershel adamantly refused, however. "I saw the Germans in 1914, during World War I, and they are decent people. I'm not going anywhere."

Oy, Hershel, Hershel — your penchant for deciding everything yourself led you astray. Rochel's pleas were futile, and she had no choice but to leave Kiev accompanied only by her two children.

She escaped to our home in Stalino before the Germans arrived. With tears in her eyes, she told Zissel that she had not managed to convince their father and younger sister to leave Kiev.

After the war, eyewitnesses related that these "decent" Germans led the Jews before a firing squad. Hershel, who was still a powerful man, resisted so strongly that it took a number of policemen to subdue him. His hands were tied with barbed wire, and a heavy wooden log was clamped to his foot with iron chains. He was then dragged to Babi Yar. Even in that condition, a minute before his death Hershel managed to grab a shovel from the hands of a Ukrainian policeman and break his skull with it. The murderers tied Hershel's daughter Dina by her long braids and dragged her before a firing squad.

We learned of the tragic circumstances of their deaths only after the war ended.

In the meantime, the Nazi occupiers were rapidly approaching Stalino, and Rochel hurried to leave the city.

"Zissel," she urged my mother, "take your mother-in-law and the boy and come along with me!" She begged her sister to flee just as she had begged her father. But again, her pleas were for naught.

"If my father remained in his home, why should I leave mine?"

Zissel argued. "They're promising on the radio that the war will end soon.[6] My husband will return from battle, and where will he search for his family? And the child is very little — only three years old — where can I go with him?"

Rochel did not manage to convince her sister. It turned out that she was wiser than the rest of her family — she did not believe the radio announcers' soothing words, and she escaped deep into Russian territory. In that way, she saved herself and her children.

I remained behind, along with my mother and grandmother.

Stalino During the War

Stalino (Donetsk) was occupied by the Nazis from October 21, 1941 to September 8, 1943. In 1941, the city's population numbered 507,000; by the end of the war, only 175,000 remained.

The Nazis hired Ukrainians to serve as policemen, and these Ukrainian officers participated in firing squads and other aktions. The cruelty of these officers often surpassed that of their employers, the Nazis.

A short while after the Nazis invaded Stalino, they gathered all the Jews into a ghetto in the White Quarry, a former mining site. The ghetto's existence was short-lived, for it was liquidated cruelly and speedily. Some of the Jews were shot and thrown into a deep mine shaft, while others were thrown into the shaft alive! Local residents related that screams and moans were heard from the depths of the mine shaft for a long time after the ghetto's liquidation.

In the protocols of a postwar criminal court hearing, the former mayor of Stalino gave testimony regarding the ghetto and the fate of its inhabitants. These records are archived under the files of the mayor and other Nazi collaborators:

6. During World War II, the residents of the Soviet Union were permitted to listen to a public radio, which was typically located in the middle of each town. The radio announcers tried to raise the people's morale, concealing the truth from the citizens. People were not allowed to use their own home radios, and these devices were confiscated.

The White Quarry was chosen as the site of the ghetto.
It was surrounded by a barbed-wire fence, and guards
were stationed all around it. In March of 1942, the police
commanders and neighborhood sentries were instructed
to round all of the city's Jewish residents into the ghetto.
Each family was advised to bring along its valuables and
jewelry, as well as food for five or six days. The Jews were
required to give over the keys to their homes to police
representatives who were charged with the "population
transfer."

Jewish families were expelled from all of the city's
neighborhoods. Those who were weak were helped
along, and the young children were carried, while the
soldiers prodded them forward with whips and rifle-butts.
Screams, moans, and cries of children were heard from
every direction. This entire population was led to the
designated place, and due to a dearth of wooden shacks
in the area, many were left with no roof over their heads.
All their valuables and jewelry were confiscated. The
assembled Jews — over 3,000 of them — were liquidated
by being shot or by being suffocated by poison gas.
Their corpses were thrown into a mine shaft in Kalinovka.
Afterward, the wooden shacks were destroyed by the
police .... The Jews were liquidated — and that is a fact. If
anyone survived, it was only by a miracle.

M. Kashdan, an eyewitness, relates: At the end of the
month of February, we were forcibly transferred to
wooden shacks in the White Quarry. It was freezing cold
in this terrible place, and unbearable hunger reigned. The
ghetto was patrolled by police officers and their dogs;
one gate served as an entrance and exit. The one thing
that is deeply etched upon my memory is the fear that
penetrated the body's every cell.

The feeling of death hovered in the spring air. On that
fateful day, April 30, I did not imagine for one second that
when I headed to work in Makeevka in the morning, I was
seeing everyone for the last time. When I returned the
following evening, May 1, unaware of what had transpired
in the interim, I met a Russian woman whom I knew.

"Where are you going?" she asked me. "You can't go there. At night, they took everyone."

The Parting

My father Moshe remained with his close friend Nikolai Olchovski, with whom he had traveled to Donbas years earlier. The two lived in neighboring houses and were drafted into the same army unit. Within a short time, the Germans dubbed this unit the "furnace of Kremenchug." Very few soldiers in this unit escaped the "furnace" alive, but fortune smiled upon my father and his friend: They fled from the Nazi clutches and made their way home.

When they approached Stalino, they learned that it had already been captured by the Germans.

Nikolai opined that the Soviet government had caused him only hardships. He was therefore unwilling to give his life for that government, and he decided to return home. Moshe also wanted to sneak into the captured city in order to search for his family, but he knew that he could not enter the city, for if he were identified as a Jew he would be condemned to death. How, then, could he find out what had happened to his family?

Nikolai promised his friend Moshe that he would take care of Moshe's family, if he would manage to find them. He then returned to the captured Stalino, while Moshe returned to the battlefront.

When Nikolai returned to Stalino, he began working for the Germans as a police officer. He participated in the *aktions* and mass killings, but he kept his promise to his friend Moshe nevertheless.

My family and I were expelled to the ghetto along with the other Jews of Stalino. Our fate would have been the same as that of the other Jews in the ghetto, except that our salvation suddenly arrived a few days before the *aktion* in the form of Nikolai Olchovski, the police officer. At the end of March, Olchovski appeared in the ghetto together with his wife Matriona and told my mother, "Zena [that was what the gentile neighbors called Zissel], you have to leave; all the Jews in the ghetto are going to be liquidated. I can save you and the child, but I can't take your mother-in-law along."

"If we can't take the old woman with us, I'm not going anywhere," my mother replied. "What will I tell my husband when he asks me where his mother is?"

Olchovski was therefore compelled to take Bubbe Faiga along as well. Years later, Bubbe Faiga would remember this incident and would emphasize, "Zissel didn't want to leave me!"

Olchovski could not hide all of us in one place; each of us had to be hidden separately, and my mother was forced to part with me, her young son.

The adult residents of the ghetto were often taken to work in the city, and Olchovski was thus able to bring my mother and grandmother through the ghetto's gate without arousing the suspicion of the guards. But what could he do with the child? For that purpose, he enlisted the help of his wife, Matriona. Matriona was a good friend of my mother and grandmother; when I was born, she had gone with my grandmother to bring me home from the hospital.

Matriona Olchovski was a tall, heavyset woman. To sneak me out of the ghetto, she tied me under her skirt, and wrapped herself in a fur coat. Her husband seated us in a wagon and drove us to a village. The inhabitants were of Greek extraction, and were more tolerant of the Jews than the Ukrainians were.

I don't remember my mother's tears, nor do I remember parting from her.

As I described in the introduction, I was first hidden in the village of Granitnoe, and then brought to a German orphanage in Starobeshevo, where Karl Schultz, the director of the orphanage took a liking to me. Eventually, he adopted me and brought me to his home in Germany. After he was killed in battle in 1944, his wife Elsa handed me over to the Nazis.

Ravensbrück

Ravensbrück was a concentration camp intended primarily for women, and the inmates there underwent fatal "medical experiments." Over 132,000 women and children were imprisoned in Ravensbrück. The children suffered unspeakable torture at the hands of the Nazis, and the fate of these tender victims was horrendous. Very few survived.

The camp was liberated by the Red Army on April 30, 1945. By then, only 3,000 women and children and 300 men remained alive.

Of Dogs and Humans

I was sent to Ravensbrück along with a large group of children. We walked for a long time to the train station, supervised by uniformed German women and their guard dogs. There were no men with us. The German women hit the children mercilessly, and seemed to us more menacing than their dogs.

At the train station, we were loaded onto freight cars and sent to Ravensbrück. I remember all of this vaguely, as though it were a bad dream.

My barracks held only boys, and the neighboring barracks held young girls. These two barracks were separated from the rest of the camp by a barbed-wire fence. The boys in my barracks served as blood donors; I don't know what the fate of the girls was. Each day, we were taken to a special barracks. German clad in white coats jabbed thick needles into our veins and withdrew our blood. It was both painful and frightening. At first I cried, but eventually I stopped crying and began submitting to the daily bloodletting obediently along with all the other boys.

The Germans did not hit or abuse us, but they gave us practically no food. The ashen-faced children perished quietly one after another. We did not talk to one another; we didn't have the strength for that. We were not interested in anything except food.

A watchdog patrolled the other side of the iron mesh fence that separated our barracks from the rest of the camp. I noticed that every day, the guard brought this dog a bowl of food, and that bowl of food captivated me. All of the inmates were terrified of the ferocious dogs that guarded the camp, but I, for some reason, was not afraid of them; perhaps this was because I had grown accustomed to a similar dog in Schultz's house. I was much more leery of the two-legged beasts who guarded us than I was of the dogs.

One day, I could no longer contain myself. Paying no heed to the dog or to his German master, I crawled under the fence toward the bowl and began devouring the food hungrily. The guard watched me in idle curiosity, certain that the dog would attack me immediately and tear me to pieces. But the dog did not touch me; I don't know why, but he even retreated from the bowl, as though waiting for me to finish eating. Only after I finished did he approach the bowl to eat. Apparently, the dog was kinder than its human masters.

From then on, I began to visit the dog and partake of its food every day. The guards could easily have shot me, but they found it amusing to watch me eating from the bowl like a dog. They rolled with laughter, pointing their fingers at me, calling me derogatory names, such as "son of a dog," and heaping abuse upon me. I understood German, and I was deeply hurt by their words. I cried, but I continued eating.

The Motherland, My Stepmother

"There is no mitzvah greater than redeeming captives."
— Rambam, *Hilchos Matnos Aniyim* 8:10

Russia's POWs

Throughout the generations, Jewish people have exerted themselves greatly in order to redeem any fellow Jew who was held captive. In the Soviet Union, however, captives were treated differently. Soldiers were expected to commit suicide rather than be taken alive, and those who were taken prisoner by the enemy were considered traitors to the Motherland. The Russians were therefore in no hurry to gain the release of those of their comrades who were prisoners of war. When they did finally bring these prisoners home, the fate of the prisoners was dire: They were either shot or sent to Siberian camps, and their families were imprisoned. Captive children did not receive better treatment.

The war with Germany ended on May 9, 1945 (5705), but it took a long time for Russia to bring home its captured citizens. I was taken to a transit camp along with other Russian citizens who were inmates of Ravensbrück. To me, the conditions in this camp seemed worse than those in Ravensbrück. In the concentration camp, the Germans had abused me, but now the inmates themselves were beating and degrading me. That was because I spoke German, the despised language.

The beatings I received for speaking German forced me to learn Russian very quickly, but my Russian was still not fluent enough for me to be considered "one of them."

We were confined inside a barbed-wire fence for over half a year, until finally, in December, we were taken back to Russia. We were transported in German passenger trains until the German border, and we were fed and treated well during that first leg of the journey. But this favorable treatment did not last long — the moment we crossed the Russian border, everything changed.

In the city of Brest (Brisk), we were transferred to Russian freight trains. The freight car I was in was filled to capacity with children; there was not a single adult among us. So horrific was the crowding that we could not move at all. I tried to push myself closer to the door, because along with the cold some fresh air entered through the gap.

The journey lasted several days, and the train halted in the train stations along the way for long periods, during which we were never allowed to leave the train. Clearly, we were considered unimportant cargo. We were given food at very infrequent intervals, and several children died in the course of the journey.

Near me, on the floor of the railroad, lay a child who was older than I was, and very thin. At the beginning, we spoke to him a bit, but afterward he fell silent and I could feel that his body was cold. I tried to move away from him, but it was not possible. We lay that way, the living alongside the dead, for the remainder of the journey.

We reached the Darnitza train station in Kiev, where we waited another two days. During this time, the doors were not opened, and we did not receive any food or water. This was in December, the height of the winter, and the cold penetrated our bones, numbing us to the extent that we no longer cared who lived and who died.

Finally, the doors of the freight car opened, and military officers appeared. (I later realized that these were NKVD[7] officials.) They grabbed the half-dead children by their collars and threw them out

7. The NKVD was the Russian Committee of State Security and the precursor of the KGB.

of the freight cars into the snow. They then kicked us in order to compel us to rise to our feet and enter a yard surrounded by barbed wire. These frightful people, dressed in Red Army uniforms, beat us and held us outdoors in the freezing cold for a full 24 hours.

Then the sorting began. I and several other children who did not speak Russian were separated from the rest of the group, and we were treated with exceptional cruelty.

The worst memory of my life is that of my return to the "Motherland" and my treatment at the hands of these human beasts.

The "Reunion"

Forty years later, in 1987 (5747), an official request from Germany reached the city of Zhitomir, where I was living at the time. Mrs. Elsa Schultz of Germany, with the help of the Red Cross, was looking for Sasha Granitni, who had lived in Germany as a child. When I noticed the request, I wondered if I was that child.

I responded to the letter, and after a short while I was notified that Elsa Schultz had arrived in Kiev and wished to meet with me. (At that time, foreign visitors were not allowed to travel to Zhitomir.)

My wife was opposed to this meeting. "What do you need this for?" she asked angrily.

At that time, meetings between Soviet citizens and foreigners were frowned upon, and such a meeting could have harmed my career. I did not listen to my wife, however, and I traveled to Kiev to meet with Elsa Schultz. If she wanted to meet with me, I reasoned, why should I refuse?

When I reached the hotel where she was staying, I telephoned her room to let her know that I had arrived. Several minutes later, an aging, heavyset German woman entered the lobby, accompanied by a younger woman. We sat on armchairs near coffee tables in the lobby.

The younger woman turned out to be an interpreter; I sensed some thinly concealed hostility in her. The older woman was tense. She leaned forward and stared at me without uttering a word. The interpreter then began to interrogate me: Had I ever lived in Germany? Did I recognize the older woman sitting opposite me?

I answered that I did not recognize the woman, but that I had lived in Germany during World War II. Hearing this, the older German woman jumped up from her place, approached me, and hugged my head tightly.

"What are you doing?" I protested. "You're suffocating me!"

She released my head and burst into tears.

"My son," she sobbed, "please forgive me! I handed you in then because it was so difficult for me to survive!"

She then began to tell me how she had thought of me all these years. "I searched for you through the Red Cross," she related, "but I was unable to find you. It took until now for me to receive a sign of life from you."

She told me that she was financially comfortable, but lonely. She had never remarried, and she had no children; she considered this a punishment from heaven for having handed me in. Now, she was inviting me and my family to move to Germany and live there with her, becoming heirs to her estate. "Jews are allowed to leave the Soviet Union already," she added.

I looked at Elsa and thought to myself, *This woman was so attached to me — and yet she sent me to a concentration camp, to almost certain death!* I understood now what her motive had been in handing me in: I was a Jewish child! Why, if not for the *bris milah* my father had given me, I would have become Elsa Schultz's son forever!

I still remembered enough German to converse with her without the help of the interpreter. I told Elsa that I did not need anything from her, and that I was unwilling to travel.

It was as though she did not hear me, however. In an attempt to awaken warm feelings in me, she began to reminisce about my childhood antics, telling me about the time I had wanted to give my new shoes to the goat. Dredging up these memories brought color to her face, and she began to appear younger. She even laughed as she recalled another incident that had happened when I was a child.

"Come, let's go to a movie," she said. "Do you remember that you promised me, 'Mama, when I grow up, we'll go to a movie in the cinema and I'll buy you a ticket for a seat in the front row'?"

How did she dare utter the word "Mama"? I had to restrain myself from interrupting her sentimental prattle, and I waited politely for the meeting to end.

When we parted, she expressed her hope that I would reconsider and accept her offer, and she kissed me warmly — just as she had done when she had handed me over to the concentration camp. All that was missing now was the bunny rabbit, the toy through which she tried to absolve herself of guilt and atone for her betrayal of me.

I have forgotten many things, but the memory of that treasonous gift pains me to this day.

For several years after that, I continued to receive letters from Germany, from Elsa Schultz. These letters included invitations for my entire family, but I ignored them.

The White Soup Tureen

After our traumatic return to the Motherland, we were held in Kiev for over a week, and then we were sent to an orphanage. In my documents from Ravensbrück, my name appeared as Alexander Granitni. The documents also stated that I had arrived in Germany from the region of Stalino, and I was therefore sent back to that region.

At first, I was placed in an orphanage in the village of Milikino. Afterward, I was transferred to Mariupol, to Makeevka, and finally to Stalino, my birthplace (formerly called Yuzovka, now Donetsk). But no one realized that I had returned to my hometown.

All the memories I have of that period are connected to food. I did not grow properly; I was shorter and thinner than other children my age. I was always hungry, and I tried to keep as close to the kitchen as possible. Fortunately, the cooks in the kitchen took pity on me: "Look how skinny you are!" they would cluck. "Skin and bones!" These women always gave me something to eat. They also became very attached to me, and that became a decisive factor in my fate.

At one point, all the younger children in the orphanage were sent to a different city, and only the children who had reached the age of compulsory education (at that time, eight years of age) remained in the orphanage. The cooks refused to part with me, however. They asked the director not to send me away, even though I was only seven years old, but rather to enroll me in school a year early.

In the orphanage, the cooks enjoyed an exteemed status, since they were involved with food, which was in short supply at the time. Their request that I remain in the orphanage was therefore honored.

It was 1946 (5706), and people were dying of hunger in the streets. The children of the orphanage received barely any food, and we were forced to fend for ourselves; it is frightening to contemplate what our diets consisted of. Our constant hunger compelled us to seek food in any way possible, and in this regard, I was saved by a dog once again.

The director of the orphanage, Boris Aharonovitch Slavin, lived with his family in a small wooden house on the property of the orphanage, and a ferocious dog guarded the house. Boris fed his dog well, even though we, the children of the orphanage, were starving. Twice a day the dog received a heaping bowl of meat and bones. The children were very envious of the dog, but no one dared approach it — we were scared of both the dog and its owner.

I was not afraid of dogs, however, and when I recalled how I had eaten the dog's food in the concentration camp, I decided to try the same strategy again. One evening, I waited for nightfall so that the director would not notice me, and then I crept toward the coveted bowl of food. The other children watched me from afar and placed their bets: Would the dog tear me to pieces or not?

To their surprise, the dog allowed me to eat from the bowl without even barking at me. Not only did I eat my fill, I also filled my pockets with "gifts from the dog" for my friends. The dog allowed one other child besides me to approach him, and we took turns eating with the dog and bringing back food to the other children. But we turned to the dog for food very infrequently, since we were terrified of incurring the director's wrath.

In the summer, Boris Aharonovitch Slavin would eat dinner outside in the open air with his family, under a lilac bush in the garden near his house. When the director and his two sons sat down to eat, a group of younger children from the orphanage gathered to watch this exciting event from the side. We stood on our tiptoes and craned our necks so that we could observe every detail.

The director's wife emerged pompously from the house carrying a large white soup tureen, which she placed on the table. Boris removed the tureen's heavy cover, and the intoxicating aroma of meaty soup wafted throughout the garden. Then Boris slowly ladled the steaming soup into bowls, and the family began to eat. Our hearts skipped a beat at the sight of this sumptuous meal, and our eyes followed every spoonful the family members took into their mouths.

Many years have passed since then, but a white soup tureen has forever remained, to my mind, *the* symbol of wealth and happiness. Any time I saw such a tureen in someone's house, I knew for certain that this was a rich home.

When I established my own home, nothing was lacking in our house — apart from a soup tureen. Perhaps that was because my house lacked the most important feature of a home: happiness.

I did eventually purchase a white soup tureen, some 50 years after my experience in the orphanage. The tureen was not for me or for my own family, but for the family that was dearest and closest to me in the whole world. That was the family of my friend Leizer. When Leizer and his wife celebrated their fortieth wedding anniversary in Jerusalem, in the company of their children and over 40 grandchildren, I decided to present them with a special gift.

That was how I found myself buying a white soup tureen. To me, that tureen epitomized wealth, and symbolized my own dream of a happy home that had never materialized.

I affixed to the tureen a photograph of Leizer's extended, unified family, and when I presented it to Leizer and his wife, I said, "You cooked an excellent soup together!"

The Wide Belt

Meanwhile, the famine raging in the area was claiming a rising toll of human life. The children of the orphanage had to fend for themselves by selling coal and firewood, which we stole from passing freight trains.

Near the city of Stalino were train tracks that led to a mine. The freight trains traveling toward the mine carried firewood, and the trains coming from the mine carried coal.

In the postwar period, there was a great deal of discarded ammunition to be found. We would collect this ammunition and fashion small, makeshift explosives by filling the rubber nipples of baby bottles with the dynamite we had gathered. The older children would then place these bombs on the train tracks.

When the locomotive of a freight train would travel over the bomb, an explosion would be triggered, forcing the train's conductor to stop the train and investigate. While the conductor would try to figure out what had happened, the smaller children would scamper out of their hiding places, climb onto the freight cars, and quickly throw to the ground whatever firewood or coal they could get their hands on. The older children would remain in their hiding places to avoid being apprehended by the police. (When the police would nab the younger children, they would beat them and then let them go. The older children were no longer considered minors, however, and they were liable to face criminal charges of theft that could land them in prison or in a camp for juvenile offenders for many years.) Once the conductor climbed back into the locomotive and drove the train out of sight, we would gather our loot, sell it, and use the money we earned to buy food.

We didn't steal only firewood and coal — we stole anything we could. Once a week, we were taken to the bathhouse, and on our way there, we passed the local marketplace. The older children would swoop down upon the women peddling their wares, shouting, "Auntie, give us money!" Brazenly, they would dig their hands into the coveted stashes of money hidden in the peddlers' pockets.

The peddler women would clutch their money bundles tightly and scream, "Help! Thieves!"

While the older children were diverting the peddlers' attention in this way, the younger children would dive under the peddlers' stands and steal bread and food from their baskets.

The hunger-filled days of my childhood made me develop a habit of never refusing a second helping, even if I have eaten my fill. During those days of hunger, I was taught never to take the last portion from the serving tray. Such an act invited a murderous, gang-style beating. The last piece on the tray belonged to the strongest kids, and the older children invariably took it for themselves.

Life in the orphanage was very boring, and hunger gnawed at us constantly. Along with my friends, I tried to escape from the orphanage many times. In the summer, we tried to escape to Moscow, and in the winter, to Tashkent,[8] which boasted abundant fruits and

8. Tashkent is the capital of Uzbekistan, formerly an Asiatic Soviet Republic.

a milder winter. To make our way to the big city, we crawled into the compartments beneath railroad cars, but the police invariably apprehended us and removed us from the trains at the stations along the way. I never did make it to Moscow or Tashkent in those years.

Nevertheless, the memories of my attempted train escapes are the best memories I have of that period, even though each time we tried to escape we were brutally beaten by the police officers who nabbed us. I used to scream, "Uncle, don't beat me with a wide belt!" The lashes inflicted by the wide belt were less painful than those inflicted by the narrow belt, and the officers — who wished to inflict the most painful blows possible — made a point of beating me with the wide belt after hearing me beg to be beaten with a narrow belt.

One day, an officer named Kozirov caught me. This officer was usually the one who came to apprehend the truant children of the orphanage, and he caught wind of my strategy. "You don't want the wide belt?" Kozirov bellowed. "Here, you'll get the narrow one!" He removed his narrow rifle belt and beat me so violently with that for three days afterward I was able to lie only on my stomach.

We were doubly punished each time we tried to flee: first, by the police, and afterward by the staff of the orphanage. The orphanage staff beat us with exceptional cruelty, subjecting us to a horrific punishment called "the fifth corner." Four fierce men — Director Slavin, and the teachers Smolov, Kartinov, and Shatalov — would throw the child from one to another like a ball. After a while, the child would fall unconscious, and the men would then expertly use the soles of their shoes to kick the child in his ears. This blow left no outward mark, but damaged the child's hearing for life. My own hearing was damaged from these blows.

In my file the police recorded nine attempts to escape. Three of these were "armed attempts": I was armed once with a grenade, once with a rifle, and once with a knife. We children felt more confident escaping when we were armed. Obviously, we could have easily been blown up along with our ammunition, but who thought of things like that? Once, a "samopal" (a hot, homemade explosive) exploded in my hand, reducing my palm and fingers to a bloody pulp. The other children helped me to bandage my bleeding hand, and I suffered for several weeks until it healed. I did not tell the adults in the orphanage what had happened, for I was afraid that they would punish me. Luckily, this incident did not maim me permanently.

From "German" to "Zhid"

When I first arrived at the orphanage, I still spoke Russian with a heavy German accent, and I was therefore nicknamed "the German." My documents stated that I was Russian, but when Shatalov the teacher brought us to the bathhouse, he realized that I was Jewish and labeled me "Zhid." After that, he never missed an opportunity to heap abuse on me. Shatalov taught in our school, and any time he called me to the board to answer questions he used the term "Zhid." This epithet clung to me until the end of my school years. (Shatalov later advanced in his career, eventually earning the designation, "Illustrious Teacher of the Soviet Union.")

At first, I did not really understand what Shatalov meant. I was not familiar with the term "Zhid," and I was not even offended. Later, however, I got the message. Shatalov was an expert at abusing children, and I personally experienced his brutality on many occasions. I never passed up an opportunity to get even with him, and I tried to take revenge against him whenever I could.

When I found out that Shatalov had installed new windows in his house, I riled up a few of my friends, and over the course of a few evenings we smashed all his windows. Shatalov guessed who was responsible for the damage, but he had no proof of my guilt, so he merely continued to torture me.

I comforted myself with the thought that when I would get older, I would settle the score with him.

Eventually, I did settle the score with him. I followed him, and observed which route he typically took. I then tampered with the iron cover of a sewer pipe situated along this route so that it would overturn when he stepped on it. I concealed the cover with wooden branches, and hid nearby in order to watch Shatalov receive his comeuppance. Shatalov stepped right onto the sewer cover, and fell and broke his leg. He had to use crutches for a long time, and when he recovered and returned to school, he nabbed me in the corridor, pressed me to the wall, and thrashed me thoroughly.

I looked straight into his eyes, and with barely restrained fury I hissed, "If you ever touch me again, I'm going to drown you."

He believed me, and left me alone.

There were only two people in the orphanage who took pity on us: the maintenance man, Uncle Fima Gurshpon, and his wife, Auntie Clara. I thought they were wealthy people because they owned a white soup tureen like Director Slavin. The difference was that Auntie Clara occasionally shared the soup in her tureen with us.

Uncle Fima had golden hands, and he was therefore treated with respect and admiration. At times, he would take me with him to the storage room where all the orphanage's possessions were kept. I was supposedly in the storage room to help Uncle Fima, but in practice I was busy with something else entirely: I waited until Uncle Fima turned his head to the side, and I grabbed anything I could find and stuffed it into my pockets, whether it was an undershirt or a pair of shoes. Uncle Fima paid no attention to my swollen shirt, and in that way allowed me to remove the stolen items from the storage room. I suspect that this was actually his real motivation in bringing me there. Just like the other children, I sold these items in the marketplace and used the money to buy food.

This arrangement helped me take care of myself for several years, and in the process I even managed to get my hands on two large leather shoes from Germany, which were a source of great pride to me. The soles of the shoes were reinforced with iron, and they never tore or let water in. The two shoes both belonged to the left foot, and they were a few sizes too big, but this was advantageous for me, because it ensured that no one stole my shoes, and my feet did not freeze.

Dangerous Games

Even among the teachers at our school there were some kind souls. When I was in elementary school, a teacher named Vera Semyonovna used to treat us to pretzels and fragrant carrot cookies.[9] When I reached the higher grades, my angel of mercy was Anna Israelevna Marchenko, the history teacher. She took a special liking to me, while I took pleasure in frightening her. I would climb out of the window of our third-floor classroom, grab hold of the wall with my two hands, and propel my body forward along the narrow outer ledge of the building. I would inch along the outside of the building until I reached her classroom window, and then I would suddenly poke my head inside and say politely, "Greetings, Anna Israelevna!"

She would clap her hands together in alarm, much to my foolish delight. Seeing that she cared about me warmed my heart, and I sought her attention at any price.

Once, when she approached my desk, I purposely knocked over the inkwell at the corner of my desk and spilled the ink on her dress. I don't know why I did this; maybe I was trying to test the limits of her kindheartedness.

9. Many years later, I learned that these cookies were a Jewish food called *imberlach*, which are made of carrots and ginger.

But she tolerated all our antics and never reported us to the principal. Apparently, she knew what the outcome of a complaint on her part would be. The other teachers were very quick to complain about us students, and the offenders would be taken to the teachers' room, where he would receive the dreaded punishment: the "fifth corner."

Our attempts to enrich our gloomy lives in the orphanage did not always end well. For instance, one of our favorite pastimes was to hang on the back of the cars of the light rail train and enjoy a free ride. Once, one of the children slipped and fell under the wheels of the train and his leg was severed. From then on, he would run after us on his crutches.

Shortly afterward, a movie about World War II entitled *It Happened in Donbas* was filmed in our city. This was an exciting occasion for us children. We abandoned all our other pastimes and trailed after the filmmakers instead.

Several years later, when I watched this movie, I was surprised to see myself and the boy with crutches on the screen during a scene in which the Germans were leading a group of prisoners of war. Apparently, the two of us had run in front of the movie cameras while they had been filming, and we had unwittingly made it onto film. By the time I saw the film, the boy on crutches was no longer living. He had died a horrible death a short time after the movie's filming, and this brief film appearance was the only memorial to his all-too-brief life.

As I watched the movie, I recalled that with his death, he had unintentionally saved my life. This is how it happened:

One day, in search of a new adventure, we hauled an old iron barrel to the top of a large terricon[10] near a mining quarry. The mound was about 400 feet tall, and we wanted to slide down its side in the

10. A terricon is a slag heap, a pyramid-like mound formed when separating coal from rock.

barrel. Each of the boys in our group wanted to slide down first, so we cast lots. As luck would have it, I won the lottery.

When I was about to enter the barrel, the boy on crutches came up to me, hit me from behind, and pushed me aside. He then entered the barrel along with his crutches. Despite his handicap, he was larger and stronger than I, so I was forced to give up my right to enter the barrel first.

The boys gave the barrel a gentle push, and it rolled noisily down the mound, skipping over indentations in the terrain, until it finally came to a stop down below. Whooping gleefully, we ran after the barrel to bring it back up to the top of the mound and take our turns rolling down. We were surprised, however, that the boy did not emerge from the barrel. When we reached the barrel, we peeked inside and saw what was left of this unfortunate child. We then fled the area, shocked to the core.

Once, on our way to school, my friend and I came across an abandoned munitions warehouse, and we crawled inside through a small opening in a wall. What a treasure trove it contained! Grenades, bullets, etc. We quickly transferred all our schoolbooks into one knapsack, and then stuffed as much ammunition as we could into the second knapsack. The knapsack became very heavy, and we had to drag it along the ground all the way to school.

We arrived in school before the bell rang, and we brought the heavy knapsack into our classroom and emptied our treasure onto the back bench in the classroom. We didn't notice when the teacher entered the room. She peeked under our desk, let out a scream, and fled into the corridor.

A minute later, the assistant principal burst into our classroom and shouted, "Collect all that junk and remove it from the school premises!"

He didn't tell us to leave the classroom immediately, nor did he call upon a munitions expert to neutralize our contraband. Unlike us naïve children, he understood very well the danger to which he was exposing us, but he didn't care that we were liable to blow ourselves up.

Listlessly, we dragged the knapsack out to the yard, wondering where we could throw our treasures so that the school staff would not be angry at us. Without thinking much, we decided to throw it into a cesspool in the outhouse in the yard. We managed to take a few steps away from the outhouse before a powerful explosion rocked the wooden hut, sending it flying upward along with all of its contents. We walked away from the site without a scratch.

The children of the orphanage did not fear death, nor did we have any compassion toward others. No one cared about us and no one loved us, so our lives and the lives of others had little value in our eyes. We were the kind of children who later grew into ruthless professional killers, of the type employed by the army and the establishment to carry out the most dangerous and gruesome assignments. If they did not return, no one would ever mourn them.

Many of the children I grew up with became criminals and landed in jail. Had I remained in the orphanage, my lot could easily have been the same as theirs. But one day, after six years in the orphanage, my life changed dramatically.

Part III
Coming Home

ברכות הורים בערב יום הכפורים.

Vintage postcard: Parents blessing their children on Erev Yom Kippur

Where Were You?

It was a day that I will never forget. I was 11 years old, and it was Election Day in the Soviet Union. (Of course, elections in the Soviet Union were a farce: There was never more than one candidate for each position, and that candidate was chosen by the government.)

Election Day was an exciting day in the orphanage. On Election Day, we received better food and new clothing, and we were taken to a voting station to perform before the voters. The atmosphere at the voting stations was uplifting, with music playing and people milling about. The people congregated mostly around the cafeteria, where rare delicacies were sold in honor of Election Day — hot dogs, oranges, mandarins — all to attract people to come vote.

As part of the Election Day festivities, the children of the orphanage would put on a performance. We were thin, clad in shabby grey uniforms, with our heads cleanly shaven, but we felt festive and important. Now, looking back, I understand that our pathetic appearance caused the goodhearted "aunties" in the audience to shed a tear and give us a rousing round of applause. We felt honored by their approval, and we were proud to have the opportunity to perform on such an important occasion.

We each received new clothing and shoes for the performance, but these treasures were taken from us upon our return to the orphanage after the performance. We therefore made sure to tear our new clothing and remove the heels from our shoes and hide them in our pockets, for if the clothing were ruined we would be allowed to keep it. Later, we would repair the damaged clothing ourselves and glue the heels back onto our shoes, and voila — we had new clothes and shoes!

On this particular Election Day, we performed in the voting

station at the school for engineers. Some of the children sang, and others danced, while I was given the role of reciting poems written by the poet Mayakovsky. I performed my part admirably, reading aloud, with expression, while moving my hands rhythmically and placing one foot to the side. I did not experience stage fright.

The moment I finished my performance and descended from the stage, a tall, heavyset woman approached me, gave me a strange look, and asked, "Tell me, child, what is your name?"

"Sasha Granitni," I replied, certain that she had been impressed with my recital of the poems.

She continued to stare at me, without any pretense of politeness. Then, she said, "No, child, you have another name. Tell me, do you have a mouse-shaped birthmark on your right thigh?"

"I do," I said, wondering how this woman could possibly have known that.

"Show it to me!" she commanded.

I was embarrassed. But the woman did not wait for me to obey her — she proceeded to lift my right pant leg and looked at my birthmark. Then she burst into tears.

"You have a family," she told me. "A father, a mother, a grandmother — come, I'll take you to them."

I released myself from her grip. "What are you talking about?" I protested. "I'm not going anywhere with you."

But the woman grabbed me and dragged me out to the street. I did not want to fight with her, so I decided to go along with her and see where she was taking me.

We had walked only about 20 steps in the street when a diminutive older woman, wearing a kerchief on her head, emerged from a neighboring courtyard. The woman who was pulling me called out to her, "Faiga! Faiga!"

"What do you want, Motia?" the older woman asked.

"Faiga, look who I'm bringing you!"

"Who?"

"It's your grandson!"

"Which grandson?"

"Moshe's son."

"Motia, what are you talking about?" the older woman cried out. "Even the bones of Moshe's son no longer exist."

"Look at his face," the woman insisted. "He resembles his grandfather."

"I myself don't remember what my husband looked like," the old woman retorted. "And you remember?"

They went on arguing this way, while I stood at the side and listened.

"Do you remember what the boy had on his right leg?" Motia finally said. "We brought him home from the hospital together, remember?"

"Of course I remember!" the old woman retorted. "When my daughter-in-law Zena[11] was expecting, a mouse ran past her. She became very startled and grabbed her leg. When the baby was born, he had a birthmark on his right leg."

At that point, Motia and Faiga pounced on me and brought me into the courtyard from which Faiga had just emerged. Paying no heed to my protests, they again examined my birthmark, and then they both burst into tears.

I didn't understand what was happening, and I wasn't sure whether to run away or stay there.

Crying, they took me by the hand and brought me into the house.

As we climbed the stairs to the balcony, the door of the house opened, and a younger woman, short, plump, and pretty, appeared in the doorway. She looked at me and froze. Her eyes widened, and then she said softly, "My son, how I've waited for you! Where were you all this time?"

My heart skipped a beat. Not believing what was happening, I asked, "How do you know that I'm your son?"

"I know," she insisted. "You're mine!" She said these words with such conviction that my doubts melted away. My knees trembled, and I could not move.

---

11. Zissel was called "Zena" in Russian.

That was how I was reunited with Mama.

The two women who had brought me stood at the side and wept, while my mother and I stood there speechless, just looking at each other. She was afraid to come over to me and give me a hug, and I was afraid as well. Even afterward, for the rest of our lives, we were both embarrassed to express our feelings to each other. I have regrets about that to this day.

Mama brought me into the house and seated me next to a large table. She placed a plate of food before me and went to call her husband.

Her words were short and to the point. "The boy was found!" she said excitedly.

She did not ask me any questions, nor did she examine my birth-mark.

I was hungry, but my throat was dry. I ate slowly, trying to take in my surroundings.

I liked the house. It was clean and neat, and the atmosphere was warm and pleasant, with a fragrant aroma wafting through the air. There was a beautiful engraved cupboard next to the wall, and an ancient wooden box in the corner (that would later serve as my bed); carpets were hung on the walls, and lace doilies adorned all the furniture, even the footstool of the sofa.

A short while later, Papa arrived. He was a giant of a man, and he held my head with his large hand. Like my mother, he did not examine me at all.

"My son," he exclaimed, "where have you been?" He had a strong, rolling voice, suited to his physique.

"Why do you think that I'm your son?" I asked warily.

It was hard for me to believe that these were my parents. Maybe it was a mistake, and they would just throw me out when they learned that I was not who they thought I was. It had happened many a time that a child was taken from our orphanage by a family and then sent back, and there was no child in the world more piti-able than he. Everyone ridiculed them, and they were beaten by the teachers and the children of the orphanage alike, as though they were responsible for having been sent back.

"I know that you're mine!" Papa embraced me and gave me a kiss.

I was seated at the table near Papa, and food was served again. Papa asked Mama to bring vodka, and he poured himself a shot and downed it in one gulp. He then downed a second shot of vodka, and a third. I don't remember ever seeing Papa drink after that, except for on one other occasion.

Who was the woman who recognized me and returned me to my family?

She was Matriona (Matia) Olchovski, the same woman who had smuggled me out of the ghetto.

Who Am I?

I stayed in my parents' home that day until it was late, and then Papa accompanied me back to the orphanage. He entered the home of Director Slavin, despite the late hour, while I ran back to my friends. I felt bad about one thing: I hadn't managed to ruin my festive clothing, and when I returned to the orphanage the new clothes were taken from me immediately. At any other time, I would have been terribly distressed over this, but tonight I had other things to think about.

I was very excited, but I tried mightily to keep my news a secret and not tell anyone that my family had been found, at least until the matter would be resolved one way or another. I did not manage to control myself, however, and I told my secret to my best friend. This friend immediately revealed my secret to the other children, and I was beaten roundly as a result. The beating was obviously rooted in jealousy, although the children claimed that I was being beaten for having betrayed and abandoned them in favor of my family. What hurt me the most was the fact that it was not only the children who bothered me habitually who were beating me now, it was also the children whom I had considered my friends. Now, I was a stranger to all of them.

The following day, I went to school as usual. When I emerged from school after dismissal, I saw an older woman standing near the gate. It was Bubbe Faiga. Apparently, she had come to bring me home. Embarrassed to approach her in front of the other boys, and afraid of being punished by the children of the orphanage, I slipped out of school through a back door. Bubbe Faiga stood waiting at the gate until the school was empty, but she did not see me.

I wandered through the city restlessly for several hours. Finally, I could not contain myself, and I ran to the house where my newfound family lived. In the evening, when I returned to the orphanage, I was beaten brutally.

From then on, I found myself in a no-win situation. Whenever I went to my family, I paid for it with a beating at the hands of my friends. In an attempt to appease the children of the orphanage, I would bring them Bubbe Faiga's tasty cakes. They ate the cakes, and then they beat me anyway. I did not tell my family anything about these beatings, for they could not help me in any case.

I myself did not know where my place was. In order to remove me from the orphanage, Papa had to prove that I was his son, and this was no simple matter. Like many other children in the orphanage, I was registered as a Russian, while my family was Jewish. And no official would agree to change my status from "Russian" to "Jewish."

The pieces of evidence that proved my identity conclusively were archived documents from the trial of Nikolai Olchovski, the former Nazi police officer who had rescued my family from the ghetto.

At the end of the war, Olchovski and other Ukrainians who collaborated with the Nazis and participated in mass killings were brought to judgment. The sentence for crimes like these was unequivocal: death by shooting. What saved Olchovski's life was the testimony of Bubbe Faiga during his trial. Speaking Yiddish, with the help of an interpreter, Bubbe Faiga testified that Olchovski had saved a Jewish family. Thanks to her testimony, Olchovski's death sentence was commuted to 25 years in Siberia.

Motia, Nikolai Olchovski's wife, would frequently say that Bubbe Faiga had saved her husband's life.

As long as Olchovski was in Siberia, Papa helped his wife Motia and their two daughters. After Olchovski finished serving his sentence and returned home, he built a high fence around his house and declared that he wanted nothing to do with the Soviet authorities.

The documents from Olchovski's trial stated that Olchovski had hidden a Jewish child in the home of a family living in the village of Granitnoe, and that family had handed the child over to a German orphanage. The documents also stated that a German named Schultz had taken the child from the orphanage to Germany. The orphanage of which I was currently a ward possessed documents stating that in 1944 Sasha Granitni had been brought to a concentration camp by Elsa Schultz.

In this way, the circle was closed, and it was proven that I was not Sasha Granitni, the Russian, but Shepsel Gutman, the Jew.

Papa's acquaintances advised him to keep me registered under my current status. "It's better for him to remain registered as a Russian, with a Russian surname," they said. "It will make his life easier."

Papa's answer was unequivocal: "He's a Jew, and he has to know why he's being beaten! He'll carry our family name."

When I was asked in court what I wanted to do, I replied, "Let it be as my father requests."

The court did not agree, however, and Papa had to bribe the people in charge, plying them with money and vodka in order to convince them to register me as a Jew. He did not manage to have them change my name to Shepsel — *that* they refused to do at any cost.

"There is no such name," they told Papa, and they gave me the name Semyon. I continued to be called Sasha in school and at home, though. Only Bubbe Faiga called me by my real name: Shepsel.

Russia's "Jewish Problem"

וַיֹּאמֶר הָמָן לַמֶּלֶךְ אֲחַשְׁוֵרוֹשׁ יֶשְׁנוֹ עַם אֶחָד מְפֻזָּר וּמְפֹרָד בֵּין הָעַמִּים בְּכֹל
מְדִינוֹת מַלְכוּתֶךָ וְדָתֵיהֶם שֹׁנוֹת מִכָּל עָם וְאֶת דָּתֵי הַמֶּלֶךְ אֵינָם עֹשִׂים
וְלַמֶּלֶךְ אֵין שֹׁוֶה לְהַנִּיחָם (אסתר ג:ח).

Then Haman said to King Achashverosh, "There is a certain people scattered abroad and dispersed among the peoples in all the provinces of your realm. Their laws are different from every other people's and they do not observe the king's laws; therefore it is not befitting the king to tolerate them" (Esther 3:8).

In his work, The History of the Jews in Russia, *the Russian historian Iulii Gessen writes the following:*

The first group of Russian laws regarding the Jews was passed in 1804. For nearly 100 years, the spirit of these laws did not change, and the Jew remained an illegal entity. The only solution to the "Jewish problem" that was acceptable to the czarist regime was mass conversion.

The person who set the tone for these laws was the famous Russian poet and justice minister Derzhavin, who "investigated" the condition of the Jews and in 1802 presented the czar with a "reeducation" program to be imposed on the Jews by force. This program constituted the basis for cruel legislation.

Derzhavin suspected mutiny at every turn, and he was doubtful "whether the Zhids are capable of benefiting the state."

Derzhavin named "Talmudism" as the main cause of the Jewish problem. He explained that even the Jewish custom of covering one's head was rooted in the fact that they "consider themselves superior to all other peoples." Jews, he said, accumulate wealth not for the same reasons as all other people, but for the sake of "rebuilding the Temple in Palestine."

"We must also credit to [the Jews'] slyness the fact that many of them have similar names — there are many Moshes, Avrahams, Leibs, Chaims, etc. In addition, they all wear the same black garment, and that is what creates confusion and causes the distinction between them to be blurred — particularly when they are counted or when there is a need to distinguish between them for monetary [tax] purposes and investigations."

Derzhavin suggested that Russian epithets be appended to the Jews' names — pejorative nicknames like "Zamislovaty" [sly one], "Diky" [wild one], and the like to facilitate the census and for the purpose of law and order. At the beginning of the twentieth century, Jews in Russia did not have surnames; instead, they used names and titles that were often connected to their occupation or place of residence. During this period, however, Russian Jews began to assume surnames.

Fargess!

W hen I rejoined my family and began telling them about my life, Mama and Bubbe Faiga cried incessantly. Auntie Motia, who had found me and brought me home, used to interrogate me when she visited as well, and then all three of them would cry. If other friends or relatives would come, the scene would repeat itself: They would ask me questions; I would answer; they would cry; I would be silent.

Only Papa did not interrogate me and did not ask me any questions, for he did not want me to dwell on my past. Once, when guests arrived and the questions began, he could not contain himself. He closed his eyes tightly, as though he was experiencing a sharp pain, tightened his fists, pounded on the table, and cried out, forcing back tears: "*Fargess* [Forget it]! Enough! There's no more talking about this. Zissel, bring a cup of vodka quickly."

Mama ran to bring him a cup of vodka, and he downed it in one gulp. This was the second and final time I ever saw Papa drink vodka; the other time had been on the day I was found.

Papa's word was law in our house, and from that day on, the questions ceased.

Papa entrusted me to the devoted care of Mama and Bubbe Faiga, hoping that their kindheartedness would melt the ice and enable me to feel like a part of the family. Nonetheless, he personally oversaw and took an interest in my daily life. Often, he would call home from work to find out what I was up to.

Already during the first few days after my return to my family, a strong bond formed between me and my mother and grandmother, who doted on me and demonstrated tremendous concern for me. I was glum and withdrawn, however, and I did not trust anyone. I was easily startled by any sudden move, like a wild animal. Mama and Bubbe Faiga understood this very well.

It took a long time for me to become accustomed to my parents' house, and during that time I refused to submit to authority. I did not want to follow the daily schedule of the house, and many times I ran back to the orphanage to sleep.

The nights were especially difficult for me at home. When everyone retreated to their rooms to sleep, it was quiet and dark in the house, and sadness engulfed me. I was used to living in a group, and cruel and crude as that group was, I was part of it; I was never alone.

In the orphanage, I had to be on guard every night to ensure that I did not fall prey to some prank. At times, I myself played pranks on other children. When you weren't the victim of the prank, it was very funny.

One of our pranks was called "guitar" or "bicycle." We would choose a child who was in a deep sleep as our victim, stick pieces of cotton wool between his fingers or toes, and then set them afire. The fire would spread through the cotton and the poor sleeping child would begin shaking his hands violently, trying to get rid of the burning sensation. We called this "playing the guitar." If his feet were afire, we would call it, "riding a bicycle."

In our group, it was dangerous to be left alone, without a friend, for even a minute: You always had to guard your back. The children were therefore willing to give up their last morsel of food just to make friends with someone.

I was very well acquainted with the rules of our group, and I knew no other set of rules. Strange as it sounds, I felt closer to the children of the orphanage than to my parents. I had grown up with these children, and I was more interested in them than in my family. It is not surprising, therefore, that I did not wish to move to my parents' house.

In my parents' house, when I was alone at night, lying on clean, comfortable linens placed over the wooden box, I whimpered like a puppy. At those times, I thought that it would have been better if my family had never found me.

The Hooligans' School

I was torn between my family and the orphanage. When Bubbe Faiga admonished me, I ran to the orphanage, and when I was beaten in the orphanage, I ran home. My parents did not force me to stay with them. I was very stubborn, and had they forced me to do anything, I would have done exactly the opposite.

For half a year, I could not find my place — not at home, and not in the orphanage. It was a very difficult period for me.

When Papa finally managed to prove that I was their son and to make all the legal arrangements, he told me, "It's enough running around — now you'll stay at home."

By instruction of the director, I was no longer allowed to enter the property of the orphanage; perhaps Papa had requested this. In any event, the children of the orphanage beat me savagely when I was in their presence. So I had no choice but to become "domesticated."

I may have become domesticated — but I was not tamed. To the children of the orphanage, adults were the enemy, and I harbored a powerful desire to cause trouble for adults.

After I joined my family, I continued to behave the way I had behaved in the orphanage. But Papa never hit me — except for one occasion, and that was because of Mama. She was washing the floor one day, and she crawled under the bed. The bed was heavy, and Mama — who was a heavyset woman — was unable to extricate herself from underneath it. I stood at the side, watching her and laughing; it did not even occur to me to help her. Just at that moment, Papa arrived. He lifted the bed, freed Mama, and gave me a slap.

Bubbe Faiga occasionally hit me with her stick as a punishment for the pranks I played on those around me. She had her own methods of child-rearing, and she tried every tactic she knew to tame her unruly grandchild.

At times, Bubbe Faiga asked me to watch my five-year-old brother, hoping that this would arouse warm feelings in me toward him. Having to watch him only made me angry, however, for I chafed at any attempt to curtail my freedom. I would tie my little brother's foot to a tree to make sure that he would not run around my legs or disturb my soccer game. So happy was he to come along with me that he bore this treatment silently, without complaint.

My parents had hopes of turning me into a "normal" Jewish child,[12] and they even bought me a violin and hired a music teacher to teach me. Initially, I agreed to this arrangement out of curiosity, but the moment the violin reached my hands, I hurried to trade it with another child for a pair of skates. Disregarding the fact that the skates were mismatched, I tied them onto my shoes with string and skated blissfully on the ice. Eventually, the child who received

12 At that time, Jewish children were expected to learn to play a musical instrument and to excel in their general studies. This would enhance their prospects of earning a livelihood later in life.

my violin in exchange for his skates became a professional violinist.

My parents gave up on teaching me to play the violin after this incident. They did not even become angry at me for having traded it; this was far from the worst trouble I caused them.

One of my pranks landed on Papa's head, almost literally. One morning, when Papa was on his way to work, he passed my school at a time when a test was supposed to be administered, much to the students' chagrin. I quickly devised an innovative way to avoid having to take the test: Before the teacher entered the classroom, I took the box containing all the inkwells that we used to dip our quills in, and threw it out the window of the third floor, onto the street.

The box landed precisely at Papa's feet, splattering him with ink from head to toe. He was forced to return home to shower and change his clothing. Papa was very angry, and declared that he would no longer walk past the "hooligans' school." From then on, he maintained a safe distance from the school building.

Fortunately for me, he never did discover who had thrown the box of inkwells out the window.

Unpunishable

Mama

Even after I joined my family, I remained an angry, restless street kid, and I incessantly annoyed and harassed the people around me. Now, as an adult, I realize that I was in need then of a good psychologist. But who could think about trivial things like that during that Stalinist postwar period? At that time, people were concerned mainly with survival.

Mama had a very gentle, kindhearted nature, and she never became angry at me, no matter how naughty I was. Instead, she tried to win me over with words and awaken my conscience and good sense. Her attempts were futile, however.

Owing to Mama's soft nature, Bubbe nicknamed her, "Zissel *Lekach*" (*lekach* is Yiddish for "honey cake").

Bubbe and Mama understood each other without having to utter more than half a word. Their conversation was interspersed with light humor, and this amusing banter created a very pleasant, comfortable atmosphere in the house. The two of them complemented each other perfectly, and I enjoyed their good humor and the respectful way they treated each other.

The moment I entered the family, however, their harmonious relationship was swiftly disrupted. When I was involved, Bubbe Faiga's absolute control over the household evaporated, for Mama stood her ground and would not yield to anyone in matters that had to do with me.

Once, I threw a rock at one of the Jewish kids in our neighborhood and split his head open. This boy was the grandson of Bubbe's friend, and his parents came to our house to complain. Bubbe shouted at me angrily, and insisted that Mama punish me. But Mama cut her off in mid-sentence. "Go into your room, Mama," she shouted at her. "I'll take care of him myself."

This was the first time I ever heard Mama raise her voice to Bubbe.

After the neighbors left the house, Mama announced in that same uncharacteristically vehement tone, "No one will have the privilege of seeing me punish my son!"

Bubbe slunk behind Mama's back and quietly slipped away into her room.

All her life, Mama carried in her heart an unbearably intense burden of guilt for what I had suffered, and that made me unpunishable in her eyes. When I was exceptionally naughty, such as the time I split open the other boy's head, she would sit down beside me and cry bitterly, "*Vey iz mir* [woe unto me]! What will become of you when you grow older? You threw a rock and cut open the head of a child you don't even know — why? Why should the neighbors have to come and complain about you? I'm not going to hit you, but if I tell Papa, it will be terrible!"

When my little brother misbehaved, Mama didn't cry. But if I was the one who made trouble, she would cry bitterly. I wasn't afraid of anyone, but Mama's tears made me feel ashamed, and I took pity on her. I think that was the only thing that reined in my behavior somewhat.

Mama and I had a special bond that is difficult to describe in words. This bond was forged the moment I returned home, and it endured for the rest of our lives.

Mama always knew when something happened to me, even if I was far away, and I had a similar sense about her. Even when I was an adult, she would not go to sleep at night until I returned home. She would stand by the window and wait up for me, no matter how late it was. During all the years I lived in my parents' home, I never had a key to the house, even though my younger brother did. Mama would always tell me, "You'll come home and I'll open the door for you."

She continued to wait for me all her life. Apparently, she still carried inside her the pain of our separation. Once, when I was already living in a different city and I came home for a few days, I visited a friend and stayed there overnight. When I returned home in the morning, I saw Mama standing by the window. She had stayed up the entire night waiting for me.

Years later, I was vacationing with my elder daughter in the Carpathian Mountains, when I suddenly sensed that something was wrong. "For some reason, I'm worried about your grandmother," I told my daughter. "I'm going to the post office to call her."

My brother answered the phone when I called and told me that my mother had suffered a heart attack and was in the hospital. That very night, I traveled back to Zhitomir, where I was living at the time, dropped my daughter off at home, and hurried to the airport. By the morning, I was already standing beside Mama's hospital bed in Donetsk, having traveled a distance of over 1,000 kilometers (600 miles).

Papa

Mama and Bubbe tried not to tell Papa about my shenanigans, for they did not wish to cause Papa distress. To me, Papa was a threatening figure, but that did not deter me from continuing to make trouble; that was the only way I knew how to get what I wanted.

Papa paid close attention to what I was doing, but he never punished me — except for the time he slapped me for laughing when Mama was stuck under the bed.

When I joined the family, I did not hide the fact that I smoked —I was proud of it, in fact. Like other children in the orphanage, I smoked cigarette butts that we found in the streets. Once I began living at home, I would request or even steal cigarettes from Papa.

Papa was the director of a department in a large store, and I often joined him at work, ostensibly to help him move merchandise. I was *really* there to steal cigarettes and candies. I would bring my loot to the children of the orphanage, trying to prove to them that they were more beloved to me than my father was.

Papa realized that I was stealing, but he did not scold me. The next time I asked him for a cigarette, however, he said, "If you want to smoke, you can smoke your own cigarettes. I've stopped smoking."

"But I don't have money!" I protested.

"That's your problem," he replied. And he indeed stopped smoking.

A short while after I made my appearance, a severe quarrel erupted between Mama and Bubbe; it's possible that the quarrel had something to do with my behavior. When Papa returned home from work that day, the two of them ran to him with tears in their eyes, each one complaining about the other.

They spoke Yiddish, so I did not understand much of what they were saying, but I was sitting at the side and I saw everything.

"Zissel, go out," Papa said to Mama calmly. "And you, Mama, sit down," he told Bubbe.

Bubbe Faiga told him something animatedly. He listened to her, and then said, "If you have complaints against my wife in the future, please tell me and I will deal with it myself."

When Bubbe Faiga left the room, Mama returned and sat in her place. The same scene repeated itself: Papa told Mama, "If you have a problem with my mother, please tell me, and I'll take care of it myself."

I was very impressed with the way Papa dealt with this situation.

The next day, I came home from school at five o'clock in the evening, and I heard Bubbe telling Mama, "Zissel, it's almost time for Moshe to come home from work!"

No hint of yesterday's argument remained. The two of them hurried to put themselves together and beautify themselves in advance of Papa's arrival.

This was an example of Bubbe Faiga's feminine wisdom: She believed that a woman has to be pleasing to her husband. In keeping with this advice, Mama never met Papa in a housecoat. Before going out to greet Papa, she always put on a dress, makeup, and high-heeled shoes.

In the Right Time!

Bubbe

Bubbe Faiga had an amazing influence on the people around her. She devoted her entire day to helping people, and the neighbors loved her and honored her greatly.

She was short in stature, thin, and sprightly, and she never used a cane when she walked. Her cane was used for disciplinary purposes only. When the gentile neighbors fought in the street, or if a drunken husband hit his wife, people would hurry to call Bubbe Faiga. When she would arrive, she would hit the aggressors with her stick, and the fight would be over. It sounds strange, but that's how it was.

When the neighbors would argue, they would come to Bubbe Faiga to mediate their conflicts. Before hearing the claims of the two sides, she would place her hand inside the deep pocket of her dark, wide skirt, and remove a large, ancient five-kopeck copper coin from the czarist period. Then, she would say in her lilting Yiddish accent, "Yours is *rol*, and yours, *reshka*."[13]

Bubbe Faiga would throw the coin into the air, and the neighbor whose side the coin fell on would stay inside and present his claims, while the other neighbor would go out and wait behind the door. After listening to both parties separately, Bubbe Faiga would usher both of them inside and issue her ruling.

"You are incorrect on this count," she would tell one party, "so you have to pay him three rubles."

She would turn to the other party and say, "And on this count you are wrong, so you owe him two rubles."

Then, she would conclude, "And you each owe me one ruble."

And both sides would be satisfied with her ruling.

In addition to coming to Bubbe for mediation, the neighbors would also come to her for her sage advice.

In the yard of our house was a cellar where we stored potatoes, pickled vegetables, wine, and Bubbe Faiga's samogon (homemade vodka).[14] Samogon was a widely accepted currency — you could use it to pay for all sorts of services.

When one of our thirsty neighbors would come to Bubbe to borrow money for vodka, she would say, "I don't give money for vodka. But if you can't control yourself, go into my cellar and drink as

---

13. These were the two sides of a coin in the Russian vernacular, roughly the equivalent of "heads" and "tails" in English.
14. Production of samogon was illegal. The right to produce and sell alcoholic beverages belonged exclusively to the government.

much as you want. Just make sure to leave on your own two feet, because I don't plan to remove you from there."

She never checked how much the neighbors drank or what they took from the cellar, and they greatly appreciated the trust she placed in them. Surprisingly, they never stole anything from Bubbe Faiga — even though stealing was de rigueur among the general population. On our property, if an apple or apricot fell from the tree to the ground, no one dared to touch it, even as the neighbors' trees were stripped bare by thieves.

During that period, every family on our street had at least one member who had sat in jail for theft or fighting. Any time the police arrested someone in the neighborhood, the neighbors would call Bubbe Faiga. She would go to the office of the police chief and put up such a fuss that the police would occasionally release the detainee just to avoid having to deal with her.

She devised ingenious ways to avoid hurting or embarrassing people. When guests came to our house, Bubbe Faiga never asked whether he wanted to eat. Instead, she would say happily, "You came just at the right time — I was just about to sit down to eat. Come sit with me and keep me company."

Even the most bashful people could not refuse this offer, and they sat down to eat with her. Knowing that Bubbe Faiga had just finished eating prior to the guest's arrival, I marveled at the way she always managed to sit and eat again with her guests.

At times, the Greeks who had hidden Bubbe Faiga and Mama during the war would come from their village to visit. Bubbe Faiga would stuff their handbags with food, shower them with gifts and money, and set the table with the best foods she had in the house. Mama would sit with them and eat, but Bubbe Faiga would stand the entire time and wait on the honored guests.

Bubbe's "Children"

Bubbe spoke only Yiddish, although she knew Russian and Ukrainian as well. She addressed everyone in Yiddish, even when she was in the grocery or the marketplace, and, wonder of wonders, they understood her! I don't recall anyone in our anti-Semitic city ever making a disparaging remark in response to Bubbe's Yiddish. Because of Bubbe Faiga, some of our gentile neighbors actually began speaking Yiddish.

After the war, there were no preschools, and the young children wandered the streets with no supervision. Bubbe Faiga gathered all the children of the neighborhood, kept them under her watchful eye, and fed them. In this way, the children learned to speak Yiddish.

Bubbe claimed that she did not know how to pronounce gentile names, and she would change the children's names to suit her taste: Slavik became Sarik; Alyosha became Yossi (this name clung to him to the extent that even his Ukrainian parents called him "Yossik"); Oleg she renamed "Solomon," owing to his cleverness and cunning, and this name stuck to him permanently.[15]

These children were known in the city as "Bubbe's children." When one of these children misbehaved in school, and the school summoned his parents, the child would run to her and cry, "Bubbe Faiga, help!" Bubbe would then tie a large shawl over her usual kerchief and head to the school. There, she would explain that she had come in place of the parents, who were at work.

She would say that she didn't understand Russian, so they would bring her an interpreter: Anna Israelevna. Bubbe Faiga would listen patiently to all the accusations leveled against the child, and she would always say, "It's not so terrible. He'll grow up a year,

---

15. Eventually, Oleg was appointed to the position of Deputy Agriculture Minister in the Ukraine.

he'll become a year wiser, and then he won't do silly things like this anymore."

In the evening, the neighbor would ask her, "Faiga, you were in the school — what did Solomon do there already?"

She would answer, "They said that there's no child in the world who's better than your Solomon!"

From the time I moved in with my family, the children of the orphanage harbored a grudge against me. My lot would have been bitter indeed, if not for my classmates who were "Bubbe's children." These children protected me from the children of the orphanage and did not allow them to harm me.

The world outside our house was harsh and brutal. The local children fought with the children of the orphanage; the children of one street plotted against the children of a different street. The concept of gratitude was nonexistent — on the contrary, if you did someone a favor, that person would repay you with evil. In this ruthless environment, our house was a lone island that was governed by different rules, rules that were unknown to me and unheard of during that period.

Part IV
Stranger

*Graduates of Shepsel's elementary school class. Shepsel is second from right;
in the middle, holding a bouquet of flowers, is the teacher Shatalov.*

Anti-Torah Edicts

From the czar's edicts (mid-19th century):

"Even to Siberia, when serving a criminal sentence, the Jews should not be allowed to take their wives with them, so that they do not proliferate and harm the Russian heartland through their Judaism."

The czarist government concluded that the true reason for the Jews' religious extremism and isolationism was Torah study. All attempts to extinguish the light of Torah failed, whether the authorities tried to conscript Jewish children to the army through the Cantonist laws or to expel the Jews from their towns. Consequently, only one other method of preventing Torah study remained, and that was "Enlightenment":

"For this purpose, the cheders must be replaced with Jewish elementary schools in which the students will learn the Russian language and other secular studies. With time, this will cause the Jews to abandon their faith."

It should be noted that the vast majority of the Russian population was illiterate at that time. The government made no efforts to educate these ignorant masses, choosing instead to focus on promoting secular studies and education among the Jews — who were already literate and learned — in order to cause them to abandon their heritage.

With Utmost Secrecy

Despite the ban on Jewish observance imposed by the Soviet authorities, my parents' home was a hub of religious activity. In our home, Jews congregated for Shabbos and Yom Tov prayers;

matzos were baked; and *brissin* took place for children whose parents were afraid to have the ceremony performed in their own homes. Each of these activities was punishable by many years in prison.

Life was not easy for my family, and my arrival complicated things even more. Before I joined the family, they had to fear being discovered by outsiders; now, they also had to hide their religious activities from their son, who was a product of a Soviet orphanage and school. For a long time, I did not suspect anything, and my parents were forced to employ various strategies in order to keep me in the dark. They had good reason to be fearful, too; I could easily have told my friends what was going on in our home, and my friends were all would-be Pavlik Morozovs.

Pavlik Morozov: Informer 001

In the Soviet Union, informants young and old were enthusiastically encouraged for their "patriotism," and Soviet citizens were expected to inform on one another as a matter of course. In this way, the authorities prevented any sort of "foreign thoughts" and instilled fear and unquestioning obedience into the population. People accused of entertaining "foreign thoughts" were arrested and even killed.

The following is an excerpt from the documentary book, Informer 001: The Myth of Pavlik Morozov, *written by Yuri Druzhnikov in the 1980s:*

Pavlik Morozov, a member of the Pioneer youth group (for youths ages 9-14), denounced his father to the authorities in the 1930s and was killed by his relatives for doing so. At least that is the official version of the story. What actually happened was that the young informant spied on all the people in his village, and the number of people killed or harmed as a result of his actions and denunciations reached double digits. He was secretly killed by government agents in order to concoct an excuse for beginning a murderous campaign throughout the country. He was necessary as a role model: The existence of family was troublesome to the Communist Party, and the informant son had torn the family apart from within.[1]

Judgments like these (similar to that of Pavlik Morozov) were planned in advance, with neither the victim nor the participants having any inkling what their role in the spectacle was. Before a judgment began, the authorities did not search for a guilty party, but rather for an appropriate person to be convicted as the murderer or felon. During these trials, the informant children testified against their family members. The authorities devised a plan in which the new generation would wipe out the old. In the leadership convention of the Communist Party, it was said in the name of Stalin, "Pavlik has to become a supreme role model to all the children of the Soviet Union."

… It was far easier to convince children that a despicable act was a brave act under the new system, and in this way, a mass network of informants was created.

Statues of Pavlik the informant were erected, streets and schools were named after him, and opera and poems were composed in his honor. The author of the book Pavlik Morozov *describes one of these poems:*

The idea behind this plan was to convey that when Pavlik Morozov betrays his father, he knows that he will have a new father:

> *Father — a cherished word*
> *The nation expresses its love*
> *To Stalin, with this word.*

If he has a new father — i.e., Stalin — why would he need his old-fashioned biological father? Of the two fathers, the child chooses the one who will lead him into an "enlightened future."

---

1. The communists viewed the family unit as a threat, since families are united and strong and preserve traditions and values antithetical to communism. The communists therefore had a strong interest in breaking up families, and causing children to denounce and turn against their parents was an ideal way to accomplish this.

From the newspaper Pionerskaya Pravda *(Truth for Young Pioneers), 1933: "Millions like Pavlik are studying in schools ...."*

From Pionerskaya Pravda, *1936: "Two hundred children are traveling on vacation to the Crimean Peninsula, to the beautiful Artek summer camp for pioneers."*

In this way, the vacation spot on the bank of the Black Sea became the official vacationing spot for young "volunteer informants."

At the beginning of the 1970s, the Soviet press published an article containing a confession of a former counselor in the Artek Pioneer camp. This counselor worked in Artek in the 1940s, and she didn't dare to tell her story for over 30 years.

One year, she said, the thousands of campers in attendance during the three summer camp sessions were all children who had imitated the "courageous"

act of Pavlik Morozov, informing on their parents and causing them to be executed. As a sign of appreciation for their bravery, these children were sent to this vacation village. During the daytime hours, the children tried their hardest to appear brave and patriotic before their friends. But at night, this camp counselor recalled, she was afraid to even enter their rooms, because there were dozens of children there sleepwalking, fitfully moaning, crying, and calling for their mothers.

In the town squares and parks, in the schools and orphanages — everywhere, in short — statues of Stalin were erected and his picture was hung on the walls. In school, we recited in unison the chorus, "Thank you, Comrade Stalin, for our happy childhood." We also sang, "Stalin is our father, he's our battle flag." And we all believed that this was true.

My parents were reunited with me after I had been thoroughly brainwashed, and they therefore had good reason to be afraid of me. They understood the danger from the start, and my presence in the house forced them to take emergency measures.

The first time I entered my parents' house, I noticed that the wall of their living room was adorned with a beautiful maroon velvet wall-hanging embroidered with lions and clusters of grapes. A few days later, when I returned home from school, I saw that the rug was gone, and in its place hung a large picture of Stalin, surrounded by a heavy gilded frame. I was very pleased with the picture, thinking that it added a distinguished dimension to the house.

"What a nice picture," I commented approvingly. "But why did you take down the rug? You could have hung the picture somewhere else."

I did not receive an answer. The truth was that the picture had been hung there for me, in an attempt to divert my "Pioneer Scout" eyes. Every Shabbos morning, men came to our house to pray in the living room near the picture in the gilded frame. This did not surprise me; I was accustomed to seeing people gathered near this type of picture, both in the orphanage and at school.

The moment I left for school, the Jewish visitors moved the picture of the great Leader and withdrew the *Sefer Torah* from its hiding place in the wall. (Prior to my arrival, the *Sefer Torah's* hiding place had been covered with a *paroches* — the beautiful velvet wall-hanging I had seen.) They then began to *daven* Shacharis of Shabbos. At the conclusion of the prayers, they returned the *Sefer Torah* to its place and covered it again with the picture. Had the authorities discovered the *Sefer Torah*, all the people present would have been thrown into jail.

I believe that it was none other than Bubbe Faiga who came up with the ingenious strategy of exploiting people's absolute reverence for the Leader in order to keep me unaware of what was actually going on. She always managed to find creative solutions for problems. As I learned a short while later, Bubbe managed to fool not only me with the picture of Stalin, but also an enemy who was far more dangerous than I.

The Strange Hut

There was a small hut in our yard that served as a summer kitchen.[2] One section of the hut was reserved for storage, and no one but Bubbe ever entered that section. When Bubbe would enter, she would always lock the door behind her. I was very curious to know what she kept there. *It must be something very special and tasty, if no one is allowed in*, I reasoned.

Once, Bubbe forgot to lock the door when she entered the mysterious part of the summer kitchen. I sneaked in after her, and she did not tell me to leave. I looked around, but to my disappointment, everything was clean and empty! With the exception of a few bottles of Bubbe's homemade wine, there was nothing edible there.

This part of the summer kitchen was attached to the back portion of the chimney leading from the summer kitchen's stove. The chimney was covered in ceramic tile, and the same ceramic tile also covered a small, square pool of water dug out of the floor of the hut. The water in the little pool was barely waist-high, and three steps led down into it.

"What is this for?" I wondered.

"It's for washing the vegetables before they are preserved," Bubbe replied without battling an eyelash, as she rubbed a rag over the already clean floor.

In truth, I never saw vegetables in that part of the summer kitchen, although I did hear Bubbe Faiga give the same answer to a

---

2. The summer kitchen was used to prepare food during the hot summer days and to store food for the winter.

curious neighbor who stuck her nose into the hut and wondered what it was used for.

Men were not allowed into the summer kitchen in the evenings — it was the women's domain during those hours. When darkness fell, women would come to Bubbe, usually in pairs — a younger woman and an older woman — and they would stay there until it was late.

Sometimes, I peeked into the window of the illuminated hut and saw Bubbe reading something to the women from a book. There was a samovar on the table, and it appeared to be an innocent women's gathering.

The strange hut

The roof of the hut was built in such a way that rainwater descended from the roof through a drain and entered a pipe that disappeared underground. Nearby was a deep pit that was covered with bars. In the winter, when I would shovel snow in the garden, Papa would ask me to throw the clean snow into that pit. I didn't probe into the reasons why they needed snow there in the winter or why they needed rainwater there in the summer.

The answer to this mystery became clear to me only about 40

years later when I moved to Israel and began working as a janitor in a mikveh. That was when I finally understood what the purpose of the pool in Bubbe's summer kitchen was, and why rainwater and snow were needed there.

A Jewish-owned brick factory. Vinnitza region, end of 19th century.

Ban on Jewish Garb

During the nineteenth century, the czarist regime decided to ban traditional Jewish garb, on the grounds that it "prevents the Jews from all contact with Christians." At first, a tax was levied on Jewish garb: Merchants had to pay 50 rubles a year, and an additional five rubles to wear a yarmulke. For comparison's sake, a riding horse cost five rubles; a work horse cost up to 10 rubles; and a Cossack racehorse cost 500-600 rubles.

In 1851, an edict was issued proclaiming that "Any difference between the garments of the Jews and those of the indigenous population must be eliminated."

Only the elderly were allowed to wear their traditional clothing. It was forbidden to grow a beard or peyos or to

appear in the street wearing a tallis or tefillin, and these
edicts were enforced by the police.

— *R' Mendel Futerfas*

Take Off Your Hat

For a long time, my parents managed to conceal from me the fact that my family was observant. After all, I did not know how other families lived, and I thought that what I saw in my house was normal.

Papa's head was always covered. In the summer, he wore a hat or a cap, and in the winter, he wore a fur hat. I noticed that Papa did not remove his hat even at home.

"Papa, take off your hat," I urged him once. "It's hot in the house!"

"My head freezes when I'm not wearing a hat," Papa replied. As always, he tried to joke his way out of the situation. He resorted to humor any time I asked him a question that he could not answer directly. He certainly couldn't tell me that Jews were required to cover their heads.

It was the same way with other mitzvos. Before Shabbos, Bubbe would buy a live chicken — we never ate meat or chicken during the week — and she would instruct me to take the chicken to Uncle Yasha (Yaakov) Friedman to have it slaughtered. I brought the chicken to Uncle Yasha, not realizing that he was a *shochet*.

Every Friday, Bubbe and Mama lit candles, covered their faces with their hands, and whispered something. For some reason, Mama always cried at this time, and Bubbe quietly whispered, *"Guttenyu, Tattenyu meine tayere, fir meine kinder tzu Torah deine* [Hashem, my dear Father, lead my children to Your Torah]."

Once, during the winter, the candles were not lit in the house, but were lit instead in the window of the summer kitchen. Every night for the next week, more and more candles were added. Papa, Mama, and Bubbe would stand near the window of the house and gaze at the candles, and they would call me over to join them. "Look, come see how nicely the candles are burning!" they would tell me, without explaining that the purpose of lighting the candles was to publicize the Chanukah miracle.

"Why did you light the candles in the summer kitchen, instead of in the house?" I wondered.

Even Bubbe didn't know what to answer. Of course, the reason was because they were trying to hide the Chanukah candles from outsiders; they were afraid of me as well.

I was very happy with this holiday they called Chanukah. For one thing, Bubbe fried delicious potato latkes. For another, she gave me a small bag and told me, "Go to the houses of our relatives, and they'll give you Chanukah *gelt*." Indeed, wherever I went, I was given money. It was great — I became rich overnight!

My family was very scrupulous about keeping kosher, and the kitchen was always under Bubbe's watchful eye. She prepared all the food herself, and did not allow anyone else to set foot into the kitchen — even Mama. If it ever happened that a neighbor asked to borrow a pot when Bubbe was away and kindhearted Mama could not refuse, Bubbe would become very angry.

"Zissel-*Lekach*!" she would say indignantly. "If you can't say no, tell them to come to me. You have nothing to do with the kitchen. Now we have to throw away the pot."

If people asked to borrow kitchen utensils from Bubbe — who always treated everyone warmly — she would place her hands on her hips and reply cynically, "And maybe you also want to borrow my socks?"

With time, even the most unperceptive neighbors got the message: You could ask Faiga for anything — except kitchen utensils.

I loved being around Bubbe when she was preparing food, because she always gave me something good to eat.

Once, I complained, "Why do you always give me a roll with jam to eat in school? The other children who live at home always bring bread with lard! I don't want jam anymore — give me lard!"

This was too much even for Mama.

"*Vuss* [what]?" she shouted. She was about to admonish me, when Bubbe Faiga stopped her. "Zissel, *shveig* [be quiet]!" she ordered.

"You want lard — you'll get lard," she told me.

Mama looked at her very strangely, but Bubbe calmly went down to the cellar and returned with a yellowish piece of fat. (It was goose fat — schmaltz.)

"Here's your lard," she said. "Tomorrow you'll have it for school."

"But where's the skin?" I demanded, sensing that there was some deception here. Lard, I knew, was supposed to have skin with black bristles.

"The skin?" Bubbe responded with equanimity. "You know that Uncle Yasha is a furrier. He tans hides, so I give him the skins. If you want lard, take it!"

The following day, I proudly brought a sandwich with "lard" to school and gave it to my friends to taste.

"The Zhids' lard is much tastier," my friends said approvingly. "It practically melts in your mouth. It must be because the Zhids feed their pigs bread, not slops like everyone else."

This comment was far from innocuous. During that period of intense hunger, feeding animals bread was considered a crime. The newspapers featured "exposés" of crimes like these on an almost daily basis, and even I understood that my friends' accusation was very dangerous to my family.

A Ruble for a Prayer

I was awed by Papa, who was tall, strong, and quiet. He left the house early every day and returned late at night. I did not know what he was involved with, but I saw that people treated him with great respect. Apparently, he carried on his shoulders the heavy burden of running an underground Jewish community.

When I awoke in the morning, I would see Papa praying, wrapped in his *tallis* and tefillin. When he returned home in the evening, I would be in bed, but still awake. Papa would sit down beside me, take a book in his hand, and tell me about Avraham, Yitzchak, and Yaakov. I was very drowsy, and it was hard for me to keep my eyes open, but I struggled to remain awake. The memories of these moments that Papa spent beside me are extremely precious to me.

I did not know then that Papa was reading to me from the Torah; I thought that he was telling me fairytales, and I found them fascinating. But the moment that Papa would sit down to read to me, Mama would come into the room and say in a disapproving tone, "Don't confuse the child — he has to concentrate on his studies!"

Why is she upset? I wondered to myself. *What's wrong if Papa tells me these stories?*

Presumably, Mama was opposed to my studying Torah because she wanted to protect me from the dangers that religious Jews faced during that period. Educated in Soviet schools, Mama herself had not known much about Judaism before she married Papa. She had learned a great deal from Bubbe after she married into a religious family, but the central tenets of *emunah* were a matter of uncertainty in her mind.

To this day I regret that my relationship with Papa remained stilted. How badly I needed a close relationship with him! Perhaps my life would have turned out differently had we managed to forge a closer bond .... .

Owing to the complexity of the laws of kashrus in the kitchen, Bubbe Faiga did not trust Mama to keep a kosher kitchen. Nevertheless, she tried to share her Jewish knowledge with Mama.

Every Shabbos, I witnessed the following scene: Bubbe would sit with her *sefarim*, reading from a *Chumash*, and she always managed to find a *chiddush*.

"*Zissel, kim aher, ich hab gefunen eppes nayes* [Zissel, come here, I found something new]!" she would call out excitedly.

Zissel would smile patiently. "Mama, what *chiddush* could you have found in there already? You've been learning from that *sefer* for 90 years already!"

Bubbe would wave her hands despairingly in Zissel's direction. "*Oy, Zissel, du farshteist gornisht! Shepsel, kim aher* [Oh, Zissel, you don't understand anything! Shepsel, come here]!"

I would sit down beside Bubbe, and she would tell me what she was reading in the book. Mama would become very upset. "*Bubbe mayses! Farklop nisht kindt der kup* [Old wives' tales! Don't confuse the child]!" she would complain. "These are ancient customs; better that the boy should do his homework and earn a medal. He needs to study in order to be accepted to university. He has to learn the 'Torah' of math and the 'Torah' of physics!"

Mama used the word "Torah" to refer to any branch of knowledge.

Each time this scene repeated itself, Bubbe would raise her finger heavenward and answer Mama with the same cryptic sentence: "*Zissel, Zissel, nuch kimt a tzait* [Zissel, Zissel, a time will yet come]!"

I loved Mama dearly, but in my eyes, Bubbe's authority was a notch above Mama's. What's more, I noticed that everyone living on our street submitted to Bubbe Faiga's authority. Even Uncle Fedia the steel-smelter, a mountain of a man who was feared by everyone, obediently and reverently fulfilled Bubbe's instructions. So when there was a disagreement between

icht benschen.   הדלקת נר שבת

Vintage postcard

Bubbe and Mama, I sided with Bubbe. Besides, I enjoyed sitting beside her and listening to her lilting voice tell stories about the village of Vachanovka and about my grandfather Shepsel Wolf.

Bubbe accorded me special treatment, for she thought that I possessed a spark of the soul of her late husband, Shepsel Wolf, whose name I carried. I was the only person to whom she was able to speak at length about her late husband, for I was eager to hear what she had to say about him.

She told me that Reb Shepsel Wolf would sit in shul poring over heavy *sefarim* from morning to night. The Jews of Vachanovka revered him greatly, and often came to him for advice. "He never had to run after anyone," she recalled. "The people always ran after *him* — all because of the wisdom contained in the *sefarim* that he learned."

Bubbe wanted me to understand the difference between the *real* Torah and the "Torah" of mathematics.

Bubbe Faiga's mantra was that an action is worth a thousand words, and she made sure to involve me in every aspect of running a Jewish home. In deference to my stubborn nature, she never compelled me to work — instead, she made business deals with me. Before Purim, for instance, I would manually grind poppy seeds with a hand grinder for Bubbe's hamantaschen. The work was tedious, but while I ground the poppy, Bubbe would tell me something about the holiday. And the main thing was that for every kilogram of poppy that I ground, she paid me a ruble — which to me was a lot of money.

Bubbe also used money to lure me away from the orphanage, during the initial period when I still felt torn between my family and the orphanage. To ensure that I would not run back to the orphanage, she would come to school and tell me that my help was needed in the house. After I would do the work she requested, she would pay me for it.

In addition, Bubbe gave me a ruble for every prayer that I learned by heart. Bubbe would write the Hebrew words of the prayers in Russian letters for me and I would memorize them, even though I did not understand a word of the Holy Tongue.

Why did I, a Soviet Pioneer, agree to memorize these prayers? Because I saw that our Tatar neighbors prayed in the Tatar language, and it was important to me to be like everyone else. If my Tatar friend prayed in an unfamiliar language, so could I. Besides, Bubbe Faiga paid me handsomely for this.

When I needed money, I would go to Bubbe Faiga and say, "Bubbe, give me a ruble!"

"Learn a prayer and I'll give you a ruble," she would answer. When I wasn't in the mood to learn a new prayer, I would mumble words that I had memorized previously. But I could never fool Bubbe: "That's the prayer you told me last time," she would say decisively. "If you want a ruble, you have to learn a new prayer."

At this stage, Mama would intervene. "Why does the child need to learn this? Better that he should review his studies."

Bubbe was resolute, however, and I learned the unfamiliar words.

Thanks to Bubbe, I learned the *Shema* and the morning blessings by heart, and these prayers remained engraved upon my memory forever. Many years later, my knowledge of these prayers played a crucial role in my fate. As Bubbe used to say, "*Nuch kimt a tzait* [A time will yet come]!"

Vintage postcard

Pesach in Siberia, end of 19th century. A minyan of Cantonists are hosted by a rabbi exiled from Poland.

Jewish Children

Because the attempts to forcibly subdue the Jews' religious observance were unsuccessful, the czarist government decided to target what was most precious of all to the Jews: their children. A document from the czar's offices dated 1820 contains a recommendation that daughters of Jewish parents be taken away, housed in dormitories, and married off at the age of 12 to Christians living in the new settlements of Siberia. "There is no reason to suspect that these girls will disseminate their Jewish faith in the settlements. The daughters of the Jews are not strong in matters of faith, and they will not be able to influence the settlers, who are all former criminals ... and are known as devout Christians."

The authorities knew that the girls' Jewish education was minimal — unlike that of the boys, who were taught Torah from the age of the three.

This recommendation regarding Jewish girls did not come to fruition. But for over 30 years, beginning in 1827, tens of thousands of Jewish boys were kidnapped from their parents and turned into soldier-slaves: Cantonists.

— *The Russian historian Iulii Gessen* (The History of the Jews in Russia, *1916)*

Shabbos, Shabbos

I had an additional source of income: preparing for Shabbos. On Shabbos, Bubbe did not allow any of us to use water from the tap; apparently, she was concerned that opening the faucet triggered a pump. For the same reason, she closed the bathroom in the house on Shabbos, and we had to use a wooden outhouse and cesspool in the yard.

On Thursday, after I returned home from school, I would draw water from the well and fill two large oak barrels for use on Shabbos.

Mama would cry, "The child needs to do his homework!"

"It's not so bad that he should earn some money," Bubbe would respond. She would pay me three rubles for each barrel I filled.

Bubbe ran a kosher Jewish home, scrupulously adhering to every nuance of halachah. She was similarly stringent about every aspect of mitzvah observance. This required her to work very hard. She did most of the work herself, not relying on anyone else; Mama only helped her.

Bubbe ran a mini-factory of sorts. In the fall, she made her own wine in industrial quantities — not only for our family, but for other Jewish families as well. The wine was poured into huge 50-liter bottles made of dark green glass, and these bottles were placed into straw baskets filled with sawdust and stored in a special corner of the summer kitchen that was kept strictly under lock and key. One bottle of wine was designated for Pesach, and no one was allowed to come near that bottle.

At the end of the summer, Bubbe would prepare jars of cherry compote. This compote served as dessert at the end of each of the Shabbos meals, bringing a whiff of summer into our house during the frigid winter days.

Everything that Bubbe did during the week was somehow connected to preparing for Shabbos. Her weekday food was tasty, but its preparation seemed almost incidental. Thanks to Bubbe's ingenuity, the Shabbos foods became special to me, even though I did not understand most of what was going on around me.

Early Thursday morning, I knew what day it was even before I opened my eyes, because I could smell the delicious aroma of fresh bread wafting through the house. On Thursday, Bubbe would bake large challos for Shabbos — I called them "braided rolls" — and she would bake bread then for the rest of the week as well.

Bubbe and I also prepared "bird rolls": She tied strips of dough into knots and I decorated them with "eyes" made of raisins. Admittedly, some of the "eyes" made their way into my mouth, but Bubbe didn't scold me. She had her own reasons for luring me into the kitchen: She wanted to accustom me to the idea of Shabbos.

The crispy "bird rolls" were distributed during the Friday night meal, and I looked forward to this moment all week.

It was fascinating to watch Bubbe preside over her kitchen as she prepared for Shabbos. The gefilte fish she prepared was fit for a king. With the deftness of a magician, she rolled the skin off the fish in one piece, from head to tail, just as one would remove a sock. After that, she separated the soft flesh from the bones, leaving only the head on the fishbone. Then, she would prepare a batter from the flesh of the fish and fill the "sock" of fish skin from bottom to top. The fish now appeared whole once again, as though it had been created in this stuffed state.

Bubbe would cook the fish for a long time, and when it was ready she would transfer it to a platter and place a round piece of carrot in its mouth. The fish was served in all its majesty at the Shabbos table, and Papa would slice it ceremoniously with a large knife.

The Shabbos soup was called "*yoch mit oiglech mit lokshen* [chicken soup with eyes and noodles]." Bubbe's *lokshen* practically melted in your mouth. To prepare them, Bubbe would stretch a dough very thin and throw it into the air until it became transparent as lace. Then she would slice the dough into noodles and set them aside to dry.

The main course of our Shabbos meal was "*esek fleish* [sweet and sour meat]," a heavenly dish prepared with honey, plums, and cherries. Shabbos was the only day of the week that we ate meat or chicken.

From Friday until Shabbos morning, a pot filled with beans, potatoes, and meat was kept in a hot oven that cooled down slowly. This was our *cholent*.

My parents didn't explain anything about Shabbos to me, and they never forced me to come to the Shabbos meal. They did, however, insist that everyone in the family eat together on Friday night. "Whoever comes late, doesn't get food!" they warned.

Given the choice between playing outside with the boys or coming home to Bubbe's delicacies, Bubbe always won. Frustrating as it was to me to take leave of my friends and their games, I would run home every Friday night when sunset came. I wasn't the only unfortunate boy who had to leave the games early: Another boy named Yoske also ran home when I did, for his family kept Shabbos as well.

When I came home, I found Papa sitting at the head of our long table, which was bedecked with a white tablecloth. Around the table sat other men, our guests. A small table was set for the women, who sat separately in the next room, near the oven.

Papa closed his eyes and sang in a low, stirring voice, "*Shabbos los zach, Shabbos auf der gantzen velt, luss zach auf Yidden der Shabbos* [Shabbos is entering, Shabbos throughout the whole world, Shabbos is entering for all the Jews]."

It seemed as though the world around us relaxed when Papa sang this melody. Even I lost interest in running around and playing outside when I heard Papa singing.

Papa poured dark red wine from a small glass jug into a silver goblet, which had long ago blackened and was slightly dented. Papa made *Kiddush*, and then cut the crisp, golden challah and distributed slices to each of the people present. That was when Bubbe gave me my coveted "bird roll."

Papa wanted me to sit beside him, as befitted the firstborn. But I felt lost in the company of the men, and after sitting beside Papa for a short while, I silently stole away to where Mama and Bubbe sat. I reveled in the pleasant, warm atmosphere that reigned near them, and they indulged me, heaping the best portions onto my plate.

I did not sense that there was anything unusual about our Shabbos meals, because to me they seemed quite similar to the holiday meals of our gentile neighbors. In this regard, I thought we were just like everyone else — our gentile neighbors also gathered around the table for festive meals sometimes. The difference was that they sang very loudly, and their parties typically ended in a brawl. In contrast, our guests sang quietly and slipped away inconspicuously when the meal was over.

It Shall be Called "Matzah"

Clandestine Matzah Baking

Beginning in the year 1937 (5687), the Soviet authorities permitted the baking of matzah in government bakeries only — which meant that any matzos baked legally were inevitably non-kosher and invalid for Pesach use. Matzah baking therefore became an underground activity, and Jews who presided over this clandestine matzah baking were subject to government persecution.

In later years, between 1957 and 1966 (5716-5726), the Soviets closed down more than 100 shuls that had survived World War II. In 1961 (5721), the authorities

banned matzah baking even in communal bakeries,
except for those of Moscow, Leningrad, the Asian
Republics (such as Uzbekistan), and the Caucasus. From
1963 (5723), the ban on matzah baking was extended to
Moscow and Leningrad as well.

In June 1963, a show trial was held for several Jews
who had baked matzah illegally, and these unfortunate
Jews were convicted of profiteering through the sale of
matzah. In the Ukraine, Jews who proclaimed in shul on
Pesach, "Next year in the rebuilt city of Jerusalem," were
thrown into jail and convicted of disseminating Zionist
propaganda.

Before I rejoined my family, I did not know what the word "matzah" meant. I thought that "matzah" meant "skinny," because in school, "matzah" was the nickname of a skinny Jewish child named Siomka (a corruption of the name Semyon, or Shimon). When Siomka actually brought matzos to school instead of bread, I called the matzos "crackers." Seeing these matzos, the other children would say, "Look, for Siomka it's already Pasha [Easter]."[3]

In our house, we baked matzah for our own family and for other Jews as well. I didn't dream that this was illegal, and I eagerly participated in the process.

We prepared for the baking of the matzos well in advance. During the winter, Papa brought home sacks filled with wheat. He bought this wheat in the village where the Greeks who had hidden Mama and Bubbe during the war lived. I helped Papa drag the heavy sacks to the attic, and we placed the sacks along the length of the oven's chimney so that the wheat would dry out.

In the springtime, shortly before Purim, Bubbe sent me up to the attic with a stack of paper envelopes. Each envelope was numbered, corresponding to the number of sacks of wheat in the attic. I had to take a handful of wheat kernels from deep inside each sack, place the kernels into the envelope with the corresponding number,

---

3. In Russian, the same word is used for "Easter" and "Pesach."

and bring the envelopes containing these samples to Bubbe, who took a kernel from each envelope and threw it onto a rock. If the kernel bounced off the rock with a "ping," like a small stone, she knew that the kernel was dry and suitable for Pesach use.

After this test, the sacks of wheat were brought into a special room in the summer kitchen that was opened only before Pesach. There was a special oven there for baking matzah, and only Papa, his brother, Bubbe, and I were allowed to enter. The Russian neighbor who was hired to cut firewood for the matzah oven brought the wood no farther than to the threshold of the summer kitchen, and one of us carried it into the kitchen.

My job was to grind the kernels of wheat into flour, using ancient millstones. One of the millstones was large and round, and had an opening into which the smaller round millstone with a handle was inserted. The kernels of wheat were placed into the space between these two stones, and I turned the handle of the smaller stone to grind them. Only about a cup of wheat kernels could be ground at one time, so the process of grinding the wheat into flour was long and arduous. But Bubbe Faiga gave me a ruble for every kilogram of flour I ground.

Bubbe Faiga supervised my every action carefully. Before I began to grind the wheat, she made me wash my hands, and after I washed my hands she checked whether I had dried them well. Only after I passed Bubbe's inspection would she allow me into the summer kitchen. She would then lock the door behind me, leaving me alone, and I would grind as much flour as I could. When I wished to leave the summer kitchen, I would ring a bell, and Bubbe would come to free me. When I went back into the summer kitchen, the entire process would repeat itself: I would wash and dry my hands again, Bubbe would inspect them, and she would lock the door behind me.

Papa and his brother baked the matzos themselves; sometimes Uncle Yasha the *shochet* helped as well.

When the matzos were ready, they were placed into white pillowcases, and I distributed them to Jewish families. Papa hung the pillowcases containing the matzos designated for our family on special hooks beneath the ceiling of the summer kitchen, where they remained until Erev Pesach.

In advance of the first Pesach seder of my life, Bubbe taught me the *Mah Nishtanah*. When the seder night arrived, I recited the Four Questions, as is customary, and I then "stole" the *afikoman*. When I returned it, I was compensated handsomely, much to my satisfaction.

To Protect the Children

Once, Papa called me and my brother into a room. He asked us to sit down, and sat down beside us, his face wearing a grave expression.

"Children," he said, "I want you to know this: You are circumcised Jews."

"Why did you have to circumcise us?" my brother asked.

Usually, when Papa did not want to answer a question, he joked his way out of it. For instance, when I asked him why he always wore a hat inside the house, he joked that his ears were cold. This time, however, his face did not wear a hint of a smile. He looked into my eyes and said very seriously, "So that the children should not be lost!"

This answer satisfied my younger brother, and he ran back out to play with his toys. He was too young to understand, anyway. The answer was directed primarily at me, even though I did not understand much then, either.

My younger brother knew nothing about my turbulent childhood, and to this day he is unaware of my past. In our house, my early childhood was a taboo subject, for my parents knew that discussions of this nature could only cause problems. They thought it was better to forget, and I forgot.

Only many years later, after I met with Elsa Schultz, did I understand what Papa had meant when he had said the words, "So that the children should not be lost!" Had I not been circumcised, I would have remained with Elsa Schultz and been lost to the Jewish people forever.

Once, after a *bris* was held in our home for a child of a family I did not know, I noticed that Bubbe gave a gold coin to the *mohel* and another gold coin to the father of the baby. Bubbe would always give a gold coin to relatives of ours who made a *bris* for their children, in order to encourage them to fulfill this mitzvah. I recall that when one of our relatives said that he was not planning to perform a *bris* for his son, Bubbe told him emphatically that he would not receive a gold coin. At the end, he did the *bris*. After all, a gold coin was worth a great deal at that time.

Communicating With Space

The date of my bar mitzvah was approaching, but Papa did not know how to explain to me the significance of this event.

Preparing me for my bar mitzvah was no easy task, for my teachers in school taught that humans descended from apes, and I believed them implicitly. I thought that people who still believed in God were backward, and I assumed that they clung to that outdated belief only because they had not had the good fortune of being educated in Soviet schools.

Papa did not dare to speak to me openly about my upcoming bar mitzvah, for fear that I would tell my friends about it. He therefore waited for an opportune time, which came when I brought home a tattered volume about ancient Egypt. This book contained pictures of pyramids, sphinxes, and hieroglyphics. One of the illustrations showed people who had long, thin, antenna-like branches on their heads. Intrigued by this picture, I showed it to Papa and asked,

"What are these?"

Papa decided that this was the right moment to introduce me to tefillin. "These illustrations depict the connection between man and outer space," Papa replied. "I also have 'antennas' like these," he added, and showed me his tefillin. "Would you like me to place these on you?"

"But why?" I asked.

"So that you can feel the connection with space."

"Sure!" I declared, and allowed Papa to tie the black tefillin straps onto my arm and head. I stood and listened for a long time, but I did not feel any connection to space. I was sorely disappointed. *These antennas must be too old to work,* I thought to myself.

When Papa asked me the next day if I wanted to lay tefillin again, I vehemently refused. Papa did not force me. There was still some time until my bar mitzvah, and he hoped that he would manage to convince me to lay tefillin before then. It never did happen, however. On my thirteenth birthday, the second day of Rosh Hashanah 1952 (5713), Papa was arrested.

Prison

Just when I was starting to acclimate to family life, just when my stubborn, aggressive nature was beginning to mellow, my life was overturned once again.

On the night of Rosh Hashanah, prayer services were held in our house, and late that night there was a knock on our door. When Papa opened the door, men in black coats burst into the house and began a search.

When they entered, I was sleeping on the wooden box in the living room. They sent me away, opened the box, and emptied all its contents onto the floor. I was not frightened of these police officers; I had never been afraid of the police.

Bubbe called me into a side room, and placed a wide fabric belt filled with something under my shirt. She then instructed me to slip out of the house and run to Auntie Motia Olchovski.

"Leave the belt with her and tell her that our house is being searched," Bubbe told me.

I did as she instructed, and then I returned home. Everything in the house was overturned. Officers in civilian garb were taking apart the floorboards and tearing the upholstery from the sofa and the chairs. They went up to the attic, leafed through all the books, and combed through all the items in the closet. They did not dare to approach the picture of Stalin, however, and maintained a reverent distance from the spot where Bubbe Faiga had ingeniously hidden the *Sefer Torah*.

The officers were particularly interested in ancient Hebrew books such as *Chumashim* and *siddurim*, and they confiscated these books. "These are my books," Bubbe protested when she saw them holding these books. The officers relented and allowed her to keep some of the books, for what could they do to an old woman who knew no language other than the forbidden Hebrew tongue?

The money that we kept on a closet shelf was untouched, as was Mama's jewelry. Apparently, the search and subsequent arrest were connected to our Jewish observance.

Toward morning, when the search concluded, the officers took Papa away. Papa seemed to have lost weight overnight. He approached me to say goodbye, and gazed at me as though he was parting from me forever. He hugged me tightly and gave me a kiss.

The officers took Papa outside, and we ran after them until they ushered Papa into a black vehicle and drove off.

We returned to our house, which was in shambles. Clothing, books, and torn wallpaper were strewn all over the floor. Mama sat and wailed bitterly, but Bubbe seemed concerned about something else entirely. She moved around the house quickly, concentrating intently. After a while, she approached me gravely, and for the first time I sensed that she was addressing me openly, as a very close relative; perhaps this was because she saw how distressed I was over Papa's arrest. Without hiding anything from me, she went over to the picture of Stalin, moved it from its place, opened the secret hiding place behind it, and withdrew a large package wrapped in strong canvas.

"Shepsel," she requested, "take this up to the attic. There, behind the Pesach dishes, is a hiding place. If you see that there is still sand strewn on there and that the officers did not touch that spot, you should open the hiding place, place the package inside, and then cover it again with sand. But if you see that the hiding place is open, come back to me and I'll give you a different place to hide the package."

At this point, I was no longer surprised by anything, and I did not ask any questions. I simply did as Bubbe asked.

The closet in the attic that contained the Pesach dishes was completely overturned, and some of the dishes were broken. The hiding place had not been touched, however, and I concealed the package inside it. I did not know then that the item I had hidden away was a *Sefer Torah*.

When Pesach came, Bubbe refused to use the dishes that had survived the search, and she insisted that we buy new dishes — even though our financial situation that year was very difficult.

Bubbe was visibly relieved when I told her that I had hidden the package. Now that the *Sefer Torah* was safely hidden, Bubbe headed to the police station to find out what had happened to Papa. She took our neighbor Auntie Vera with her, but did not allow Mama to come along. "You're too soft," she told Mama. "They'll manage to get everything out of you."

The following morning, Bubbe was arrested. She was held in prison for two days before being released. When she returned home, she behaved just as she always did, as though nothing had happened. She did not say anything about her imprisonment in my presence, and it was only by coincidence that I overheard a conversation she had with Mama. The two went outside to talk at a time when I was sitting in an apricot tree, hidden by the branches, and they did not notice me.

Bubbe spoke Yiddish, but by then I was already proficient in that language. She told Mama that during the interrogation she had been asked who visits our house, whether Jews congregate there for prayers, and about the matzah baking.

This conversation was not intended for my ears, but now I finally understood — better late than never — that I had to be careful with what I said.

Every morning, Bubbe and Mama would leave the house, as if they were going out to work, and would make their way to the police station and the prison to inquire about Papa. But each time they received the same ambiguous answer: Nothing was known about him. This answer did not bode well, for it may have signaled the worst. One can just imagine how worried Mama and Bubbe were.

Later, we discovered that Papa was still alive. He was not being held in prison, but in the underground dungeons of the KGB. Very few people emerged from those dungeons alive, but hearing this news ignited some hope in us nonetheless. The dungeons were situated beneath the playground that was next to the Pioneer's House. I had wandered around that park many times, never dreaming that right there, beneath my feet, Papa was being tortured.

The Son of the "Enemy of the People"

After Papa's arrest, I did not attend school for several days. When I did return to school, the Russian language teacher entered the classroom and announced, "Children, you should know that Gutman's father is an enemy of the people, and has been arrested."

I expected to be terrorized by the other students, but to my surprise, none of my classmates gave me a hard time. Some of the children were not interested in ruining their relationship with me, since I was a good student and I allowed them to copy my homework. Others were simply unimpressed by stories about jailed relatives, since almost every family had at least one member who had sat in jail for stealing or fighting. And so the children did not bother me after Papa's arrest; only the adults ridiculed me.

Papa's arrest was very difficult for me. Mostly, I pitied myself: I had finally found a family, and again I was orphaned! Mama was disconsolate, too. The only one in the family who managed to maintain a cheerful demeanor was Bubbe Faiga. She never mentioned the word "prison," and she tried to shore up everyone's spirits.

"Zissel, don't cry," Bubbe comforted Mama. "We have to be happy. Moshe is on a journey, and he will return."

Everything in the house was different now. No one came to us to pray. Before Pesach, Uncle Yasha (Yaakov) baked matzos at our house, but not in the same quantities as in previous years. There were no matzos for me to distribute, and I did not earn any money from Bubbe that year.

Our financial situation was exceedingly difficult. At times, we did not even have bread in the house. Bubbe and Mama bought bread only for me and for my younger brother; mainly for him.

Outwardly, Mama behaved as though nothing had happened. She still left the house looking perfectly groomed — wearing a wig, makeup, and high-heeled shoes — and walking in a slow, dignified manner.

Sometimes, when Jewish acquaintances met her in the street they would ask, "Mrs. Gutman, your husband is in prison — perhaps you need money?"

"*Gelt* [money]?" she would respond confidently. "*Bai mir gelt vi mist* [Money is as plentiful as garbage to me]!" She was too proud to accept money from anyone, even though the soles of her elegant shoes had holes.

To support the family, Mama began to sew coats and pants with warm linings, and Bubbe and I sold these items in the marketplace. Our merchandise found customers speedily, for the stores were empty. Trade like this was forbidden, however, and was deemed "profiteering." The police hunted down profiteers mercilessly, but this was not the first time I had fled the police, and they did not catch me with the merchandise even once.

Our ruse was very simple: Over her clothing, Bubbe wore a coat Mama had sewn, and she sold it off her own back, while I stood not far away with a bag of additional merchandise. After Bubbe sold one coat, she would don another and sell it as well. If the police apprehended her, she began screaming so loudly in Yiddish that her voice could be heard at the other end of the city. While she distracted them, I managed to vanish in seconds.

For every item we sold, I received a ruble from Bubbe.

At around that time, the following incident occurred: Mama gave me three rubles and sent me to buy bread. Some youths who were bigger than I caught me, threw me to the ground, and beat me. One of the youths, Tolik Litvinov, forcibly seized the money that Mama had given me. This Tolik never missed an opportunity to conspire against me, even though I was a friend of his younger brother Lyoshka (Alexei), the one whom Bubbe Faiga had named "Yossi."

Tolik was a ruffian, and a few years later he was thrown into prison together with his friend. My friend Lyoshka was also imprisoned.

Because Tolik stole Mama's money, my entire family remained without bread. As I rubbed angry tears from my eyes, I told him that I would get even with him.

He laughed. "How can a weakling like you get even with me?" he taunted.

The truth was that Tolik was bigger and stronger than I was, and I had never dared to threaten him before. But this time it was *Mama's* money! She had relied on me, and now I couldn't buy her bread! I was covered with mud and choking with anger.

For several days, I conspired against Tolik, until finally I came up with a plan. I climbed onto the entrance gate leading to his house, and waited for him to return home. When he passed through the gate, I threw a rope around his neck and jumped to the other side of the fence while holding the rope in my hand. He barely escaped strangulation; it was only with the help of the passersby that his life was saved. I managed to scare him thoroughly, and from then on he was careful not to start up with me. His friends caught me and beat me, but by then I had already made myself a name among the hooligans.

"Don't start up with that Zhid," they told one another. "He'll find a way to get even."

From the Mouths of Babes

The Doctors' Plot

In 1952 (5713), a plot was hatched under Stalin's personal direction for the purging of all the Jews of the Soviet Union. Throughout the country, lists of Jews were prepared, and plans were made for the Jews to be expelled to Siberia and Birobidzhan. A portion of the Jews were to be disposed of along the way (in train "accidents" and pogroms) and the remainder were to die a "natural" death from cold or hunger.

To set the stage for the mass liquidation of the Jews, the authorities contrived a case named the "Doctors' Plot," in which Jewish doctors were accused of having intentionally poisoned Russian leaders and the general population. The accused Jewish doctors were to be hanged in Red Square.

It was only Stalin's sudden death on March 5, 1953 that prevented this satanic plan from being implemented. This miracle took place on the day of Purim, only a few days before the plan's scheduled implementation.

That year, Stalin died. When his death was announced on the radio, Mama wept. "What will be with us?" she worried.

"Don't cry, Mama," my 6-year-old brother comforted her. "This uncle died, another will take his place."

"*A kind zugt emes* [A child speaks the truth]," Bubbe noted quietly.

Heavy mourning descended upon the entire country. There were those who, like Mama, mourned Stalin's death genuinely, out of the naive belief that the entire country depended upon this tyrant. Others merely feigned mourning, out of fear that they would be suspected of disloyalty to the country.

The day after Stalin's death, an honor guard was posted in our school near a sculpture of Stalin's head. Only students who excelled were given the privilege of participating in this honor guard and waving their hands above their head (that was the official salute of the Pioneers). Every fifteen minutes, a new shift of students was posted near the sculpture. The teacher on duty appointed me to the honor guard, since I was an outstanding student. Sensing the importance of the moment, I stood frozen in place, my hand waving the salute.

At that moment, Alyochin, the assistant principal, emerged from the teachers' room. When he saw that the son of the "enemy of the people" was positioned among the members of the honor guard, his face darkened from anger. He leaped toward me, grabbed my collar, threw me out of the honor guard, and commanded me to return to my classroom. In my place, he stationed a different student, a child who was average or below but happened to be the first student Alyochin encountered after he banished me.

I was confused, and could not understand why Alyochin pushed me away and humiliated me before all the students of the school. Wasn't I an outstanding student?

Unable to get even with Alyochin, I decided to settle the score with the innocent child whom Alyochin had stationed in my place. I provoked my friends into beating him, "so that he wouldn't stick his nose into a place that wasn't his."

After Alyochin threw me out of the honor guard, I realized with lightning clarity that as hard as I would try to succeed in school — whether by excelling in my studies or by demonstrating my Pioneering enthusiasm — I would never become "one of them," a comrade among comrades; I would always remain an outsider. Now, I understood that I belonged to my family.

From then on, I kept my distance from the children of the orphanage, and joined forces with "Bubbe's children," the neighbors, who never hurt me. I even started to protect that other Jewish child, Siomka, on occasion.

Revenge

The following is an excerpt from the book Voices in the Silence, *the memoir of Basya Barg. Basya's father, Rabbi Meizlik, was arrested in Kiev in 1951 (5711), and was released from prison after Stalin's death.*

Of course the miracle was because of Stalin's death, just as Mama had hoped. The whole KGB went into a panic at the news. Now that the tyrant was gone and fear of him fled, all the prisoners might be released any day, there might be a revolution, and the judged might suddenly become the judges. Everyone remembered how the Czar's secret police had been tried and shot by the Communists; now it might be the KGB's turn to pay for its crimes. So they thought it best to free all the prisoners — quickly — and Tatteh was among the many who went free that very day.

… They grabbed him and forced him into the car and drove off to the central jailhouse, near Bodgan Chmielniczki Square …. The prison cells were in the basement of a tall building, next door to the "interrogation rooms," meaning torture chambers. Tatteh was put through the works. They wanted to know whom he baked

> matzos for, who came to the mikveh, who came to eat
> at his table on Shabbos, and what they talked about ....
> The interrogations and torture went on for two full years,
> but Tatteh remained steadfast through it all. They got no
> names out of him, not a scrap of incriminating evidence
> against anyone. They simply couldn't break him.
>
> The whole time he never even saw his tormentors,
> because in Russia everyone was a paranoiac. They knew
> that at any time the tables might be turned and their
> victims might be interrogating them, so they took care to
> keep in a dark corner while a spotlight was aimed at their
> victim's face, effectively blinding him.
>
> Tatteh was imprisoned in a dark cell for the whole two
> years, never knowing day from night. There was only
> one way he could tell when a day had gone by, and that
> was when they brought him his daily ration of bread and
> water — twelve ounces of bread and a quart of water a
> day ... they had also brought him some soup or stew each
> day, but he had left it on the tray, untouched.

Stalin's death saved Papa. After being held in prison for nine months without trial, he was freed on May 11, 1953.

Papa was thin and worn out when he returned home. His health had deteriorated, and it took a long time before he regained his strength. He never told us where he had been or what he had endured; at least, I don't know any details of his imprisonment. The only detail he disclosed upon his return home was that our Jewish neighbor Krutonog was an informant, and we should be careful around him.

Who would have dreamed that Krutonog, an old friend of Papa's, was an informant? Why, Krutonog had even served as the *sandek* at my brother's *bris*!

A short time before Papa's arrest, Krutonog had purchased the house attached to ours. This house had previously belonged to a gentile neighbor named Ivan Ivanovich.

For years, my parents had maintained a strong friendship with

Ivan Ivanovich and his wife, who were religious, upstanding people. On Shabbos, Ivan helped our family by serving as our "Shabbos *goy*," lighting and extinguishing fires when necessary, and never accepted money for these services. As believing people, they viewed this duty with reverence. Even after he sold his part of the house and moved into a different neighborhood, Ivan would come to our house on Shabbos to help us. This went on for a very long time. "If I don't help you, who will?" he would ask.

The windows of Ivan Ivanovich's part of the house faced our yard, and it was impossible to hide from the neighbors what was going on in our house. On the holidays, when many Jews gathered at our home to pray and the space inside the house was insufficient, the congregants would go outside: The men would pray in the summer kitchen, while the women would pray outdoors.

When Ivan decided to sell his house, he approached Papa and said, "I don't want to sell to a stranger. After all, a neighbor is closer than a brother! Maybe you can find a purchaser who meets with your approval, and I'll sell the house to him at a discount."

Papa arranged for Ivan's house to be sold to Krutonog, a colleague of Papa's whom he trusted. But a mere two months after Krutonog became our neighbor, Papa was arrested.

When I learned that Krutonog had informed on Papa, I vowed that I would make his life so miserable that he would not be able to live near us anymore.

Papa dismissed that notion, however. "Don't you dare think of it, or I'll teach you a lesson," he warned me.

But when my desire for blood was kindled, there was nothing that could stop me. At the end, I achieved my goal, and Krutonog moved away.

During the entire summer, I stubbornly climbed up to the roof and relieved myself into the chimney of his house. When I tired of climbing up to the roof several times a day, I simply filled two buckets from the cesspool of our outhouse and poured their contents into his chimney. When Krutonog began to light his ovens in the autumn, an unbearable odor pervaded his house, and he was forced to move elsewhere.

Many years later, when I was a college student, Papa reminded me of the incident. "Do you think I didn't know that you did it?" he asked reprovingly. "I wanted to punish you at the time, as you deserved, but I never had the chance. When I left to work, you were still asleep, and when I returned home, you were already sleeping! And it is forbidden to awaken a Jew, for while he sleeps his soul ascends to heaven, and if he is suddenly awoken his soul is liable not to return."

I chortled. "Really, Papa, what soul?"

Krutonog moved, but I didn't forget about him. He wasn't going to be free of me so easily, I vowed.

Together with my friends, I broke all the windows of his new house, using the same strategy I had employed when I broke the windows of the teacher Shatalov's house. Still, my desire for revenge simmered, and a short while later I finally had the opportunity I craved.

One day, I overheard my parents saying that Krutonog was planning to hold an elaborate wedding for his daughter in his backyard. My parents were invited, and they were compelled to attend, so as not to arouse suspicion. It was very dangerous to reveal an informant's identity, and my parents had to maintain the illusion that they were unaware that Krutonog had informed on them.

This, I decided, was my chance to finally get even with Krutonog. I wove a plot together with my friends, and when the wedding began, we hid behind the fence of Krutonog's yard holding paper bags filled with sand. We watched the proceedings through a hole in the fence, waiting for the moment when all the guests would be seated around the beautifully set tables.

Krutonog had prepared a sumptuous banquet indeed. It was a feast for the eyes, and a prime target.

Krutonog, dressed in brand-new festive clothing, beamed as he made his way between the tables. "Please help yourselves, honored guests!" he announced, turning to the guests.

This was the moment I was waiting for. I motioned to my friends, and from behind the fence we threw our bags through the air, aiming them directly at the tables. The bags exploded loudly, strewing sand all over the serving platters filled with goose meat, salads, and caviar. Krutonog ran to the street to apprehend the perpetrators, but by then we had vanished without a trace.

In the evening, when my parents returned home, they related that hooligans had spoiled Krutonog's celebration. They were good people, my parents, and they even took pity on Krutonog.

As for me, I lay on my improvised bed, the wooden box, and rejoiced at Krutonog's disgrace. At least I had settled the score with him somewhat.

Estrangement

For a full year after Papa was freed from prison, Bubbe did not allow the picture of the deceased Stalin to be removed from the wall — "in case something happens." Now, I knew why.

When Papa returned home, Jews began to convene once again at our house for the Shabbos prayers. Bubbe had her own reserved spot for the services: She prayed in the corridor near the room where the *minyan* was held. If I entered the corridor during the prayers, she sent me to the room where the men were.

Famed Soviet singers, such as Alexandrovich and Horowitz, prayed in our house on occasion. When these singers came to perform in our city and sought a place to pray secretly, the Jews directed them to our home. I remember that when one of them came to pray in our house, we covered the windows with quilts so that the people outside should not see what was going on.

During that period, my brother fell gravely ill. Mama and Bubbe prayed tearfully, and he recovered. This incident affected Mama deeply, and she subsequently stopped arguing with Bubbe about religion. Instead, she would sit beside Bubbe and pray. Bubbe said that if Mama would pray to Hashem, I would graduate school with good grades and be accepted to university.

It seemed that now, nothing stood in the way of my forging a close relationship with Papa. I remembered longingly how he had cared for me before his arrest, how he had observed my every action, and how he had learned Torah with me despite Mama's protestations.

But Papa's attitude toward me changed dramatically after he returned from prison. I don't know what they revealed to him during the interrogations or what he heard at that time, but I sensed that he was a changed man after his imprisonment. He became very distant, and I felt an estrangement between us. He no longer read to me from the *Chumash*, and he did not ask me any questions.

Papa would gaze at my red Pioneer's tie penetratingly, without saying a word. I realized that he did not like it, and in order to please him, I stopped wearing the tie in the house. On my way home from school, I would remove my tie and hide it in my pocket. Even so, however, Papa treated me like a stranger. This was very painful to me.

Why had Papa suddenly become estranged from me? Why didn't he trust me? After all, Bubbe and Mama had told him how I had helped them after his arrest, and how I had hidden the *Sefer Torah!* *They* trusted me — why, they had even divulged other family secrets to me!

I did not understand then that my innocent conversations with my friends may have caused Papa's arrest in the first place, and were liable to land him back in prison even after his miraculous release. The father of one of my friends was a government prosecutor, and the mother of another friend occupied a high-ranking position in the police.

In 1954 (5714), Papa received a notice from America informing him that a relative had bequeathed an inheritance to him. At that time, just having relatives living abroad was considered extremely dangerous. Papa immediately replied that he had no relatives abroad, and renounced the inheritance.

In Strangers' fields

That year, matzos were once again baked in our house for Pesach. I did not like the Pesach holiday, for I was not interested in distributing packages of matzah. Besides, the food on Pesach was not tasty, and food, to me, was the most important yardstick in life. All of the other holidays were "tasty": On Purim, I enjoyed giving my friends hamantaschen, and on Chanukah, donuts. Bubbe gave me large quantities of these goodies to distribute to my friends in school, and my friends were delighted to receive them. "Bubbe baked cookies!" they would announce joyfully when I presented Bubbe's delicacies to them.

But what did I have to offer them on Pesach? Crackers! For the Russians, Easter was a "tasty" holiday. When we visited Auntie Marusia around this holiday, I saw that she had prepared an airy cake and colorful hard-boiled eggs. Once, I even brought home a piece of Russian Easter cake, but Bubbe instructed me to throw it away and never to bring home things like that again.

Bubbe Faiga understood my need to be like everyone else, and she started preparing a special Napoleon torte made of *matzah brei* (matzah dipped in egg and fried). She would give it to me and say, "Go give your friends a taste of *our* 'Pasha.'"

When I brought this delicacy to school, my friends remarked, "If Bubbe Faiga baked this, it must be a real Jewish 'Pasha.' But Siomka's mother doesn't know how to make anything, and that's why they have tasteless crackers."

Siomka, as I mentioned earlier, was a thin, weak, homely child who was nicknamed "matzah." The other children conspired against him and bullied him incessantly, and I was also among his tormentors.

I was just as anti-Semitic as the other boys, or perhaps even more so, since I always had to prove that I was on *their* side, against the Jews. I used every opportunity to show my friends where my allegiances lay, and Siomka and his family were the perfect scapegoats.

Siomka's father tried to protect him, but this only fanned the flames of our hatred toward him. We made the lives of Siomka and his family miserable.

Siomka's family earned a living by raising martens and nutrias for their fur. Caring for these hungry animals and cleaning up after them was difficult work, and we only made it more difficult.

Our band of hooligans stole into their yard during the nights and opened the doors of the cages, setting all the animals free. When Siomka's father caught us, he twisted our ears, causing us severe pain. Once, he caught me and twisted my ears so badly that I could not go about my daily routine. I viewed my own prank with forbearance, and I thought that Siomka's father had had no justification for hurting me. I could not forgive this offense, and I began plotting how to get even with him.

In Siomka's yard, there was a huge, ferocious German shepherd dog tied with a chain. Siomka's parents were afraid to come near it; they would serve it food from afar using long tongs, and the dog would tear the tongs with his teeth. I was not afraid of dogs, and I knew that dogs obeyed me, so with the help of a friend, I pulled this huge dog to the roof of Siomka's summer kitchen. I tugged at the dog's collar and my friend pushed it from behind. We then tied it with a chain to the chimney and left it there. *Let them try to get it down*, I schemed.

The dog yelped all night, and its owners ran around it helplessly, much to our delight.

This did not satisfy me, however, and I came up with yet another prank against Siomka's family: Once, my friends and I stole a case of yeast from the grocery. Each of us took as much yeast as we could carry and brought it home, in order to prepare samogon.[4] I took my share of the yeast, but since I could not bring stolen goods into our house, I threw all of my yeast into the cesspool of the outhouse in Siomka's yard. It was summer, and the heat quickly activated the yeast. Within a short time, the cesspool began to bubble and overflow, until it flooded the entire yard. What a sight! My friends and I split our sides laughing.

In our neighborhood lived the K. family, a Jewish family whose son Joseph had learned to play the violin. (Today he is a famous singer.) Joseph's mother dressed her chubby *wunderkind* in a velvet suit with a bowtie. The effect his appearance had on the children of the street was similar to the effect a red cloth has on a bull, and Joseph became our favorite victim. To stave us off, his parents were compelled to take turns accompanying him to the music school that he attended. But the moment Joseph appeared on the street alone, we attacked him, beat him, and smeared him with mud.

Joseph's mother changed a ruble into 10-kopeck coins and gave these coins to her son, hoping that he could use the money to pay off the hooligans, but it was to no avail. The hooligans took the money and continued to beat him.

Once, Joseph's father asked my father, "Why do the hooligans always beat my son, and they never beat your son?"

"Let him beat them back," my father replied.

"How can he defend himself against a whole group?" Joseph's father remonstrated, very logically.

That night, Papa asked me, "Why don't you protect Joseph?"

"How can I protect him?" I protested. "He's bigger than me!" I lowered my eyes, hoping that Papa wouldn't discover that I myself was one of the hooligans.

---

4. Samogon is a homemade liquor made with yeast.

A Distinguished Zhid

Once, when I was still living in the orphanage, I was invited to the home of another boy in my class. Visiting a family was a rare treat for me, and I was delighted to accept the invitation.

Apparently, the day I visited was some sort of Christian holiday, because the priest visited the house that day as well. He was ushered in with great respect, and the family served him a shot of vodka and gave him the best food they had to offer. Afterward, the parents brought their children before him and asked him to bless them.

The priest blessed the children, while waving the large cross that hung from his neck above them. Suddenly, he noticed me standing among the children, and the sweet smile disappeared from his face at once.

"What are you doing here?" he barked angrily. "I will not bless you! Jews are evil — get away from here!"

I turned around, seeking protection. But my friend's parents averted their gaze, and no one protected me.

I left the house, deeply wounded. By now, I understood why Jews were hated. But what did that have to do with me? After all, I was registered as a Russian! In my mind, the nickname "Zhid" seemed to have no connection to the word "Jew," since in Russian, the two sound completely different.[5] I was actually proud of my nickname, for I thought it implied a person who was smart and strong, just like me. My archenemy, the teacher Shatalov, never called me by my name. "Zhid, go explain it to them," he would say when he called me to the board. I would stand up and explain the lesson, for I was the only one in the class who understood it.

When I returned to my family, the children of the orphanage taunted me and said, "Nu, Zhid, you found Zhids?"

---

5. "Zhid" is the derogatory term for Jew; the proper term is *Yevrei*.

I was not insulted. My parents were handsome, strong, distinguished people — "Zhids," in my mind — not hated, weak, fearful, sniveling Jews like Siomka and his family.

I continued to live with this illusion, until my parents explained to me that "Zhid" and "Jew" were one and the same. But by this time, the pejorative "Zhid" was permanently attached to me.

Mischief

Near us lived a Jewish family: Uncle Grisha (Gershon), Auntie Genia (Henia), and their son Iylushka (Eliyahu). The three of them had survived the war by hiding with partisans. Iylushka was an only child, and his parents pampered him in any way they could. Every morning, Auntie Genia would urge him to drink warm milk, and she would say in her gentle, singsong voice, "Iylushka, drink milk, and I'll give you 20 kopecks. You'll be able to go to the cinema!"

We, Iylushka's friends, found this very amusing. Each morning, we stood under Iylushka's window and waited for the moment when Iylushka would receive his hated milk and his 20 kopecks. When the moment came, he would lower the cup of milk to us through the window, and we would drink it gladly. In this way, everyone was satisfied: The boys got milk to drink, and Iylushka didn't have to drink his milk. I didn't need milk; I was living at home by then and I no longer lacked anything. I participated in this exploit solely for the sake of the mischief.

I will never forget the date of March 16, which was when I played my most despicable prank ever. I regret this prank to this day.

Five pranksters, including Iylushka and me, decided to open the swimming season in the local park early so that we could brag about it afterward to the other boys. We ran to the park, where patches of ice still covered portions of the small pool. The ice did not stop us, however. Under the train tracks that separated the park from the pool was a large pipe. We entered the pipe and removed our clothing. After competing over who would be first to enter the pool, we splashed into the freezing water, screaming wildly. Then, we quickly jumped out of the water and ran to get dressed. Iylushka hesitated slightly as we were leaving the pool, and at that moment a mischievous idea popped into my head.

I gathered Iylushka's clothing, and we all ran away, leaving Iylushka alone and unable to leave the park. My friend Lyoshka and I went to Iylushka's mother together, and I told her, "Auntie Genia, Iylushka drowned in the pool!" I then handed her his clothes.

Iylushka's mother began to scream and cry. She ran toward the park, screaming in a terrible voice. People were shaken by her screams — Russians, Jews, and Tatars alike — and they joined her on her way to the park. A large crowd ran with her through the city, and even the fire department was summoned. The firefighters walked along the edges of the pool and peered to the bottom, while the worried neighbors gathered around.

Just then, Iylushka emerged from the pipe beneath the train tracks, shivering, blue, and frozen. "Mama!" he screamed, as he ran crying to his mother.

We, his four friends, stood at the side and rolled with laughter. When people saw us laughing, they understood what had happened, and Uncle Vania (Ivan), Uncle Yasha, and other neighbors began to chase us, shouting angrily. They could not catch us, however.

In the evening, I returned home as though nothing had happened. But when I entered the house, a strange sight met my eyes: Mama was sitting and crying, while Bubbe stood beside her, a clothesline rolled around her arm. Bubbe shouted something in my direction, from which I understood that I was about to be punished severely. I jumped back outside and hid in the attic, where I spent the entire night.

Later, I heard Bubbe and Mama searching for me and calling for me to return home, but I did not answer them. My friend Lyoshka was hiding in the neighboring attic, to escape his parents' wrath.

Two years later, Iylushka's parents were arrested and sentenced to prison for 10 years. Iylushka was left alone, and my parents took him into our house. He lived with us for some time, until relatives of his from a different city took him in. Iylushka's parents sat in prison for five years, and then they were released.

A Pesach "Gift"

I lived at home for a number of years, during which I warmed up to my family and grew stronger physically. Like all my friends, I joined the Komsomol[6] when I reached the age of 14, as was customary in Soviet schools.

Papa did not approve of my activities in this organization. To him, belonging to the Komsomol was even worse than wearing a Pioneer's tie. But his disapproval meant less to me than my desire to be like everyone else, and I decided that my family would have to become "like everyone else" as well.

In our school, we had a compulsory class on atheism. Armed with the knowledge I acquired in this class, I realized how "antiquated" and "backward" my parents' beliefs were, and I embarked on an atheist propaganda campaign in our house. I apprised my friends Tolik and Valerka of my planned campaign, and they strongly urged me to carry out my plan; apparently, they had the active encouragement of their parents, who were high-ranking Communist officials.

"Show that you're a true Komsomol youth!" they insisted. "Jews don't eat lard. If you throw it into their food, the Jews won't eat it."

So badly did I long to find favor in their eyes that I devised a plan that was more nefarious than any they could have thought of. "In our house, the Pesach matzah is stored in cloth bags," I told them. "I'm going to put lard into these bags."

---

6. The Komsomol was the Soviet youth organization. A person who did not belong to this organization had virtually no chance of being accepted to university, for he was considered politically untrustworthy.

"Yo!" they enthused. Finally, I had managed to elicit their whole-hearted approval. "Watch what happens when Pesach comes," they goaded me, "and tell us about how they have to stop celebrating the holiday because they have no matzah to eat."

My friends thought of a problem with my plan, though. "Where will you find lard?" they asked.

"We have lard in our house," I told them.

"Yours is no good," they said. "We'll bring you ours." They understood what my "lard" was, while I in my naiveté did not distinguish between lard and schmaltz.

These "friends" brought me a large piece of lard, complete with skin and black bristles. For such an important purpose, they did not skimp.

Before Pesach, I ground the wheat, sifted the flour, and distributed the matzos to other Jewish families. As always, Bubbe duly compensated me.

The white pillowcases containing our matzos hung from a hook in the ceiling, as usual. On the day before Pesach, I waited for an opportune moment when no one was home, and dropped a piece of lard into each pillowcase.

The night of Pesach arrived, and with it my long-awaited moment. The house had been scrubbed clean, the table had been covered with a white tablecloth, and the special Pesach dishes had been removed from the attic. Everyone sat down at the table, and Papa removed the bag of matzos. He opened it, and a piece of lard fell out. He ran to bring a different bag, and the same thing happened. In every bag he opened, he found black bristles.

Papa shouted at me in an menacing voice and tightened his fists. His face reddened. I had never seen him so angry. He looked as though he was about to hit me, but Bubbe said firmly and concisely, "Moshe, Pesach!"

That was enough. Papa controlled himself and sat quietly in his place.

The silence in the room was so thick, I was afraid even to breathe.

"*Ich mit em alein oitzitun* [I will take care of him myself]," Bubbe said in the same firm tone. Then she turned to me and said, "Run to Uncle Yasha and ask him for three matzos. Just be careful not to break them along the way."

I ran as fast as I could and brought the matzos from Uncle Yasha.

The seder continued as though nothing had happened, but I felt alienated. No one looked in my direction and no one talked to me; it was as though I was not even at the table.

That night, I did not ask the Four Questions, nor was I allowed to come near the matzah. The handsome "payment" for the *afikoman* was given to my brother Genka.

The truth was that my "war on religion" had begun during the previous year's Pesach seder. When my turn had come to ask the Four Questions of the *Mah Nishtanah*, instead of saying, "*Halaylah hazeh kulo matzah*," I had said, "*kulo chametz — a matzah tur men nisht.*"

Bubbe had cried, "*Oy vey iz mir* — the child is confused!" She had then made me repeat the sentence correctly.

I had not been confused, however; I had purposely switched the words of the *Mah Nishtanah* in order to mock the holiday. And by the following year's seder, I was already at a point where I was capable of hiding lard in the matzah bags.

Who Owes Whom?

The following morning, Bubbe Faiga awakened me at six in the morning, when it was still dark outside, and handed me a bucket full of potatoes. "To peel and to grate," she said crisply, in a tone so authoritative that it was impossible to argue with her. "I'll pay you a ruble a kilo."

"And how much will you pay me for grating?"

"You'll get half a ruble."

I began working energetically. We had no matzah to eat, and

potatoes had to take their place. We needed two buckets of potatoes a day — 16 kilograms!

When I finished working, I said, "Bubbe, give me the money."

"Now it's Pesach and I'm not giving you any money," she said. "After the holiday I'll settle with you."

I peeled and grated potatoes all week, mentally calculating how much I was earning and planning what I would buy with the money. I felt very rich indeed. Bubbe fried latkes, which I said were "tastier than those crackers, anyway." The way I looked at it, I had profited from my exploit in every respect: Not only had I made it clear what I thought of the Pesach holiday, I didn't even have to get stuck eating matzah all week.

When Pesach was over, I approached Bubbe for the money. "Sit down," she told me. "How much money did you earn?"

I named an amount. She listened and said, "You calculated correctly. That's what I owe *you*. Now let's calculate how much you owe *me*. Papa bought wheat and transported it to the house, and I paid you for grinding and sifting. After that we baked the matzah."

Bubbe wrote all this down on a piece of paper, and calculated that I still owed her 31 rubles — a fortune, in my eyes.

"It's not fair!" I shouted. "I'm not going to help you anymore!"

"When you need money, you'll come to me," she replied calmly.

Furious, I ran outside. But who needed money more, she or I?

A week later, I came to her and said, "Bubbe, give me a ruble."

"Learn a prayer, and you'll get it."

In this way, a Communist Youth activist was forced to learn a prayer.

My Bubbe was very wise. She forgave my "debt," and allowed me to continuing earning money from her.

After this prank, Papa became permanently estranged from me. I was very hurt by his estrangement, and I could not understand what the "big deal" was. Nor did I know how to make amends. I always did whatever I felt like doing, never thinking about the consequences of my actions. Later, when I suffered the consequences,

I would be wholly insulted and angry, blaming others instead of myself.

I don't know where my "war on religion" with my family may have led if not for our former neighbor, Ivan Ivanovich. He was the only one of the neighbors with whom Papa was friendly. Apparently, Papa complained to Ivan Ivanovich about my atheistic campaign. A short while after the incident with the lard on Pesach, I visited Ivan Ivanovich's son in their home. Ivan Ivanovich led me to the bedroom, as if innocuously, and pointed to an icon hanging in the corner. "Look at our icon," he told me. "That's our god."

"Why don't we have this in our house?" I asked him.

"Because you have a different God," he answered.

I held Ivan Ivanovich in great esteem. He was a Russian and he worked as an electrician; in other words, he was *like everyone else*. If he said that there was a God, it was worth considering the possibility seriously.

From then on, I developed a more tolerant attitude toward the fact that my parents were believing Jews.

Respect Him or Suspect Him?

Living at home for several years revitalized my body and renewed my energy stores, after the incessant hunger of the preceding years. I was still weak, however, and I did not always have the upper hand in fights with my friends. To protect myself, I trained as a boxer. Interestingly, it was none other than the teacher Shatalov, my archenemy, who sent me and several other tough guys from the school to train in boxing at the municipal community center. After training for several years, I earned the title "Champion of the Republic" in the flyweight class,[7] and at

---

7. Because a boxer's weight is an important factor in the strength of his punch, boxers are classified into 11 weight classes. Boxers in the flyweight class weigh under 112 lb/50.8 kg.

the same time I acquired the "expertise" to "solve" local problems, such as fighting.

At the end of Grade 7, all the children of the orphanage in our school were sent to trade school, and I was invited to join them. To me, the main draw of the trade school was the spanking new uniform and black visor cap that the students wore, but Papa would not allow me to study there.

"You have a home," he told me. "You'll learn in school, like all the other children."

That summer, Mama sent me to visit her sister Rochel in Kiev, so that I could become acquainted with my relatives. Aunt Rochel received me warmly, and I immediately felt as though I was among family. It seemed, however, that my destiny was to stumble into adventures even when I was not looking for them.

The day after I arrived, powerful knocks were heard at the door. The whole family was sitting at the table at the time, and Aunt Rochel paled.

"It's the OBkhSS!"[8] she whispered.

The knocks turned into heavy blows. Timidly, my uncle went to open the door. Had he not opened it, they were liable to break the door completely.

As my uncle was walking toward the door, Aunt Rochel dashed into the adjacent room and quickly returned holding a cloth package. "Wear this under your shirt and go out to the street," she whispered to me. "Don't come back until the search is over."

The package was stuffed to capacity, and was similar to the package that Bubbe had hidden under my clothing when Papa had been arrested.

By now, I was no stranger to these searches, in which plainclothes and uniformed officers would burst into a house and ransack it completely.

I sneaked out of the house as the officers were entering, and they

8. The OBkhSS was the government Department Against Misappropriation of Socialist Property, that is, theft and embezzlement of Soviet property.

did not notice me. Outside on the street, no one paid any attention to a skinny kid like me, and for several hours I wandered the nearby streets, observing from afar what was happening in Aunt Rochel's house. Finally, the police vehicle left, which meant that the search was over. Just to be safe, though, I waited until nightfall to return to the house.

The scene that greeted me in Aunt Rochel's house upon my return was a familiar one: Everything was overturned and destroyed. The main difference between this search and the search that had been conducted in my home was that this time, no one was arrested. In the midst of all the bedlam sat — my uncle, alive and well! Aunt Rochel explained that her husband had not been arrested because the officers had not found anything incriminating. Hardly believing their good fortune, my uncle and aunt sat at the table, frozen in shock.

I removed the heavy belt Aunt Rochel had given me and placed it on the table. Only then did I realize how tired I was. I went to my room and stretched out on my bed, feeling satisfied with myself at having accomplished an important mission.

Just then, I heard my uncle speaking quietly to my aunt in Yiddish. Undoubtedly, they thought that I could not hear or understand what they were saying.

"Rochel, check the belt to make sure nothing is missing," my uncle instructed. "The boy grew up in an orphanage, and he may have stolen something."

I felt as though a knife had been thrust into my back. Hurt to the core, I decided to end my visit right then. I took my handbag, sneaked out into the corridor of the house, and left with anyone noticing.

It was nighttime, and the city buses were no longer operating. I walked through the entire city until I reached the train station, and I boarded the first train of the morning that was headed toward home. During that visit, I did not manage to tour Kiev at all.

I told my parents that I had not wished to remain at Aunt Rochel's house after the search. They exchanged glances, but did not ask me anything.

Miracles

I don't know why, but I constantly found myself narrowly escaping death. One incident in which I was saved by a miracle stands out in my mind above all the others.

In 1958 (5718), when I was a Grade 10 student, I helped a friend of mine — also a child of the orphanage — to prepare for the annual May Day celebrations. My friend's job was to drape festive banners on the furnaces of the local metalworks factory. These furnaces were 40-50 meters high, and the banners that hung from them were visible a great distance away.

Around each of the cone-shaped furnaces was a narrow, winding ladder made of iron. My friend and I climbed up the ladder of one furnace that was still under construction, and when we reached the height of approximately three or four stories from the ground, we hung a red cloth banner on the furnace with the words, "Viva Mayday."

After completing our work, we sat down on the ladder and began talking. My friend sat on the rungs of the ladder, while I carelessly sat facing him on the shaky guardrail. My friend then shifted his body into a more comfortable position, resting his feet on the guardrail I was sitting on. Suddenly, the guardrail came loose. It became detached from the ladder, plunging me into a free fall along with it.

Everything went black. I know what happened afterward only from what others later told me.

I fell on my back from a height of four stories onto a concrete surface from which iron signposts jutted out. One of these posts pierced through my body in the area of my liver, poking through my clothing. Unbelievably, being impaled on an iron post actually saved my life, by slowing the pace of my fall.

Someone ran to seek help. In the meantime, my friend, who had unwittingly caused me to fall, assessed the situation correctly and did not attempt to free me from the post. Had he tried to remove me, I probably would have died.

When the ambulance arrived, the medics had no choice but to summon an ironworker from the neighboring factory and instruct him to saw through the pole beneath me. With the pole still jammed through my body, I was rushed to the hospital, where the doctors operated on me to remove the pole.

My case was so unusual that it was publicized in *Izvestia*, the major newspaper. The article described my brush with death in the typical communist style of the time, reporting that "unity between laborers — ironworkers and doctors — is what saved the life of a schoolboy."[9]

I don't know how long I was unconscious. The first person I saw when I opened my eyes was Papa, who was standing motionless at my bedside and gazing at me silently.

"You awoke, finally!" was all he managed to say. Characteristically, Papa hid his emotions.

For as long as my life was in danger, Papa came to the hospital several times a day. He would enter my room, gaze at me penetratingly, assess my condition, utter a few words, and then leave — without any show of emotion, and without asking any questions. Mama and Bubbe, on the other hand, hovered over me day and night.

As I began to recover, I became bored of lying in bed in the hospital. My classmates were preparing for their matriculation exams, and I was eager to join them. After two weeks, when I was finally able to stand on my feet, I escaped from the hospital and went home, still wearing my hospital pajamas.

I was a good student, and I hoped to receive a gold medal, which would allow me to be accepted to university without undergoing

9. Note from the author, Carmela Raiz: I recall that my father, who was a doctor, brought this newspaper home one day and said, "Read what an unbelievable miracle happened to this boy!"

any entrance exams. I did not receive the coveted medal, however, even though I knew I deserved it, for I and another Jewish girl who was also a candidate for the medal failed the Ukrainian language exam. The essays we wrote for this exam contained superfluous commas, and there was no way to prove that these commas had been added after we had handed in our papers. At the end, the medal was awarded to candidates whose nationality was more respectable than ours.

Part V

To Scale the Peak

Why I Chose to Become a Surgeon

I wanted to go to medical school, but Papa thought it was impossible. "You can't get into medical school without bribery," he said, "and we do not have money for that."

"If that is the case," I declared, "I will go *only* to medical school, and not anywhere else — but without any bribery." And indeed, I was accepted to medical school without bribery — which was astounding, considering my nationality.

Bubbe Faiga said that she wished to see the place where I was going to be studying, and she informed me that she would accompany me personally to the university on the first day of my studies.

I was horrified. "Bubbe, this isn't First Grade!" I protested.

Bubbe was insistent, however. And when Bubbe made up her mind, there was nothing you could do to change it. On the first of September, therefore, we took a taxi to the university together, Bubbe Faiga looking very distinguished in her festive kerchief, while I, her little grandson, was blushing with embarrassment. To me, it seemed that everyone was looking at us and thinking, "Look at the overgrown baby whose grandma is bringing him to university!"

While Bubbe was paying the driver and exiting the taxi, I dashed away from her quickly and ran into the building, where I blended into the crowd of students.

Once I began attending university, I opted to live in the dormitory, giving my parents the excuse that traveling to and from our house every day took too much time. The truth, however, was that I wanted to be my own master. I would visit my family for Shabbos or during the week, whenever I was in the mood of Bubbe's cooking.

I found my studies interesting, but as usual, I became embroiled in adventures.

Once, my class of fresh-faced first-year medical students was taken on a tour of the local hospital. Our professor led us from one department to another, lecturing to us as we proceeded through the hospital. We trailed after him like chicks follow a hen, taking in the hospital sights all around us. When we reached the psychiatric department, I and a friend of mine — who was thin like me — dawdled behind absentmindedly and became separated from our group. Suddenly, several of the female patients in the ward swooped down upon us. Before we could say a word, they threw blankets over our heads, wrapped us up with lightning speed, and dragged us away.

I was wrapped so tightly that I could not move a muscle, and I could barely breathe. Shouting for help was futile in any case, because my voice could not be heard through the blanket. What were these mentally ill women planning to do with us?

Luckily for us, our fellow students noticed our absence after a short while. With the help of the staff of the psychiatric department — who had plenty of experience with situations like these — the two tightly-wrapped human bundles were located under the beds in the women's room.

We were a sorry sight, my friend and I, when we were freed from the blankets. For a long time afterward, my classmates were much amused by this "kidnapping" incident. My friend and I did not find it very funny, however.

That incident caused me to lose all interest in psychiatry, and I never set foot into that department again.

When the time came to choose a specialty, I opted for surgery.

Mama was not happy with my choice, and she complained to Bubbe, "All of the neighbors' children who studied medicine chose normal specialties: Yasha [Yaakov] became a dermatologist, Boria

[Boris] became a neurologist, *a der daf a messer* [but this one needs a knife]!"

Bubbe attempted to placate her. "Some children are born with violent natures, and the Torah teaches that even these natures can be channeled into positive activities, such as becoming a *shochet* or a *mohel*. So our child will be a surgeon!"

Who Lives in Israel?

In 1962, Arab students joined our university. I made the acquaintance of one of these Arabs one day while I was playing soccer with my friends. I was the goalie, and an Arab student was wandering about in front of my eyes, which I found annoying. "Why are you walking in front of me?" I demanded. "Is your father a glassmaker?"[1]

He didn't understand my sarcasm, and he answered me in all seriousness, "No, my father's a lawyer, not a glassmaker."

I found his answer amusing, and that was the beginning of our friendship. His name was Tarik, and he told me that he was an Arab from Israel.

When I arrived home, I told my family about Tarik. "There are no Arabs in Israel," Papa said decisively. "Everyone in Israel is Jewish."

"But he says he's an Arab," I argued.

"He said that in order to be accepted to university here," Papa replied.

During those years, Papa had begun to express his wish that our family move to Israel. I did not take his words seriously, since I had no idea what Israel was or why on earth we would want to move there. But seeing that Papa was interested in my new friend, I brought Tarik home to visit on our next day off.

Papa addressed Tarik in Yiddish, and Tarik said that he did not

---

1. This was a slang expression meaning, "You're not transparent, I can't see through you."

understand. Papa then began speaking to him in Hebrew, and Tarik answered in Hebrew as well. Papa's eyes lit up.

"You see?" he exclaimed. *"Ich red mit em in Lashon Kodesh* [I'm speaking to him in the Holy Tongue]!"

Bubbe addressed him in Hebrew as well, and he answered her, too.

"Zissel, du zeist [Zissel, you see]?" Papa told Mama. He brought a *siddur* and gave it to Tarik to read.

"Give me a hat," Tarik requested. He covered his head and began reading from the *siddur.*

Papa looked at me meaningfully. "Nu, what did I say?"

Thoroughly convinced that Tarik was a Jew, Papa instructed Mama, "Give each of the boys 10 rubles and prepare them a basket of food." He spoke in Yiddish, so that the guest would not understand.

Mama and Bubbe scurried around the house preparing food and went down to the cellar to bring up tasty treats. They arranged everything in a large basket and gave it to Tarik.

From then on, no matter how much I tried to persuade Papa that Tarik and his friends were Arabs, Papa insisted that they were Jews, and he always sent kosher food for them.

After all the other Arab students completed their studies and left, Tarik remained behind at the university to specialize under the famed Professor Smuliak, who was Jewish.

When Papa heard this, he smiled knowingly. "Smuliak knew whom to keep with him!" Papa was certain that Smuliak had chosen a Jew to study under him; he naively thought that the professor was free to choose anyone he wanted.

About a year later, Tarik came and informed us that he was engaged to his colleague, the student Svetka [Svetlana]. He invited Papa to the wedding, but Papa replied firmly that he did not attend weddings of non-Jews (he meant the bride). Papa still did not believe that Tarik was an Arab, and he no longer wished to see Tarik after his marriage to a gentile.

The Second Slap

A s I related earlier, the first time Papa slapped me was when I laughed at the sight of Mama stuck under the bed. The second time he slapped me was when I was already a medical student.

One evening, I returned home, and Papa asked me, "Have you spoken to Ivan Ivanovich?"

Ivan Ivanovich, our former neighbor, was very ill, and I had promised to take him to for a medical consultation with one of my university professors.

"Oy, Papa," I said, "I forgot all about it!"

Papa was sitting at the table, and without rising from his place, he gave me such a ringing slap that I was thrown across the length of the room. Without raising his voice, Papa said, "Even if something is already in your pocket, don't promise that you're going to do it. Say, 'I'll try.' A word is not a bird, and when it flies, you won't be able to catch it."[2]

This lesson remained with me for the rest of my life.

Papa's word carried a great deal of weight, and when he promised someone something, he always kept his promise. As a result, people respected him greatly. They would say, *"Moshe's vort geven a vort* [Moshe is a man of his word]."

"A person has to have self-respect," Papa used to say. "If you say something once, you shouldn't have to say it again. And if you said it, you should keep your word."

Papa was not a talker, and I never saw him engage in idle chatter with anyone. The image of Papa that remains with me is the image of a rock-solid foundation supporting a strong building on its shoulders.

The same way the neighbors loved Bubbe and Mama, they also

2. Papa's words were based on a Russian folk saying.

revered and honored Papa, and did not come to him to discuss mundane matters. Papa, for his part, never refused to help anyone; he did not even balk at helping the neighbors drag heavy packages. Yet he never descended to the level of friendship with them.

I respected Papa because he was big and strong, although he did not demonstrate his strength often. Once, when Papa was over 70 years old, I witnessed the following incident:

In the yard of our house, workers were fixing the plumbing, and Papa told them something. He spoke with a guttural "r," and the Ukrainian worker began mimicking him, much to the enjoyment of his colleagues. Without uttering a sound, Papa lifted from the ground a metal pipe several centimeters in diameter, and bent it with his hands. He then threw the bent pipe at the feet of the mocking worker, and said offhandedly, "Try to straighten it."

The workers were taken aback. "Look at this grandpa!" they exclaimed. "It's better not to start up with him — he can twist our heads the same way he twisted the pipe!"

The Gypsy Woman

My parents knew little about my life as a student. They lived in their world and I lived in mine, and they would have been horrified to know how their son kept himself occupied.

A short while after I started attending university, I began earning money handsomely on the side, by assisting the lecturers with the design and presentation of their research studies.

My professional curiosity was awakened around this time, and I spent hours testing new theories I had. At one point, I invented a new instrument and tested its efficacy on dogs. The idea behind the instrument was superb, but for some reason, the dogs always died shortly after I operated on them. Conceding failure, I abandoned my instrument under my bed in the dormitory.

One day, Professor K., a renowned learned doctor from Moscow, came to lecture to us. His lecture was related in some way to my failed invention, and I approached him at the conclusion of the lecture to discuss this invention. To my great surprise, the honored guest took a keen interest in the details of my invention, and he quickly determined what may have gone wrong. He believed that the dogs had died because of a problem in the post-operative procedure, not because of a failure relating to the instrument itself, and he invited me to continue my experiment under his tutelage. I was delighted, and very proud.

"But they won't give me any more dogs," I explained, "because all the dogs die under me!"

"I don't have time to wait for you to experiments on dogs," Professor K. said impatiently. "We have to perform a real trial, on a human."

"But the dogs didn't survive, Professor!" I protested.

"Young man," he said reprovingly, "I am in need of an assistant who is courageous and can take initiative. I already pointed out your mistake. If you are unwilling, I will find someone else. Bring your instrument."

"I used it on dogs," I said dubiously.

"It's fine," he replied. "You'll sterilize and disinfect it."

I ran to my dormitory room and withdrew the dusty instrument from beneath my bed. In hindsight, I shudder to think of what kind of instrument this was. It had been fashioned hastily, and was extremely primitive.

Professor K. and I visited the local hospital together, and after studying the patients' medical records, the professor expressed his desire to examine several patients. A request made by this distinguished, high-ranking visitor from the capital could not be refused, and the patients were brought before him.

Drawing upon his vast medical expertise, the esteemed professor settled upon the perfect guinea pig for our experiment: an elderly, bloated Gypsy woman who had no relatives. In the event that our experiment would fail, the professor knew, no one would have any complaints about the fate of this hapless woman.

The Gypsy woman did not disappoint us. Not only did she survive the operation, she also survived the post-operative period — unlike the dogs. This enabled the professor to present his new, revolutionary invention at the upcoming medical convention in Moscow. After the convention, I saw the transcript of his speech, and I noticed that he did not mention my name at all. Nevertheless, I considered it a great honor to work with this eminent scientist.

I remained with the Gypsy woman for several days after the operation, not budging from her bedside day or night. The poor woman thought that she was receiving excellent care, and she was very touched by my "devotion."

"Doctor, my son," she murmured with tears in her eyes, trying to kiss my hand. Little did she know that this "son" was concerned with one thing only: recording the results of the medical experiment. Inwardly, I justified my actions with the argument that all this was being done for the sake of science and for the benefit of all humanity. Besides, I reasoned, the Gypsy woman would certainly have died had we not treated her.

I don't know what happened to the woman, but to this day, the memory of her appreciative, heartfelt gaze gnaws at my conscience.

The Plague

In the summer of my sixth and final year of medical school, my fellow students and I were sent, as a matter of course, to work as construction workers in the plains of Kazakhstan.[3] As a medical student, I was responsible for the health of a group of students from the Polytechnic Institute.

---

3. During those years, university students in the Soviet Union were required to spend a portion of their summer vacation doing manual labor for the State in fields, building sites, and the like.

We lived in tents, surrounded for thousands of kilometers by desolation. There was no trace of civilization anywhere.

One day, we were radioed that there was an urgent need for a doctor in a far-off village, and a small airplane was sent to fly me to that village. I took along a first-aid kit and climbed into the rickety aircraft. A short while later, the plane landed near a number of Kazakh tents, sending billows of dust into the air.

As we stepped off the plane, we were greeted by scorching heat and deathly silence. The pilot remained inside the plane, while I strode quickly in the direction of the tents, wondering why no one had come to greet us. I entered the tent at the edge of the encampment and stood there frozen, dumbfounded by what I saw: Groaning people were lying on the ground, which was mostly covered by dirty rags. I went further inside to look at these sick patients from up close, and then I immediately fled outside. Even I, a student, was able to determine at first glance that the people here were suffering from a severe and highly contagious airborne illness: the plague!

I ran back to the aircraft and radioed my findings to the center. I was instructed not to enter any other tents, but to remain some distance away from them in an area that was open to the wind and wait for reinforcements to be sent.

The plane took off, leaving me stranded in the village and surrounded by dying people. I heard their groans, but there was nothing I could do to help them. Calm as I was, I understood that my own situation was grave: I had entered the contaminated tent and breathed its diseased air!

Reinforcements arrived only the next morning. Soldiers drove up in vehicles, erected a double wire fence around the tents, and stood guard outside the fence. With them came three doctors clad in quarantine suits and wearing masks on their faces.

I walked toward them, wearing my short-sleeved shirt. Seeing me, the only living creature in sight, the doctors began running away, and commanded me not to approach them. They then entered the tents and confirmed my diagnosis. It was the plague, indeed.

The doctors gave me a protective suit and placed me in quarantine. For a week, I sat in a tent alone, but I received good food to eat. My food was placed in a container in the space between the two wire fences, and I would take it and return to my tent. The doctors remained in their tent, safely outside the fence. After a week, they allowed me to join them, and I helped them as much as I could with their horrific work.

I was taken away from the village only a month later, and I was placed in quarantine in a regional hospital for a while afterward. This affair dragged on for several months, and I arrived very late for the beginning of the academic year.

Village Doctor

In 1964 (5724), I completed my medical studies and was assigned to the Ukrainian village of Barishi,[4] which was located hundreds of kilometers away from my home in Donetsk.

Before I left for Barishi, Papa laid tefillin on me once again. This time I did not oppose him. I already knew that these tefillin had belonged to my grandfather, Shepsel Wolf. Papa laid the thin black straps on my arm according to a precise order, just as he laid them on himself every morning. It was as though in doing so he was tying me to the chain of generations — to himself, to his father, and so on. His lips moved, but I could not discern what he was saying. It seemed to me that he was praying that his son should not be lost to him again.

Thirty years later, during my first days in Israel, after I had been rescued for the umpteenth time, I arrived with my rescuer at the Belzer shul in Jerusalem. A very old man with a snow-white beard, who looked to me like Avraham Avinu, suggested that I lay tefillin, and I agreed. When he

---

4. After completing a degree in the Soviet Union, students were required to work for three years on government assignments, generally in remote areas.

began to wrap the straps around my arm, I commented, "My father used to tie them differently."

"Do you remember how?" he asked. "Show me."

I laid the tefillin as I remembered Papa laying them on me. "That's how the Litvaks lay tefillin," he said excitedly. "For the rest of your life you'll lay tefillin this way."

The village of Barishi, in the Zhitomir region, was situated 29 kilometers from the nearest highway or train station. The area was swampy, and from the end of August through June (autumn-winter-spring) you had to wear boots to wade through the muddy terrain. I thought that I would have to work in this desolate place for only three years, as was required of me, but I wound up being stuck there for seven years.

The village doctor was an important figure, and the locals addressed me respectfully as "Moyseich," or "Semyon Moysevich."

In the beginning of my stay in Barishi, I rented a room from an old Ukrainian fellow. Suspecting that I was a Jew, the old man began peppering me with questions regarding my father's origins. Attempting to ward off his questions, I told him that I was an orphan who had grown up in an orphanage. In places like this, you sealed a miserable fate for yourself by admitting that you were a Jew, and I did not have the courage to say that I was Jewish.

About a month later, Papa decided to visit me and see how I was doing. He did not inform me of his visit in advance — which would have allowed me to meet him at the train station — for he liked to investigate things independently. He found a ride to the village and approached the first old man he met and asked him where the doctor lived. Unfortunately, this old man happened to be my landlord.

"Who are you?" the old man asked him.

"I am his father."

"His father?" the old man asked quizzically. "He told me that he was an orphan from an orphanage!"

When Papa met me, he did not tell me about this encounter with my landlord. But when he arrived home, he told Mama sadly, "How can he dismiss us so easily?"

I learned of this incident only years later, when it was already too late to explain anything and there was no one to apologize to. Despite my incessant longing to be close to Papa, I always managed to accomplish the opposite.

Grandpa's Replacement

My supervisor in the village hospital was a department director who had earned the nickname "Grandpa." This nickname had stuck to him since the period of World War II, when he had served as a doctor to a group of partisans. He was a talented autodidact,[5] who had barely completed a medic's course of study, but he had vast experience and was a master at maximizing the negligible resources at his disposal.

With his battle experience and rare abilities, Grandpa could certainly have become a famous doctor. But because he was an alcoholic, he wound up in a far-flung village hospital. Many times, he was so drunk that I, a fresh medical school graduate, was forced to handle complex and unexpected medical crises independently.

Once, a woman who was expecting twins came to the hospital to give birth. Grandpa — who was intoxicated, as usual — examined her and discovered that she was actually carrying triplets. He decided to have some fun at my expense. He hid in a place where no one could find him, and fell asleep there, drunk.

The people in the hospital searched all over for him, and when they did not find him they hurried to call me. I barely knew how to deliver a baby under normal circumstances, and here I had to deliver twins! When I successfully delivered the two babies, I was very happy to have successfully met the challenge. And then I discovered that there was a third baby ....

These were Grandpa's "jokes." Even so, however, I learned a great deal from Grandpa.

5. Self-educated person.

One of the workers informed on Grandpa to the authorities, claiming that he held his position illegally, as he had no higher education. Grandpa was therefore forced to travel to Kiev in his later years and attend medical school — together with his daughter, who was studying medicine at the same time. In his absence, I was appointed senior doctor of the village and director of the hospital.

There was a dearth of medicine in the hospital, and the food supply was meager. I therefore decided to organize a private source of income for the hospital — which was not very difficult, because no one in the village came to the doctor empty-handed. Even the poorest old woman would bring me 10 eggs when she came. This was a generations-old tradition, and turning down the offerings was unthinkable. If I wouldn't accept their gift, they would think that I didn't want to treat them. And so, by the end of each week I would amass hundreds of eggs and a collection of other items for which I, a bachelor, had no need.

Once, an old woman was brought to the hospital in terrible condition. She had been suffering from a stomachache, and had decided to treat herself by taking an earthenware jug, heating it from the inside, and placing it on her abdomen, like a suction cup.[6] The jug became stuck to her, however, and sucked her belly inside its cavity. It was impossible to remove the jug from the woman's belly, and we had to shatter the jug and perform emergency surgery. After she recovered, the woman brought a calf to the hospital's yard as a sign of her appreciation to me for having saved her life. But what could I do with it?

I traded it in the village for a cow, and from then on the hospital had its own supply of fresh milk every day. Later, I built a chicken coop and planted vegetables, so that the patients could begin to receive proper food. Ironically, these efforts almost resulted in my being fired.

One day, an inspector from the center of the country arrived.

---

6. At that time, treatment with suction cups (*bankes*) was a very popular folk remedy for all sorts of ailments.

"What's this, a farm?" she thundered when she saw the livestock and agriculture I had arranged. "It's supposed to be a hospital!"

Attempting to calm her down and impress her, I brought her to see the new x-ray room that I had set up. The x-ray technician, an alcoholic, would sit in his dark room and treat patients based on the amount of vodka they brought him. Unfortunately, he had not been apprised of the inspection, and I paid dearly for that.

Seated second from right is Grandpa; beside him, third from right, is Shepsel.

The inspector entered before me. Seeing her, the technician said in his stammering voice, "Grandma, it's half a liter of vodka for half an x-ray, and a liter of vodka for a full x-ray." This was his standard price.

The inspector burst out of the room, frothing with anger and threatening me in any way she could.

I was not frightened at all, however. On the contrary — I was hoping to be expelled from the village because of my infractions, and I continued doing as I pleased.

The hospital received an ambulance for its use, but the ambulance could not move through the mud and snow. I therefore traded it for a tractor, and used the tractor to travel to my patients in all weather conditions. I was taken to task for this by my superiors, but there was little they could do, since there was no way they could replace me. Who else would agree to work in such a godforsaken place?

Once, a caller from the village telephoned me at the hospital and said, "Moyseich, run over here quickly! Our accountant has lost his mind — he crawled under the bed and won't come out!"

The accountant, Adolph Franchevitz, was of German origin — a *Volksdeutsche* — and was a wealthy, distinguished person. He was the one who paid the salaries of the people in the village. I came to his house and found him crouched under the bed. "Franchevitz, get out!" I commanded him.

I bent down to him, trying to help him emerge from under the bed. Suddenly, he bit my hand! I arranged for him to be tied up and wrapped in blankets so that he could be brought to the hospital, but he broke through the ties and dashed under the bed again.

We then summoned an epidemiologist from the center of the region. Even without approaching the patient, he diagnosed him with rabies.

I gave the medical staff instructions for caring for Franchevitz, and I took the visiting doctor out to eat in the village mess hall, where they knew how what to serve a guest of this caliber: vodka, fresh appetizers, hot borscht ....

While I was sitting at the table and chatting with my guest, we received a message from the hospital informing us that Franchevitz had died.

The regional doctor suddenly looked at me strangely. "How close did you get to him?" he asked.

"How close?" I chortled. "Look, he bit my hand!" I showed him the palm of my hand, which had bled as a result of Franchevitz's bite.

My guest blanched. "What?" he shouted. "You must take serum immediately!"

The anti-rabies serum he wanted me to take was a series of 50 daily injections in the abdomen. These injections were extremely painful, and after suffering with them for a week I became fed up and stopped taking the injections.

Once again, I suffered no harm.

Midnight Kidnaping

As the director of the hospital, I was allotted a room on the hospital grounds to live in. I greatly preferred this arrangement, which allowed me to be independent, and was also more comfortable for me — especially because the village doctor had to be on call 24 hours a day; there was no other doctor for hundreds of kilometers around.

One frigid night in January, there was a knock on my window. "Moyseich, get ready, there's someone who doesn't feel well."

"Is he far away?" I asked.

"No, he's nearby."

I took a satchel with medical equipment, threw on a coat, and headed outside, where two strangers were waiting to transport me by sleigh. I entered the sleigh, they whipped the horse, and we began traveling over the snow that gleamed under the moonlight.

The moment the sleigh entered the forest, the men suddenly placed a sack over my head and told me in a threatening voice, "Lie down and keep quiet."

They wrapped me in two fur coats — both to keep me from freezing and to restrict my movements — and laid me at the bottom of the sleigh. At first, I tried to figure out the meaning of their strange behavior, but eventually fatigue overpowered me and I fell asleep.

Our trip was a long one, and I awoke only when the sleigh stopped moving. Apparently, we had arrived at our destination — but where were we?

The men removed the sack and the coats and helped me to my feet. Looking around, I saw that the sleigh had stopped in a clearing in a black forest covered with pristine snow. The snow in the area was a bit trampled, and despite the darkness, I was able to discern some wooden huts in the area.

I was led into one of the huts. By now, I realized that I had been brought to the hideout of Banderovtsy.[7]

Inside the hut it was warm, clean, and remarkably bright. On a bed in the hut lay a sick man, writhing from side to side and hallucinating. The men who had brought me removed the quilt that covered the patient, and I saw that his leg was turning black, a clear sign of gangrene. "We have to take him to the hospital immediately to amputate his leg," I told the men. "Otherwise he'll die."

"No, treat him here," they insisted.

One of the men then approached me threateningly and said, "We know that you have a father, mother, and brother living in Donetsk. You may not tell anyone what you have seen here. Keep your mouth shut, or we'll cut out your tongue."

"Why are you threatening me?" I asked wearily. "If you want the patient to live, bring him to the hospital. I can't do anything for him here — I need medication and instruments."

Hearing this, their tone changed. "It is forbidden for us to enter a hospital," they said simply. "You'll have to operate on him here. Tell us what you need and we'll get everything for you."

I enumerated a list of items, including a rare antibiotic that was manufactured abroad. I was certain that they would not manage to acquire the items I had named, and I thought this would help me wiggle out of the mess I was in.

"Fine," they replied. "You'll get what you asked for."

---

7. Banderovtsy were Ukrainian nationalists who hid in forests after World War II and refused to submit to Soviet authority; they became bandits preying on the local populace.

They then presented me with a medical bag full of top quality, American-made surgical instruments — every surgeon's dream!

Just then, however, the patient spoke up through his hallucinations and demanded that his leg not be amputated. Apparently he was a high-ranking member of this band, and his word was law.

The men turned to me and said, "If he doesn't agree to have his leg amputated, you'll have to heal him without amputating his leg."

Their demand placed me in a very unenviable position. How was I to heal him without amputating his leg? If he were to die of gangrene, they would kill me!

They presented me with an assistant who understood a bit about medicine, and the assistant helped me and observed my actions carefully.

Having no recourse, I decided to try to heal the patient's diseased leg. I made large, long cuts down the length of the leg, improvising as I operated. I became so absorbed in the surgery that I completely lost track of the time, the place, and the danger that I faced if the surgery would not succeed.

When I finished operating on the patient, it was already after daybreak. At this point, the men brought me the antibiotic I had requested. This medication, I knew, could not be obtained even in the center of the region. *Where had they procured all of these supplies?* I wondered. *We were in the middle of a forest!*

I told the men that the patient's condition was critical, and that I needed to continue treating him every day. Addressing me in a more pleasant tone than before, they asked, "Will you be able to go without sleep every night and then work through the day in such a way that no one will guess what you are doing?"

After some deliberation, I told them that it was impossible. After all, I had patients in the hospital to treat, and if I were busy all night, my eyes would inevitably close while I was treating my day patients. We decided, therefore, that I would come to treat this patient every other night.

The men brought me back to the hospital the same way they had taken me, with a sack over my head.

This arrangement continued for a month. Every other night the men would arrive, and I would climb into their sleigh. As we would enter the forest, they would place the sack over my head, and I would fall asleep until we arrived at their hideout.

Unbelievably, my patient recovered completely after a month of treatment, and was able to walk with barely a limp. Had he been taken to the hospital, he would have left without a leg.

The Banderovtsy thanked me and compensated me royally. To me, the most meaningful gift they gave me was the bag containing the coveted American surgical instruments. I used those instruments all the years that I worked as a surgeon, and I have kept them with me to this day.[8]

Later, when I married, the Banderovtsy gave my wife a gift of a beautiful nutria fur coat, trimmed with fox fur. The coat was light as a feather and protected my wife from the fiercest cold.

I was no less interested than the Banderovtsy in keeping my nocturnal activities a secret. Otherwise, I would have been caught between a rock and a hard place: How could I have explained to the Soviet authorities why I, a patriotic law-abiding citizen, had not informed on the Banderovtsy?

My dangerous association with the Banderovtsy served me well at a later date, when I needed to obtain a rare drug from abroad. I mentioned to someone whom I suspected of having ties with the Banderovtsy that I was in need of this drug, and within a short time I received what I had requested.

Over 30 years passed before I dared tell anyone about this chapter of my life.

---

8. Note from the author, Carmela Raiz: Shepsel showed me this bag. It was small, made of brown leather. He opened it reverently, and when I looked inside I saw the instruments gleaming as though they were new.

Parting from Bubbe Faiga

Bubbe Faiga passed away in 1966 (5726). She was active and energetic until her dying day.

Shortly before Bubbe's passing, I arrived home from the village to visit my family for a few days. I could not have guessed that this would be the last time I would see my beloved Bubbe Faiga.

On her final day in this world, Bubbe Faiga went to the marketplace early in the morning and bought a chicken for Shabbos. Usually, when she returned home, she would tell Mama, "Look what a nice chicken I bought — and it was so cheap! I paid only three rubles!"

Mama would invariably answer, "When I was in the market, a chicken like this cost 10 rubles, and you always pay only three rubles!"

This was a little routine they had: Bubbe always claimed to have bought everything for three rubles. But that morning, Mama was not home, and the usual routine did not take place.

Bubbe sent me to Uncle Yasha the *shochet* to have the chicken slaughtered, and when I returned, she asked me to pluck the feathers. Together, we cut up the chicken, soaked it in water, and then salted it, to *kasher* it.

"I'm going to rest," Bubbe said then, and went to her room to lie down.

"Where's Bubbe?" Mama asked when she returned home.

"She's resting in her room," I replied.

We waited a while, and then Mama told me, "It's already late, go wake Bubbe." It was out of character for Bubbe to rest so much during the day.

"Better that you should go," I said. "Do you want her to be angry with me?"

It seemed strange to me that Bubbe was still asleep. Sensing that something was wrong, Mama and I went into her room together. When we opened the door, we found Bubbe lying on the floor near her bed, lifeless! On the chair beside her were shrouds and candles. Everything was prepared for her funeral.

Mama began to cry and scream. I called Papa, and he arrived home together with Jews who served on the community's *chevrah kaddisha*. Everything was done according to halachah: The women performed a *taharah* on Bubbe's body, wrapped her in shrouds and a sheet, and laid her on a door that had been removed from its hinges and placed on the floor.

The sight of these funeral preparations was unbearable to me. I fled the house, and began wandering through the streets and crying like a little child. How could I live without Bubbe Faiga?

In the meantime, the terrible news spread through the nearby streets. When I returned home, I found that our gentile neighbors had begun to congregate in our home. They vehemently objected to the sight of Bubbe's body lying on the ground, completely wrapped in shrouds. "What's this?" they demanded. "We can't see her face! And why is she lying on the ground? Where's the coffin?"

The neighbors were disturbed by what they perceived as a lack of honor to their beloved Bubbe Faiga, and they began to show signs of rage.

At first, Papa attempted to explain what was going on and argue with the neighbors, but Uncle Yasha assessed the situation correctly and whispered in his ear, "Moshe, there's nothing to do, we have to open the shrouds!"

Papa was forced to allow the gentile women to take Bubbe's body to a back room, where they opened the sheet, removed the shrouds, and dressed Bubbe in a velvet Shabbos dress. In the meantime, other neighbors made sure to bring a proper coffin for Bubbe.

It was frightening to look at Papa, who was deeply aggrieved that he had not managed to protect his mother's body from indignities that caused her soul distress. He tried to put a stop to these indignities, but Mama led him away into a different room, tears streaming from her eyes.

True to Russian custom, the neighbors placed the coffin on the table, and hordes of gentiles streamed through our home to take leave of Bubbe Faiga. Many of them cried bitterly, as though they had lost a close relative.

One of the Jews there said that Bubbe should be buried before dark. The gentiles did not object to this, and they finally left the house. When only Jews remained in the house, Bubbe's body was once again wrapped in shrouds and a sheet. She was then placed in the coffin, but only after several of the beams supporting the coffin were broken. This was done to ensure that Bubbe's body would be in direct contact with the ground, as the Torah says, *"Ve'el afar tashuv* — and to dust you shall return."

"Bubbe's children," the young men of the neighborhood whom Bubbe had raised, carried her coffin on their shoulders. On their way to the cemetery, they passed by the local school, where Bubbe would hurry to protect them when they misbehaved.

Years later, Mama was brought to her final rest in a similar manner, carried on the neighbors' shoulders.

In the late 1990s, anti-Semitic riots broke out in Donetsk, as in other places, and many gravestones in the local Jewish cemetery were smashed. The gravestones of my parents and Bubbe survived, however, and are cared for devotedly by one of the neighbors to this day.

After Bubbe's passing, our home was orphaned. Now, it was clearer than ever before that Bubbe had been a pillar of strength not only for our family but for our entire small Jewish community as well.

The Shabbos *minyan* continued to congregate in our house, and the prayers were held as usual, but our Shabbos table was different: We no longer had any guests. Papa had always relied exclusively on Bubbe in matters of kashrus, and now he was very worried that something would go wrong in the kitchen. Therefore Mama no longer served meat in the house, and from then on Papa ate meat only in the home of Uncle Yasha the *shochet*.

Marriage

Forced Marriage

During the years 1648-1655, Ukrainian Cossacks led by Bogdan Chmielnicki rebelled against Poland, which had sovereignty over the Ukraine at the time. They also poured out their hatred and wrath on the hapless Jews, brutally murdering an estimated 100,000 Jews who refused to renounce their faith.

The Cossacks would choose young Jewish girls for themselves and forcibly convert and marry them. One of these girls requested that the wedding ceremony be held in a church across the river, and when the festive procession reached the bridge, she jumped into the river and drowned. Another girl informed her Cossack groom that she knew how to work magic on bullets, and she convinced him to shoot her so that she could demonstrate that bullets would not harm her. He shot her, and she died. In this way, she was saved from a forced conversion and marriage.

On several occasions, I traveled from the village where I was stationed to Zhitomir, the central city in the region, in order to take care of various matters. Once, I met a young woman in the street and took a liking to her. It turned out that she was a nurse. We were headed toward the same institution, and we conversed along the way.

I suggested that we meet again after we each saw to what we had to do, and I invited her to a coffee shop. When we were seated at a table in the coffee shop, I showed her my passport, which contained my vital statistics: it said that I was single and Jewish. She told me that she was Jewish as well.

That was the main thing I had wanted to find out. I didn't have time for any other investigations, since I had to return to the village. Without further ado, I proposed marriage, and she accepted.

I didn't know anything about her, just as she didn't know anything about me. She merely mentioned that she had been raised by her grandmother, since her mother lived in a different city.

A short time beforehand, I had experienced a difficult parting from an Armenian girl whom I had wanted to marry. My father had been opposed to the match, however. "Your children have to be Jewish," he had said. "They have to know why they are being beaten."

"Why do they have to be beaten?" I had asked.

"They will be beaten regardless, and a person has to know how to cope," he had said decisively.

I had listened to him, and I hadn't married that girl.

This time, however, the girl I was planning to marry had a Jewish mother, and I therefore did not anticipate any opposition on my parents' part.

I called my parents and informed them that I was engaged to be married. My father answered cautiously, "We have to come and see."

They did not make me wait very long. A few days later, my parents arrived in Zhitomir. They knew many people there, but they preferred to stay in a hotel room, for they did not wish to be dependent on anyone.

While my parents went around visiting Jewish homes in order to inquire about my bride, I went out to meet her. In the evening, I returned to the hotel, exultant. But when I entered my parents' hotel room, I sensed that something was wrong. My parents looked very sad, and my mother tried not to look at me. I could tell from her eyes that she had been crying. What had they discovered, I wonder?

"My son! *Dos zach iz nit far intz* [This 'thing' is not suitable for us]!" Papa proclaimed decisively and concisely, in his usual manner.

He did not explain what he meant or why he was opposed to the match; it was as though he thought that his one sentence would be enough to convince me to give up my bride. Papa did not wish to speak *lashon hara* about other Jews, and he hoped that his words would dissuade me from going ahead with the wedding.

His hope was misplaced, however. I was sick of living alone in a far-flung village, and I exploded, "*She's* not suitable, and the other one's not suitable — what do I care what you found out? Maybe I shouldn't get married at all? You know what, Papa? You cooked your soup with Mama, and I want to cook my own soup!"

So I went ahead and cooked my soup. But I never did achieve the happiness that to me was signified by a soup tureen.

My parents did not come to my wedding in Zhitomir. Later, I learned the hard way that Papa was not one to speak without due consideration, and that I should have listened to him.

Career

After working in the village for seven years — well more than the three years I had been obligated to work there — I finally managed to get out together with my wife and baby daughter, who had been born in the village. We moved to Donetsk so that we could be close to my parents.

I found work in the local children's hospital, and I also worked as an ambulance doctor. Although I worked day and night, I earned only a pittance, and I could not even dream of buying my own apartment. Instead, we lived with my parents.

I knew that my mother would be able to get along with anyone, and I hoped that once we moved in my father would develop an attachment to his granddaughter and be compelled to make peace with my marriage.

Apparently, however, I didn't know my father well enough. He never did make peace with my marriage. My father simply ignored my wife. He never addressed her, nor did he ever approach my daughter. When he wanted to give my daughter something, he would tell my mother, "Zissel, give this to the girl."

The atmosphere in the house was tense and heavy.

After some time, my wife took our daughter to visit her grandmother in Zhitomir. She did not wish to return to Donetsk, and I had to move to Zhitomir to join her.

For a Jewish doctor to find work in Zhitomir was no easy task. I pinned my hopes for employment on Dr. Gorbachevski, a senior doctor and the director of the Zhitomir regional hospital. I had gotten to know Dr. Gorbachevski while working in the village, and he had taken note of me and had offered me a job working for him. I would have gladly accepted the offer, but at that time I was still obligated to remain in the village.

Now that I had moved to Zhitomir, I decided to approach Dr. Gorbachevski, hoping that his offer still held.

Gorbachevski, an elderly, intelligent Pole, received me warmly, and gave me a job as the director of a department. Considering that I was Jewish, this was a huge promotion by the standards of the time (it was 1971).

Gorbachevski was a renowned specialist in his field. During the period of the Nazi conquest, he had continued to work as a doctor, and during the Soviet regime he earned the award of "Hero of Socialist Labor." Due to his status, he could afford to hire a Jew to work as the director of a department — a daring step by Soviet standards.

Under Gorbachevski's leadership, the Zhitomir hospital accrued an all-star lineup of specialists, each of whom, for his own reasons, could not succeed in building a career in the capital city.

In the village hospital where I had worked, I had become accustomed to dealing with the staff without any trappings of respectful decorum. In Zhitomir, I continued to behave this way, not realizing that many of the people I was addressing were much older and more experienced than I was.

At our first staff meeting, I opened my mouth and began shouting at everyone. The distinguished specialists at the meeting absorbed my harsh words in silence, not daring to put the new department director in his place.

There was one exception, though. His name was Vitold Petrovich Muravyov-Apostol. His grandfather and cousins were Decembrists,[2] and he had apparently inherited the indomitable nature of his forebears. His aristocratic father had also been persecuted because of his name and his family background, except that this time the persecution had been carried out not by the czars but by the soviets.

All Vitold Petrovich had to do in order to blend in among society and build himself a career was to change his aristocratic last name — but no, he wore his name proudly, like a badge of honor. As a result, this exceptionally talented specialist was compelled to work in a regional hospital, rather than in the capital city.

At the end of the staff meeting, he approached me in the corridor. He was an elderly man, dressed immaculately and sporting a tie. His genteel mannerisms were a throwback to the days before the Bolshevik revolution.

"Semyon Moysevich," he addressed me, a tinge of irony in his voice. "You spoke so loudly that I did not hear anything!"

I repeated the entire speech I had given at the staff meeting from the beginning, so that all of the people standing around could hear as well.

The old man waited patiently for me to finish, and then repeated, "You are speaking in such a strong voice that I can't hear anything!"

Not paying pay attention to the irony in his voice, I barked, "So wash out your ears!"

---

9. The "Decembrists" were a group of Russian intellectual-revolutionaries who lived during the nineteenth century.

"I washed out my ears this morning," the old man replied, unruffled. "But you spoke in such a powerful voice that I simply can't hear. Young man — when you speak in a loud voice, *no one hears*. If you want people to listen to you, speak softly!"

Witnessing this exchange, the onlookers in the corridor could not contain their smiles. My face and my ears turned red as a tomato; I wanted the earth to swallow me up. I quickly made myself scarce, while raging inwardly at the old man. "How dare he!" I seethed. "Who is he, anyway? Some deputy department director, and I'm a director — a director! I'll teach him a lesson!"

I promised myself that I would get even with him. When I calmed down, however, I grudgingly internalized the lesson that he had tried to teach me. I modified my tone of voice and began to speak respectfully to people. And because of that, they started to like me.

Gorbachevski, my direct superior, did not hide the fact that he was a believing Catholic, and he therefore did not join the ranks of the Communist party. When it was demanded of me to join the party, I approached him for advice.

"First of all, you are a doctor," Gorbachevski said, "and doctors are apolitical."

"That's what my father claims, too."

"So listen to your elders!" Gorbachevski smiled.

What my father had actually said was, "We should stay far away from these communists; we have nothing in common with them."

This time, I listened to my father, even though I endangered my career in doing so.

Each time I received a warm recommendation to join the party's ranks, I answered that I was not yet ready to take such an important step.

I learned a great deal from my patron, Gorbachevski, and I became very close to him. He passed away five years after we began working together, however, and a Ukrainian named Peshko was sent to take his place.

Peshko declared immediately that he did not require the services of "Gutmans" and their ilk, and he appointed a person named Ilienko to replace me as department director. There was nowhere else for me to go, so I swallowed my pride and stayed on at the hospital to work as a rank-and-file doctor.

About two months later, Peshko summoned me to his office and told me, "Ilienko is not living up to the demands of the job, and people are looking for you all the time. Go back to your job as department director."

I was overjoyed, but I concealed my excitement. Who knew what Peshko would decide to do next? Today, he was appointing me director; tomorrow, he could fire me. I preferred to keep my position as secure as possible.

"No," I said, "I'm not interested. Why do I need the headache? I'll return to the post only if all of the staff members request it. But not because of your request."

At that time, it was in vogue to speak of "staff decisions," and Peshko had no choice but to call a staff meeting. Among the participants at that meeting were approximately ten Jews, whom I had hired. Needless to say, they sat quietly and did not speak. The ones who prevailed upon the director to reinstate me were full-blooded Ukrainians. By their request, I was returned to my post.

There were many speakers at that meeting, among them Vitold Petrovich Muravyov-Apostol. Over the years, we had learned to appreciate each other, and this time it did my heart good to hear his stinging words aimed at the director.

Another doctor named Philiphenko, who stuttered severely, asked to speak. "N-n-n-n-not th-th-this I-i-il-i-ienko! Without M-m-moyseich we'll have n-n-n-nothing!"

I was moved to tears that my colleagues were so eager to have me reinstated at my post.

Guttenyu,
Keep Him Alive for Me!

I can hardly describe my family life as happy. I found meaning and joy at work, not at home. I performed numerous surgeries, I busied myself with research, I wrote essays. I applied to pediatric surgery numerous techniques that I had invented for adults, and with time, I gained renown as an expert in pediatric surgery.

I needed an excellent anesthesiologist — I was working with infants, after all — and I found a talented Jewish anesthesiologist in a far-flung village. He was delighted to escape the village and begin working under me. I helped him to make living arrangements in Zhitomir, and we began working together on complex surgeries that required painstaking work.

Babies would be flown to me for treatment from places as far away as the Caucasus, Middle Asia, and the Baltic Republics. At times, these young patients were in critical condition. If I managed to save their lives, there was no one happier than I.

Once, I was informed that a plane was heading in my direction from Georgia carrying a one-week-old baby whom no other doctor was willing to treat. The baby was the only child of older, wealthy parents who had already visited the biggest experts in the field — they had chartered an airplane and flown to Moscow to see Professor Duletski, who had sent them to Professor Bayirov in Leningrad, who in turn had sent them to me in Zhitomir.

I raced to the airport in an ambulance. The more time that elapsed, the less the baby's chance of survival. Every minute was precious.

When the plane landed, I ran to see the baby. Before me appeared an older Georgian man who prostrated himself before me and cried out, "Doctor, save my son!"

I had no time for the father, though; the baby was dehydrated and withered like an old man, barely showing signs of life.

When we arrived at the hospital, I whisked the baby directly into surgery. The surgery was successful, and the baby was taken into recovery.

Suddenly, I heard a nurse call out, "Doctor, there's no pulse! And he's not breathing!"

I flew over to the monitor, which showed a flat line.

Feeling frustrated and helpless, I tore the sterile mask off my face, went out to the balcony and screamed upward, into the starry skies, "Master of the universe, why do You need him? Keep him alive for me — he's his parents' only child!"

I continued to scream and beg, until the nurse came running over. "Doctor, come quick! The baby started to breathe!"

I ran over to my young patient, and sure enough, he was breathing.

From then on, my surgical procedure was as follows: If I saw that I was not being successful, I called out to God. I asked Him for help, and He helped me. I didn't even notice that I had stopped being an atheist.

That baby survived. I kept him in the hospital under surveillance for a month until he gained strength and stabilized, and then his parents returned to Georgia with him.

The parents demonstrated their gratitude to me with majestic largesse. A short time after they returned home, I found an envelope in my private mailbox. Inside the envelope were keys and documentation for a Zhiguli car registered under my name. I went out to the street and saw a gleaming new vehicle parked near my house. I had seen it earlier, when I had come home from work, but I hadn't known then that it was mine.

Incidentally, I recently learned that the child whose life I saved by pleading with Hashem had gotten married.

Bribery

A short time after the incident with the Georgian baby, surgery had to be performed on the five-year-old grandson of Romanov, the chairman of the Communist party in Leningrad. The required operation was an easy one, even for a regular doctor, but Romanov approached Professor Bayirov, a top doctor. Romanov's capricious nature made Bayirov wary of dealing with him, so Bayirov recommended me to him as an expert in the field. A special plane was sent to fly me to Leningrad, where I performed the surgery. I remained in the hospital for several days after the surgery to monitor the child's condition, even though there was really no need for that.

A month later, when I was not home, a messenger from Romanov delivered to my house a crystal pitcher the size of a bucket. I was nervous. *Who knows?* I thought. *Maybe this is some sort of provocation?* I called Romanov in Leningrad and pretended to be dismayed. "How do you dare send a doctor a bribe?"

At the other end of the line, Romanov's highbrowed baritone voice assured me that it was merely a modest token of appreciation for my having successfully treated his grandson.

Romanov's show of appreciation did not end with that, however. A year later, I received an invitation to the wedding of Romanov's daughter. The wedding, an opulent affair held at state expense, was remembered by the Russian people with disgust for a long time afterward.

The celebration was held in one of the giant halls of the Hermitage,[10] a former royal palace that today serves as an art muse-

---

10. The Hermitage Museum in St. Petersburg is one of the largest and most prominent museums in the world. The Hermitage Museum's enormous collection is exhibited in six buildings; the main building is the Winter Palace, which served as the official residence of the Russian czars. The Hermitage Museum's art collection contains the works of many famous artists.

um. (In an interesting coincidence, the surname of the last Russian czar was Romanov as well.)

At this wedding, the royal dishes of the museum's collection were used; some claim that they were quite damaged by this use. Indeed, the communist leaders lived like kings.

Among the notables who graced the wedding with their participation was then-president Brezhnev. The huge hall was filled with security personnel, who politely but firmly seated the guests in their places and prevented them from moving around freely. I was very disappointed, for not only did I not manage to see Brezhnev (he was seated at the far end of the hall), I could not even go out to the corridor to look at the paintings and other artwork of the Hermitage. *Were we guests or prisoners?* I wondered.

An air force general from Smolensk thanked me on a less grandiose scale, but with equal extravagance. As a sign of appreciation for the operation I successfully performed on his son, he flew me several times on a plane round-trip to a stunning Finnish sauna in Smolensk — a distance of over 500 kilometers!

Officially, the patients did not pay me for my medical services, but they found ways to show their appreciation. Everyone in the hospital where I worked knew that I would summarily banish anyone who offered me money — but they also knew that patients could always approach my wife, who worked as a nurse in the same hospital. She would not banish anyone.

At some point, someone apparently slandered me to the authorities. Early one morning, when I was sitting in my office writing patients' medical records, an acquaintance of mine who worked for the OBkhSS entered. (The OBkhSS was the department that dealt with theft of socialist property.)

"Semyon Moysevich," he addressed me in a formal tone, "according to information that has reached us, you are taking money from your patients."

"If the information has reached you, it must be correct," I responded, without even raising my eyes from my paperwork.

"What?" he jumped up. "And you are talking about this with such equanimity? From whom exactly did you take money?"

"*That* I don't know."

"How is that possible?" His blood was clearly beginning to boil.

"Very simple," I said. "You see my doctor's coat hanging there on a hanger? I haven't even put it on this morning. Check the pockets — maybe you'll find money in there."

The officer grabbed the hanger, dug his hand into the pocket — and removed an envelope full of money. Beaming with joy at having apprehended me, he waved the bills at me and shouted, "Whose money is this?"

"I have no idea," I said. "I operate on many people, and I don't know which of them put the money in my pocket."

He yelled and jumped all around me, but at the end he left empty-handed. That is, with the exception of the money he confiscated ....

An Ill-Fated Climb

We had two daughters, but I rarely saw them. I hadn't the faintest idea of how to raise them, and I left that job completely to my wife and mother-in-law. I justified my behavior with the fact that I was earning a nice living and supporting them comfortably.

When I would place my monthly earnings on the table, I would watch proudly how my younger daughter abandoned her dolls to play with the crisp bills, lining them up in long rows. I endeavored to make these rows longer and longer, and I did not balk at any work offer. Work was easier for me than entangling myself in thorny childrearing issues.

The only real connection I had with my daughters was that I

would take them to the movies on Sunday, my day off. Sundays seem to drag on much longer than I could bear, however. Some Sundays, I would leave the house, place a call from a phone booth on the street to the person on duty at the hospital, and ask him, "Call my house and tell them that I am needed urgently at the hospital."

A car would be sent to bring me to the hospital, and I would be delighted to escape from the house.

When my daughters grew older, I wanted to instill in them a love for the natural beauty and splendor of mountains and forests, so I began taking them on hikes through the Carpathian Mountains. They willingly hiked along with me, and we would sleep in a tent and eat beside a campfire.

My wife was unhappy with this arrangement, however. "You are dragging the girls to all sorts of strange places," she complained to me. After that, she no longer allowed them to join me on these excursions.

She preferred to spend her vacations in expensive hotels or beachfront resorts, lying for hours on the beach and eating in restaurants. She also taught my daughters to develop a taste for these bourgeois vacations, which were a far cry from hiking with a backpack through the brush ....

My wife's idea of a vacation was intolerable to me. Once, I took my family with me on a vacation to the Crimea, to a healing resort on the Black Sea. I awoke with the dawn, while my wife and daughters were still asleep, and went to the sea. At that time of day, the water is not warm yet, and there are not very many people at the beach. As it happened, handicapped children from the local convalescent home were brought to the beach at that early hour precisely because the beach was empty then.

It is difficult for anyone to see children who are suffering, and for me, a doctor, it was even more difficult. I looked at the shriveled hands and feet of the children in the wheelchairs, and the thought that I would have to pass them every day while on vacation made me feel unwell. I went directly to the central post office, called my mother-in-law, and invited her to come take the vacation in my stead. I told my wife that I had been summoned urgently to the hospital, and I returned to work — not even realizing that I had essentially run away from my daughters.

Apparently, I was not the only person who found these "cultured" vacations distasteful. A group of thrill seekers formed in Zhitomir; they were called "Extremists." In search of adventure, these people would journey to dangerous locales, hiking through caves, diving deep into the sea, and climbing precipitous mountains. If someone had asked them why they were doing this, they would have answered that it was to satisfy their curiosity, to seek beauty, to push themselves beyond their limits, to taste life at its most euphoric.

I have since learned that when you don't know what the purpose of life is, you don't fully appreciate its value. If life is just one long pursuit of pleasure, then eventually the intensity of familiar pleasures starts to diminish and you need to look for new pleasures in order to feel fulfilled. That's why thrill seekers have to do increasingly daring things in order to satisfy their desire for excitement, and they will even risk their lives to experience the adrenaline rush of a new thrill.

After I joined the group, we began to train under an experienced mountain climber, and we traveled to a number of mountain ranges to scale towering mountain peaks. We were in Mt. Elbrus and Mt. Kazbek in the Caucasus mountains; in Pamir, Kyrgyzstan; and in the Tian Shan mountains. While in the Tian Shan mountains, I came close to reaching the "peak of triumph,"[11] but I did not manage to reach the top. I almost lost my life during that climb, in fact. This is the story.

We arrived at the Tian Shan mountains and began climbing toward the snowy peak that glittered above us in all its glory. This peak was the dream of every mountain climber. At the head of the

11. The highest peak of the Tian Shan Region is called "Peak Pobedi" (meaning "peak of triumph"), and stands at a height of 24,406 feet above sea level. It is the highest point along the China-Kyrgyzstan border.

group stood Dima (Dmitri) — famed mountain climber, accomplished athlete, and experienced guide.

We did the final, most dangerous portion of the ascent in pairs. Dima asked me to be his partner, and I happily agreed. Our entire group climbed slowly, in pairs, up the steep mountain. Dima was the leader of our pair; he affixed pegs into the rocky mountainside and I climbed after him.

Suddenly, a rock came loose together with the peg, and Dima fell. He flew past me and remained hanging on the other side of the rock, tied to me by an emergency security rope. The rope was tied to my waist, and the weight of Dima hanging beneath me caused the rope to cut tightly into my back, chafing my skin and pinning me with my face to the rock.

The other pairs in the group saw what had happened, but they were unable to help us. It was not possible for them to come near us, and they continued climbing, leaving us hanging in midair. Our only hope for rescue was by helicopter.

Dima had a two-way radio with him, and he managed to make contact with the base and ask for help. Now, everything depended on how quickly the rescuers would arrive. It was frigid up on the mountain, and we were liable to freeze to death if we remained motionless.

Dima dangled in the air several meters beneath me, swinging like a pendulum, as the rope connecting us slowly sawed into my back. The rope was also rubbing against the edge of the rock, threatening to tear at any moment. Dima, who was an experienced mountain climber, assessed the situation correctly and shouted to me from below, "Cut my rope! Why should we both die?"

He could have cut the rope himself, as he had a knife with him. In order to keep his mind off these unsavory thoughts, I began to loudly regale him with all sorts of stories and old jokes, whatever came to my mind — the main thing was to avoid silence. He also tried to make conversation and recall all sorts of things. We spoke for as long as we had the energy, in that way banishing the icy stillness around us. Slowly, however, our voices weakened, until we finally fell silent. In the silence, we were helpless, hanging above the abyss like flies trapped in a spider's web. Little by little, I became numb to the cold, and I began to feel apathetic — a sure sign that my life was ebbing away.

After five hours, a helicopter finally arrived, and rescuers extricated us from the rocky mountainside.

Dima and I were hospitalized for several days with hypothermia. I was able to lie only on my stomach, for the rope had cut deeply into my back and had rubbed the skin away, leaving a permanent scar.

We lay on adjacent beds. After we recovered a bit, Dima asked me, "Why didn't you cut the rope?"

"How could I have slept at night afterward?" I replied.

The Tefillin Straps

My relationship with my wife was very troubled. Often, after we argued, I would drive to the airport and fly to Donetsk (a distance of about 600 miles). I would stop at the doorstep of my parents' house, lean on the doorpost, and look at my mother. Seeing her, a weight would be lifted from my heart.

"My son, did something happen?" my mother would ask.

"No, everything is fine," I would answer. "I just came here to look at you." I didn't want to cause her pain, so I didn't tell her what was happening back home. I would sit at the table in my parents' house for a short time, and after about an hour I would be back at the airport. By the evening, I would be home.

One day, during the winter of 1984, my mother called me and said, "Come quickly! Papa is ill!"

I flew to Donetsk immediately. When I arrived, I saw that Papa had suffered a major stroke, and I realized that there was nothing that could be done for him.

"Mama, he's about to die," I said sadly.

"That I can see myself!" she shrieked.

She grabbed my collar with her two hands and suddenly began to shake me with a force I had not anticipated. "I didn't invest all those years into your studies to hear that! He has to live!"

I summoned my friend Grishka (Gregory), a neurosurgeon, and he arrived quickly together with a few of our former classmates, who by this time were accomplished physicians.

A group of five doctors worked on my father's motionless body for about an hour and a half. They managed to stabilize his breathing and heart function and do whatever they could for him, but Papa remained paralyzed. It was impossible to move him, so doctors and nurses had to come care for him every day. In addition, a specialist came by every two days. Mama paid them all handsomely.

Papa regained consciousness, but was unable to speak. He lived this way for another year.

When I visited together with my family, Papa would not allow my wife to even approach his bed. Seeing her, he would sigh and stir in his bed, trying to move away from her. He never did make peace with my marriage.

In 1984, Papa passed away.

I took his tefillin as a keepsake, and I placed them in a closet and forgot about them. One day, I noticed that my daughter was using thin black straps to tie ice skating blades to her shoes. The straps looked familiar to me, and I asked her where she had found them.

She pointed with her finger, and I saw that the *batim* of Papa's tefillin no longer had straps. I took the straps away from her and bought her new ice skates that did not have to be tied. The tefillin straps were lost, but the *batim* containing the *parashiyos* miraculously survived.

Could I have imagined then that in a few years, in Jerusalem, I would be offered a fortune for these tefillin, and I would refuse to sell them? Or could I have imagined that I would one day lay tefillin with a blessing every day, as my father and grandfather had done?

"Professional" Work

In my days as a student, I took an interest in the technique of restoring faces to skull bones, and I was quite successful in that field. Once, I was given an academic assignment that involved restoring the face of a Soviet tank operator who had been burnt to death in the first Donetsk tank that exploded during World War II. I didn't know how to restore the look of his hair, so I placed a tank operator's helmet on his head.

After I finished my work, his family members were invited to see it. Two women — one old, one young — arrived; they were his mother and his sister. The older woman looked at the restored face and fainted. Apparently, I had succeeded in restoring his face quite accurately. This incident convinced me that restoring faces according to the skull bones was a real science, not just a frivolous exercise.

Now, in Zhitomir, I found a use for my old hobby. I was offered work as a consultant in legal medicine, and at times, my work involved facial restoration using skull bones. I can't say that this was pleasant work, since it involved encountering criminals and their victims, but the pay was respectable. In this job, I amassed a great deal of experience in facial restoration.

My expertise in this area led to an amusing incident that took place shortly before the celebrations held to mark the 1000-year anniversary of the acceptance of Christianity by the ancient Russian monarchy, whose seat had been Kiev. The authorities decided to "revive" several historical heroes, in order to breathe new life into the flagging spirit of nationalism. For this purpose, they invited a small group of experts in the field, and I was included.

There was a shrewd fellow in the group named Kublenko who sized up the situation very well. We were brought to the Vladimirski

Church, where high-ranking church officials took turns impressing upon us, each in his own way, the great historical responsibility that was incumbent upon us, and attempted to imbue us with an appreciation of the "holiness" of the objects we were restoring. The most senior of these church officials peppered us with questions about facial restoration using skull bones.

"Is this form of restoration reliable?" he queried.

"Absolutely reliable," Kublenko answered, with inflated self-assurance.

I smiled quietly to myself.

Kublenko surreptitiously dug his elbow into my ribs. When we left, he said, "What are you laughing about? At least we'll earn some money!"

Indeed, I thought. *What did I care whether it was reliable?*

We were brought to a room and given glass boxes containing skulls. On one box was written, "Dolgorukiy." (Dolgorukiy was the founder of the city of Moscow; he was also known as "Yuri the Long-armed"). On the second box was written "Nestor the historian." This box was given to me. *Fine*, I thought. *I'll restore Nestor.*

Each day during the course of this assignment, we were transported to and from Kiev to do our work.

I worked on Nestor's skull for a long time, doing my best to restore his face. When I showed Kublenko the gaunt elder that I had managed to create, he was pleased. "I have an idea," he told me. "Let's sit Nestor up."

This wild idea appealed to me; it was reminiscent of the antics of my youth. We dressed Nestor in a thin wig and stuck a small beard on his face. From the monks' exercise room we took a punching bag, wrapped it in the black garb of a monk, and seated it in an armchair. We then attached Nestor's head to this "body" and placed an open book on the table before him. The effect was quite impressive. *Kublenko sure knew how to present his merchandise,* I thought.

Shortly afterward, one of the church officials entered the room

— he was actually the person who was supposed to pay our wages. He saw "Nestor" sitting and let out a groan.

"Heretic!" he barked at me. He waved his hands and ran out of the room.

Kublenko quickly disappeared, leaving me alone. I was sure that a scandal would now ensue and that the church officials would declare that a Jew had abused the holy bones.

There was no scandal at all, however. In fact, the opposite was true: A few minutes later, the head priest arrived with a colleague. The two looked at Nestor and whispered to themselves, paying no attention to me. One of them ran to bring a camera, and they took pains to photograph the lifelike figure from all angles. At this point, Kublenko suddenly reappeared, as if out of nowhere. Apparently, he understood his clients better than I did.

A few months later, when we were brought to the church to restore additional faces, I noticed a framed photograph of Nestor hanging on the wall. I decided to let bygones be bygones and not to remind anyone that I had been called a heretic for bringing Nestor to life.

The appetite of the people of the church had been whetted by the initial restorations we had performed. This time, they said that they had found the bones of Iliya Muromets[12] in their digs. Legend had it that Muromets had been killed by a spear blow to the chest. I don't know whether the remains I was given to work with were his, but I did see that there was a spear-shaped hole in the breastbone. According to these bones, however, it seemed that Iliya Muromets was not as well-built a hero as folklore claimed; he was no more than an average-sized man. We stuck a face on his skull, straightened him up, and gave him a marketable appearance.

The people who had ordered the work paid us and asked, "Are you certain that this is genuine?"

"We give our work with a guarantee!" Kublenko said firmly. I could barely contain my laughter.

12. A hero of Russian folk tales.

When we left, I asked Kublenko, "How do you know whether he actually looked like that?"

"Let them check," he replied with a smile. "All the better!"

The Meeting

Once, I was summoned to the offices of the KGB, where I was asked to join a committee whose job was to unearth graves of Nazi victims in order to verify the number of people who had been murdered in the Nazi mass killings.

For me, this was a very difficult assignment to accept, and I tried to decline by saying, "It's difficult for me to be objective, since my relatives were killed by the Nazis."

My refusal was not accepted, however. "So what?" I was told "It wasn't only Jews who were killed during the war."

Only people who had been thoroughly investigated and deemed "trustworthy" were chosen to be part of committees like these, since in the Soviet Union everything was considered classified information, and almost any matter was considered a national secret.

As part of this committee, I visited Katyn, where the Soviets had taken Polish officers to be killed. Generally, however, the mass grave excavations we attended were those of Jews. I tried to deal with the grisly sights we encountered in a professional manner, without allowing myself to become emotional, for otherwise I would not have been able to continue carrying out my work.

After seeing a number of these mass graves, I thought that nothing could shock me anymore. But what I saw at Babi Yar, in Kiev, shook me to the core.

While we were digging at Babi Yar, a colleague called me over to a pit that had been opened. Apparently, he had located something unusual.

"Come here!" he beckoned. "Look!"

When I approached the place where he was standing and saw what he was pointing to, I was dumbstruck. At the edge of the pit were bones of a left foot, to which a wooden log was clamped with iron chains. According to the stories I had been told, this was how my grandfather Hershel had been killed!

My face must have blanched, because my colleague looked at me in astonishment and asked, "What happened to you? We've seen every shocking sight imaginable already!"

My voice suddenly became hoarse. "I think we've found my grandfather," I said.

If those were indeed my grandfather's remains, I hope that he will forgive me, for I was unable to do anything for his bones. I didn't even know then to pray for the elevation of his soul, nor did I know anything about the existence of the *neshamah* or its connection with the body in the grave. To me, death was just like that black pit, with no continuation and no reward or punishment.

The Court Jew

... To a Nation You Never Knew

An apostate Jew who converted to Christianity once came to R' Chaim Volozhiner and said, "I don't understand. I lived near the gentiles, and they looked down on me. I tried to put an end to their contempt by drawing close to them and eating and drinking with them, but they continued to despise and scorn me. I took the next step — I stopped keeping Shabbos and observing the mitzvos — but they continued to hate me. I decided to cross the red line, and I converted to Christianity. But despite all the steps I took, I feel that they continue to hate me. Why is this?"

R' Chaim answered, "About this, the Torah says [Devarim 28:36-37], Hashem will lead you ... to a nation you never knew — neither you nor your forefathers — and there

*you will work for the gods of others — of wood and
stone. You will be a source of astonishment, a parable,
and a conversation piece, among all the people where
Hashem will lead you."*

I became a high-ranking Soviet official, and was given a plum
apartment in an OBKOM (Russian Federation) building. A security guard was stationed at the entrance to the building to protect the peace of the distinguished residents. The building's lobby
housed a special mailbox into which, each morning, the residents
would drop a list of items they needed. In the evening, the requested items would arrive, neatly packaged, at their doorstep.

In addition, I had a dacha (a private summer home in a rural
area), a car with a private chauffeur, and connections with influential, prominent people.

I didn't have Jewish friends. I was afraid to develop ties with
Jews, for fear that they would ask me to find work for them or for
their relatives. I preferred not to hire Jews to work for me, because
if a non-Jewish doctor would make a mistake, it would be his mistake — but if a Jewish doctor would make a mistake, the entire
Jewish people would be blamed. And the blame would fall first and
foremost on me, as the Jewish doctor's superior. If I did hire a Jew
to work under me, he had to be the best of the best in his field.
(Today, many of the gifted Jewish doctors who worked for me live
and work successfully in Israel.)

I was the only Jew among the high-ranking officials with whom
I had to maintain friendly relations. This made me the scapegoat
for all their anti-Semitic sentiments. After these officials indulged
in food and drink, the atmosphere would relax. Thoroughly intoxicated, the officials would not be able to restrain their contempt for
Jews, and it would become my responsibility to defend the Jews.
For them, this was the most entertaining part of the routine.

Once, someone in the group said, "Tell me, Semyon Moysevich.
Why do the Jews' eyes bulge?"

Everyone chortled, imagining to themselves what I was going to answer. To them, this was the best show in the city, almost like a chicken fight. I had to make sure not to let them get the better of me, but also not to insult them, for if I were to insult them, they might take revenge on me later.

"And tell me," I replied, "why are the eyes of the Ukrainians sunken in?"

"I don't know, you tell us," came the answer. Curiosity registered on drunken faces around me.

"The reason the Jews' eyes bulge is because the Jews have so much intelligence in their heads that their brains push against their eyes. You Ukrainians, on the other hand, have very little intelligence, so your eyes are sunken in!"

The outburst of laughter my answer evoked assured me that my answer had been well-received.

Another night, they asked me, "Maybe tell us, Moyseich, why do the Jews love money so much?"

"Indeed, they love money," I responded. "A Jewish father lifts his son up in his hands, and what does he tell him? 'When you'll grow up, Yankele, you'll be wise!' A Polish father tells his son, 'Raise your head high, Janek. Polish pride, Janek!' And what does a Ukrainian father tell his son? He bops him on the forehead and says, 'Sheep, sheep, boo-o-o-o, Waneichka!'" [This was a common baby game in the Ukraine.]

The entire group erupted in laughter.

That night, I returned home from the evening entertainment together with my friend and neighbor Ivan, who was the director of a factory that manufactured and polished marble and granite. Unlike the other officials, Ivan was a true friend of mine, and would have been ready to go through fire or water for my sake.

Even before I managed to close the door of my apartment, I heard loud noises and shouting coming from Ivan's apartment. Ivan was a calm, levelheaded person, and I wondered what could be happening in his house. I went out onto my porch and saw, through Ivan's window, that my friend was in a rage.

"Can you imagine?" he shouted to me. "I come home and what do I see? My mother-in-law is holding my son in her arms and what is she telling him? 'Sheep, sheep, boo-o-o-o, Costicoo!' I'll show her what a 'sheep' is! I'll throw her out the third-floor window!"

I could not hold myself back, and I burst out laughing.

Red Wine for Chernobyl

Once, I was summoned to the offices of Ministry of Health in Kiev. "We are appointing you to participate in the Committee for Emergency Situations," I was told.

This meant that were there to be a serious emergency or disaster anywhere in the country, a special airplane would fly me to the site along with the other members of the committee.

It did not occur to me to turn down this assignment; on the contrary, I was thrileed by the opportunity to break away from daily routine and run to where the action was.

I still chased adventure with the same enthusiasm that had led me as a child to risk my life by squeezing myself onto the back of a train headed for Tashkent.

Back then, I had not managed to reach Tashkent, but as a member of the Committee for Emergency Situations I was sent to Tashkent in 5726/1966, after a very severe earthquake hit the area.

Some years later, I also visited the city of Spitak, Armenia, which was completely destroyed by an earthquake. I can't say that we rescued anyone there; the most I can say is that we showed our presence.

My love of adventures and of earning extra money almost resulted in personal tragedy. When the Chernobyl nuclear reactor exploded, I was summoned to participate in the evacuation of the civilian populace. I asked my wife if I could go, telling her that the daily wage would be three times higher than the normal wage. My wife supported my decision to go to Chernobyl, and on May 3, several days after the explosion, I arrived in Chernobyl (Pripyat).[13]

Ordinary citizens of the Soviet Union had no idea what was happening in Chernobyl. "Hostile" radio stations in the west reported that the Swedish population was in a panic, because radiation levels in Sweden — thousands of kilometers from the site of the explosion — had been drastically elevated.

We paid no attention to these hostile radio stations, however. Our minds had undergone such profound brainwashing that we were not affected by the foreign reports at all.

I roamed, carefree, around the city of Chernobyl in a short-sleeved shirt, as though I had come for vacation. I even went to see the smoking ruins of the reactor; I wanted to get as close as I could and see what was going on there.

Fortunately for me, as I was on my way toward the reactor I met my cousin Izzia (Isaac), who was wearing a protective suit. Izzia was a physicist who held a doctorate in science, and he had been involved in the planning of the reactor. Unlike many others, he understood very well what was happening in Chernobyl. When he saw me, he screamed, "What are you doing here? Where is your family?"

13. The 1986 explosion of the Chernobyl nuclear reactor was graded level seven — the highest possible level of radiation assigned by the International Atomic Energy Agency. (Incidentally, this tragedy happened on the *seder* night, close to midnight — the time when Jews read in the Haggadah, "*Shefoch chamascha al hagoyim* — Pour out Your wrath upon the nations.") The authorities hid this information from the population, knowingly preventing them from taking protective measures, and thus reducing their chances of survival. Radio stations in the west made a big commotion about the explosion, and neighboring countries endeavored to protect their citizens. The Soviet authorities, however, in an attempt to confuse the "enemy" (i.e., foreign countries), lied to their own citizens and pretended that nothing had happened. The day after the tragedy, when the fire was raging and the radioactive radiation was at its peak, May Day parades were held in Kiev, only 90 kilometers from the site of the disaster, exposing both adults and children to peak levels of radiation. On display at the Chernobyl Museum in Kiev is a KGB document dated June 1986 whose first sentence reads: "The information revealing the true reasons for the tragedy is classified as secret."

"I am here on assignment as a member of the Committee for Emergency Situations," I explained. "My family is in Zhitomir."

"Tell them right now that they should travel as far away as possible! My family has already left."

Izzia told me that a terrible disaster had taken place, and that its effects were difficult to predict. He had been sent to the blazing reactor together with a group of experts, who had tried to measure the level of radiation being emitted. But their measuring instruments could not stand up to the intense radiation.

It was a miracle that I met Izzia, since thanks to him, my life was saved and my daughters' health was preserved. I called home and instructed my family to fly away from the area as quickly as possible. I hurried to complete the evacuation of the populace, filling the buses to capacity. I allowed people to take only money and valuables with them; there was no room for additional baggage.

No one could help Izzia, however. He passed away a short time after he returned from Chernobyl.

A few days after I completed this assignment I was summoned to the offices of the KGB. A high-ranking official began shouting at me and stamping his feet. He blamed me for having created unnecessary panic by rushing to evacuate the population of Chernobyl and ordering the people to take only valuables with them.

I was furious, for I understood that not only had the authorities lied to us, they were still continuing to lie! I had nothing to lose, so I answered him in kind, shouting right into his smug face, "I fulfilled my medical obligation — which is to save people's lives!"

A higher-ranking official who was present at this "meeting" and who was wiser than the other official intervened, out of fear that information would become public. Seeing that I was not afraid, he hurried to apologize to me. But his apologies were of no help at that point. After I had returned from Chernobyl and undergone medical testing, I understood that the people had been duped, and that I had been deceived as well.

The extent of our naiveté is apparent from the following story: While I was still on my "lucrative" assignment in Chernobyl, my friend Ivan heard from someone that red wine helps protect against radiation. Without thinking much, my loyal friend loaded cases of red wine into his car and drove to Chernobyl (a distance of 78 kilometers). He was stopped at a roadblock and told that entry into the dangerous area was forbidden. Not one to be easily deterred, Ivan put up a fuss, insisting that his friend was in Chernobyl and he could not leave him alone in distress. I was called down to the roadblock, and came down with a friend.

"Let's put the cases into my car," I suggested to Ivan, "and you'll drive back."

"Take me with you," he replied. "I want to see what's happening there."

And so Ivan traveled with us to see the burning nuclear reactor. To neutralize the radiation, we drank from the "healing" red wine.

Locating the Berditchever's Grave

Love for His Fellow Jew

R' Levi Yitzchak of Berditchev (1740-1809) always tried to paint Jews in a favorable light, both before people and before Hashem. Once, R' Levi Yitzchak saw a Jew smoking a pipe on Shabbos. "My son," he said gently, "surely you have forgotten that today is Shabbos."

"No, I haven't forgotten," he responded.

"Then perhaps you don't know that it is forbidden to smoke on Shabbos?"

"I know very well."

R' Levi Yitzchak raised his eyes heavenward and exclaimed, "Master of the universe! See how truthful your people are! This Jew could have lied, but even at the risk of looking like a rasha in my eyes, he is still careful to speak only the truth, as You have commanded!"

Once, Ivan and I were sitting and playing chess when my emergency telephone rang. On the line was a senior Communist Party Local Council official.

"Semyon Moysevich, would you be able to find five Jewish doctors?"

I was used to all sorts of unusual and bizarre requests, but this time even I was surprised.

"We'll find them," I said. "But why do you need Jewish doctors?"

"A visitor from America took ill suddenly, but he won't allow just any doctor to treat him. He insists on having only Jewish doctors attend to him."

Hearing this, Ivan told me, "I'm coming with you. I want to see an American."

At that time, Americans were a rare breed in our region.

I gathered five Jewish doctors, and together with Ivan, we traveled to the hotel where the ill American was staying.

The American lay on his wide hotel bed, groaning from pain. He was a stocky, middle-aged man with a beard, a yarmulke, and *tzitzis*. This was the first time in my life that I saw someone wearing *tzitzis*. I had seen my father wearing a *tallis* when he prayed, but not *tzitzis*.

When we entered, the patient asked to see our passports. He checked them, and when he was satisfied that we were indeed Jewish, he allowed us to examine him. It turned out that he was suffering from a gallstone attack, and we treated him quickly and effectively.

The American knew how to speak Russian, and I asked him, "What are you doing here?"

"I came to find the grave of R' Levi Yitzchak of Berditchev," he replied.

"Did you locate it?"

"No."

Ivan spoke up. "You didn't search well enough. If you give me a bottle of vodka, I'll find it for you."

The American became very excited. "I'll give you a case of vodka if you find it!"

"For a case of vodka I'll stop all the work in my factory and we'll all search for it!" Ivan enthused.

The American did not know that the simple-looking Ivan was actually a high-ranking, influential person, at least by our standards. His talk of vodka was merely for effect; it was known throughout the world that in Russia, nothing moves without vodka.

I set out with Ivan the next morning, and we went to pick up the American (who by then had recovered) from his hotel. Together, the three of us traveled to Berditchev, a distance of 35 kilometers from Zhitomir. In Berditchev, Ivan headed straight for the municipality building. There, all of his requests were met, out of deference to his status as the director of a large industrial complex. He asked to see the records of the old cemetery, and he made notes to himself on a paper.

"Let's go to the cemetery," he ordered.

At the cemetery, Ivan retained the services of the gravediggers to help us find the ancient grave of R' Levi Yitzchak, which occupied a tiny slice of the massive local cemetery. The gravediggers brought us to the area in which the grave was located, and the three of us — the American, Ivan, and I — covered every inch of ground in order to find the Rebbe's grave. We wandered between tombstones that looked as though they were about to fall, due to the ravages of time, until suddenly I was struck by a sobering thought. "Ivan, do you know how to read Hebrew?"

"No."

"Neither do I. So what are we looking for?"

"You're right," he answered. "I guess we lost a case of vodka."

We decided to give up and turn back. As we made our way through the brush, however, I heard Ivan shout, "Sasha![14] I found it!"

"What could you have found?" I grumbled. I went over to where

Ivan was standing, and saw a large tombstone surrounded by several smaller tombstones. On the map of the ancient cemetery, there was an area that looked exactly like this: several graves neatly arranged in a semi-circle around the grave of R' Levi Yitzchak.[15]

We called the American, who

Tomb of Rabbi Levi Yitzchak of Berditchev came running. He cleaned the dust from the tombstone with his hands, read the inscription on the grave and burst into tears. After that, he jumped to his feet and began to dance.

Ivan looked at him worriedly and motioned to me with a whisper, "Look, he's gone mad!"

When the American calmed down a bit, Ivan said to him, "Bring the case of vodka!"

The American pulled from his pocket a hundred-dollar bill — enough to buy many cases of vodka — and handed it to Ivan. He was obviously unfamiliar with the accepted local practices.

"Why are you giving me this green paper?" Ivan roared. "Take the car and bring me a case of vodka, as we agreed!"

The American had no choice but to travel back to the city and bring vodka. In the meantime, Ivan decided to celebrate the event in his unique way, without waiting for the American. He had some food with him, and he cut three slices of bread, added something

14. During the time he spent in the orphanage, Shepsel was called "Sasha (Alexander) Granitni," and his close friends continued to call him Sasha.

15. Author's note: In earlier times, there had been an *ohel* above R' Levi Yitzchak's grave, and the local Jews knew where the grave was located. Apparently, however, they were afraid to have any contact with a foreigner, and that was why this American could not find an escort from among the local Jewish population.]

that Jews don't eat, and poured three cups: one for me, one for himself, and one for R' Levi Yitzchak. He placed the cup on the Rebbe's grave, covered it with bread, and said, with utter sincerity, "This is for you, Rebbe!"

We drank. In the meantime, the American returned with the case of vodka, as promised. He drank a cup of Ivan's vodka with us, but he did not touch the food.

"Even though he's an American, he knows how to drink like one of us," Ivan noted with satisfaction.

We returned to Zhitomir and took leave of the American, who returned to the United States a short while later.

From the time we found the grave of R' Levi Yitzchak, something changed in Ivan. He suddenly had a powerful desire to visit the graves of Jewish *tzaddikim*. I was compelled to accompany him, and we visited all the graves of the famous *tzaddikim* in the region. After that, we traveled to the grave of Rabbi Nachman of Breslov in Uman.

Rabbi Nachman's grave was located in the yard of a local farmwoman, who made a lucrative business out of it. She would tie a head-butting goat or a biting dog to the grave and charge the visiting Jews an "entrance fee" in order to remove the aggressive animal.

When Ivan and I drew near to the grave, we discovered a huge dog chained to the grave. The dog would not allow us to approach.

"Take away the dog," Ivan shouted at the owners of the house.

The farmwoman's son came out of the house, totally intoxicated, and requested money with which to buy a bottle of vodka. Ivan gave him the money without any argument. But the fellow left without taking away the dog. Then the farmwoman came out and demanded payment as well. Apparently, this was how they were accustomed to milking the hapless Jews who came to visit the Breslover's grave.

Ivan was not one to tolerate this kind of bureaucracy, however. He was a strong, well-built man, and he approached the grave, grabbed hold of the chain that was tied to the dog, and strangled the animal. Then he cast the dog aside together with the chain.

The farmwoman began to scream and ran to call the police. A small police jeep arrived, with two policemen inside. They were not interested in determining who was guilty and who was innocent; they were certain that the people they were arresting were Jews, for who else would come to visit this grave?

The policemen shoved us roughly into their vehicle and drove us to the police station. There, Ivan presented his documents, which showed that he was the director of the factory. We were immediately released, with a thousand apologies, and the farmwoman was roundly berated. "You're at fault," they told her. "Since when do people chain a dog to a grave?"

We returned to Rabbi Nachman's grave, and Ivan poured three cups of vodka, as usual. The first cup was for Rabbi Nachman. He placed that cup on the grave, and then poured vodka for the two of us. "Here," he told me, "we have remembered his soul."

A year after the American's visit, the *gabbai* of the shul in Berditchev called me. "Semyon Moysevich, we have to meet," he said.

We did not discuss anything important on the telephone. Everyone knew that the authorities eavesdropped on phone conversations.

"If this is in regard to work for your daughter-in-law," I told him, "there is nothing to discuss. If it's about something else, you can come." (His daughter-in-law was a doctor.)

When the *gabbai* arrived, he told me, "Do you remember that you searched for the grave of R' Levi Yitzchak of Berditchev? Now, we need marble to repair his tombstone."

"What does that have to do with me?" I wondered.

"Your friend Ivan is the director of the marble factory," he replied, "and you hold sway over him."

I called Ivan. "Someone here needs your help."

"Does he have vodka?" Ivan inquired.

The *gabbai* nodded quickly. "Vodka, samogon, cognac — we have everything!" Apparently, he was well-prepared for the meeting.

"If so, you can come," Ivan answered.

We arrived at the factory and sat down in Ivan's office. Ivan loved samogon, and he immediately poured some for himself and drank it. We had no choice but to taste some, for otherwise, we would not have made any headway.

Ivan summoned his bookkeeper, who calculated how much a good-quality piece of black granite for the tombstone would cost. The figure he arrived was 18,000 rubles. [At that time, one could purchase three cars with that amount.]

"Is that price acceptable to you?" Ivan asked.

"Yes," the *gabbai* answered.

We left. As we were walking down the stairs, the *gabbai* let out a heavy sigh. "Where am I going to get that much money?"

"So why were you quiet before?" I asked him. "Come, let's go back."

We went back to Ivan's office, and I said, "Ivan, what happened to you? When did you ever see such sums of money in a synagogue?"

"You Jews don't lack anything," Ivan responded.

"We're no different from you," I told him. "We need a better price."

Ivan summoned his bookkeeper again. This time, he echoed my words, saying, "What did you do here to these people? When did you ever see such sums of money in a synagogue?"

"But this is the best-quality stone!" the bookkeeper argued.

"So calculate it as though it were inferior quality."

The bookkeeper made the calculation again, and this time the price was 8,000 rubles. Ivan promised to include the labor in that price — namely, erecting the tombstone.

"This price is acceptable to you?"

"Yes."

"But if you come back to me again, I'll throw you out the window!" This was a common threat of Ivan's.

Ivan did not disappoint us. The tombstone and the *ohel* above it were erected by the agreed-upon time.

At a later time, the authorities — who were probably intimidated by American public opinion — ordered a monument from Ivan to memorialize the Jews of Berditchev who had died in the Holocaust. The monument stands to this day, and is made of the same black granite as the tombstone of the Berditchever Rebbe.

The final Request

In 5748/1988, a nationalistic movement called "Rukh" formed in the Ukraine. Jewish homes began to receive letters containing a message to the effect of, "Go to Israel, or we'll get rid of you." There was talk in the city of a possible pogrom.

One morning, Ivan came to me looking very worried and said, "A woman and her daughters, a grandmother and a mother-in-law, they all came to my house to hide! They want to kill the Jews with lashes inside!" He was so worked up that his words came out in a rhyme.

"And what about you?" I asked him. "They're planning to kill the communists, too, you know."

Ivan smiled meaningfully. "I have a rifle."

The pogrom did not happen, but Ivan did not live much longer. This is the story of Ivan's death:

When the *ohel* atop the grave of the Berditchever was completed, Jews came from America for the unveiling of the tombstone, and they invited Ivan and me to a restaurant. We sat at separate tables: The table where Ivan and I sat was filled with the restaurant's appetizers, while the Americans ate what appeared to be canned food, not restaurant food. They even brought their own bottles of wine, wrapped in black paper so as to preserve the wine's kosher status. With them was the American who had searched for the grave together with us. He was the one who had invited us to the restaurant, and he sat at our table and drank a shot of vodka with us.

Ivan was in very good spirits. He considered himself the "*baal simchah*," for he had helped to find the grave and had erected the tombstone. So joyous was he that he downed two bottles of vodka. For him, this was nothing; he was able to drink a whole bucket of vodka. I had not seen Ivan so joyous in a long time.

We returned home late that night. I had just lain down to go to sleep, when Ivan's wife called me in a panic and said, "Come quickly, something happened to Ivan."

I jumped out of bed and burst into Ivan's apartment in my pajamas. Ivan was lying on his stomach on the floor, unconscious. He had experienced a major cardiac obstruction. I called an ambulance and accompanied him to the hospital. I did not budge from his bedside day or night, and I carefully observed the treatment he received.

I wracked my brain trying to think of how to help Ivan. As a doctor, I understood that Ivan was about to leave this world; as a friend, I could not come to terms with that.

On the second day, Ivan awoke and opened his eyes. When he saw me, he motioned with his hands that he wished to be disconnected from the respirator so that he could talk. I insisted that his wishes be honored.

After the tube was removed from his mouth, Ivan asked everyone but me to leave the room.

He began speaking in a weak voice. "I am about to die. When I die, I want to buried in accordance with the customs of the church."

"Ivan," I said incredulously, "all your life you were a member of the Communist Party! They will certainly want to attend your funeral and give speeches."

"First let them carry out the religious ceremony," Ivan whispered, "and then the members of the party can come with their speeches."

"Ivan, I'll try," I said, feeling as though I was going to burst into tears at any second.

With a great deal of effort, Ivan inhaled and continued, "Soon you are going to go to Israel."

At that time, I was not even thinking about such a possibility.

"When you travel," he requested, "take a handful of earth from my grave and bury it in the holy city."

I promised to fulfill his request.

He finished speaking, and his soul departed.

It turned out that Ivan had been correct. In his last moments on this earth, he had been granted an extra measure of intuition, and he had understood better than I that whether or not I wanted, my fate was intertwined with that of my people.

About two years later, I made *aliyah*. I kept my promise to Ivan, bringing a handful of earth from his grave and burying it in the holy city of Jerusalem.

The Blow

The Chernobyl disaster turned our comfortable, orderly lives upside down. Zhitomir was within the region that was affected by radiation, and everything — food, water, air — became contaminated. Out of concern for our daughters' well-being — our elder daughter was studying in university, and our younger daughter was still in grade school — my wife and I decided that our only recourse was to make *aliyah*.

In February of 5751/1991, I saw my wife and daughters off on their way to Israel. My elderly mother-in-law remained under my care. She had to undergo a cataract operation, and we planned that I would stay with her during the operation, finish whatever business I had to see to in Russia, and then travel with my mother-in-law to Israel to join my wife and daughters.

Truth be told, I was not emotionally ready to leave Russia, and I kept delaying my departure. My work as a surgeon was what gave me meaning in life, and I was frightened by the thought of having to give up my professional career.

My wife did not try to hasten my arrival, nor did her letters from Israel give me reason to be optimistic about the move. "Don't count on being able to work as a doctor here," she wrote. "I really would not want you to have to work as a street cleaner."

I thought that she was concerned about my future. I was concerned, too, but my family was of primary importance to me, so I finally made plans to join my wife and daughters.

When I notified my wife of my approximate *aliyah* date, I received a letter from her in response informing me that she did not want me to come to Israel. "Forget about me and consider it as though I don't exist," she wrote. "The girls are already grown, and they don't need you. They have their own life."

That was a massive blow to me. Shocked, I answered my wife that I would come to Israel because I wished to breathe the same air that my daughters were breathing. Perhaps they would still need me in the future?

With time, however, I understood that my wife wanted to have nothing to do with me. Nevertheless, deep in my heart I nurtured the hope that things would work out after I arrived.

On the eighteenth of September, I performed my last surgery. Reverently, I arranged my instruments in the small, precious satchel. Would this be the last time I worked as a surgeon? How I hoped that I would need these instruments in the future! Why, without surgery I was like a bird without wings!

I flew to Israel two weeks later.

Part VI

Yaakov's Ladder

אִם יִהְיֶה נִדַּחֲךָ בִּקְצֵה הַשָּׁמָיִם
מִשָּׁם יְקַבֶּצְךָ ה׳ אֱלֹהֶיךָ וּמִשָּׁם יִקָּחֶךָ.
וֶהֱבִיאֲךָ ה׳ אֱלֹהֶיךָ אֶל הָאָרֶץ אֲשֶׁר יָרְשׁוּ אֲבֹתֶיךָ.

(דברים ל:ד-ה)

If your dispersed will be at the ends of heaven,
from there Hashem, your God, will gather you in
and from there He will take you.
Hashem, your God, will bring you to the Land
that your forefathers possessed.

(*Devarim* 30:4-5)

First Steps

The First Day

My wife met me at the airport and we traveled together to Yerushalayim, where she had rented an apartment. We sat silently on the bus beside each other the entire way, as though we were strangers. Outside the window, the breathtaking scenery of the mountains of Yerushalayim whizzed by, but I didn't see any of it. I wanted only one thing: to have a family again.

When we arrived at the apartment, my younger daughter was not there. It turned out that about half a year earlier my wife had sent her to a boarding school on a kibbutz.

"Why did you send her away from home?" I complained.

"What right do you have to criticize me?" my wife interrupted me coldly. "We were here alone, and you were far away. I managed as best as I could."

The Second Day

The following day, when my wife came with me to arrange my documents, I learned that I was not entitled to any financial benefits as a new immigrant, since the money my wife had received upon arriving in Israel had been intended for the whole family, including me. This fact may have hastened the end.

In the evening, my elder daughter came home. This was the first time I had seen her since my arrival, and I began asking her how she lived and what she was doing. My questions sparked a stormy argument, during which it became clear to me that I no longer had any family.

In my despair and pain, I began screaming at them, not being very careful with my words. They ran into the neighbor's apartment across the hall, leaving me alone.

After a short while, the police arrived. They brought me into the neighbor's apartment, from where my wife had called the police. The owner of the apartment said something to the police officers while pointing to me. I did not understand a word.

The officers then took me to the police station. No one there understood Russian, and I sat in the corridor all night.

The Russian Compound

The Third Day

The next morning, I was ushered into a police vehicle and taken to Bikur Holim Hospital, where my head was x-rayed. I could not understand why they were putting me through these tests. After the x-ray, I was taken to a psychiatrist, who asked me if I was suffering from a head injury. Luckily, the psychiatrist spoke Russian, and I was finally able to explain myself. I told him that I was a doctor, and I asked him the reason for these tests.

He explained that the night before, when I had been arrested, the police had been told that I was mentally ill and posed a threat to the public. That was the reason for the tests.

After I was shown to be "normal" and no menace to society, I was brought back from the hospital to the police station. At this point, a young Russian-speaking officer appeared. He was a dark-skinned, kindhearted Bucharian Jew named Misha (Michael). He spoke to me, understood what had happened, and took me in a police car back to the address where I had been arrested the day before. We knocked on the door together, but no one answered. Apparently, no one was home. This was at two o'clock on a Friday afternoon.

I had to leave together with the officer, but I did not lose hope. I still did not understand what had happened. "Misha," I told the officer, "It's almost Shabbat! [That's what I had been told in the police station.] Why should you waste your time here with me? Go home.

I'll wait here myself until they come back."

Misha smiled. "Just don't get into any altercations here," he told me good-naturedly. "Don't shout and don't be unruly."

"Okay," I told him. "I'll try." Had I only known how things were going to play out ....

The officer drove off, and I left the building and waited near the entrance. I stood there, not knowing what to do. I had no money and no papers — all of my belongings had been left in the apartment.

Just then, the elderly neighbor who had called the police the day before exited the building. When he saw me, he recoiled and hurried away. A short while later, I saw him returning together with — my younger daughter! He had apparently gone out to meet her at the bus stop in order to prevent her from bumping into me.

I dashed over to her. "My daughter, my sweetheart!"

But the neighbor pushed me with his shoulder and the two passed right by me. I followed them. What had he managed to tell her during those short minutes? That I was dangerous?

They entered his apartment and the door slammed in my face.

I felt as though I was living through a nightmare. I began knocking on the door. "Open up!" I begged. "My daughter, my daughter!"

The police arrived immediately. How fast they came sometimes! One of them pulled my arm forcefully. "Come!"

I was completely irrational by then, so bent was I on being reunited with my daughters. "Leave me alone, my daughter is in there!" And then I pushed the police officer.

I pushed a police officer! I could not have imagined then how severely such an act was viewed. The moment I defied police authority, I was classified as a dangerous criminal, and the police were free to do to me as they pleased. The officers jumped on me, pulled my hands behind my back, and handcuffed me. They then grabbed me by my collar and by my feet, and threw me like a sack of potatoes toward the neighbor's apartment, my face against the stone tiles. One officer sat on my back, while a second chained my feet. Now that I was well trussed, so that I could not move my body or even lift my head, the officer pulled my two handcuffed hands upward so sharply that my shoulders let out a "click" sound. The pain was unbearable, and I screamed aloud. I was sure that my joints had been dislocated.

Then I saw my wife and my two daughters. I began to cry and to beg their forgiveness if I had offended them even slightly. I was prepared to endure any degradation for the sake of reconciling with my family and maintaining a relationship with my daughters. But they remained silent.

The officers dragged me from the apartment and drove me to prison. The name of the prison was purely symbolic — it was called the "Russian Compound," even though no one there spoke any Russian. The officers did not understand me, and I did not understand what they wanted from me.

I was placed in solitary confinement, my case pending investigation. I didn't care that a police dossier had been opened for me, or that I had been arrested twice in less than 24 hours, or that I had opposed the police, or that I been taken to prison this time, not to the police station.

All I cared about was that I had lost my daughters. How could they have given up on me so easily?

In prison, I had plenty of time to think, and the thoughts that went through my mind were painfully bitter. Hadn't I run away from my daughters, opting to wander through mountains and forests in the company of other people who had also escaped from their families, rather than to go on "cultured" vacations with my daughters? Was I not the one who had taught my daughters to view money as the ultimate value? Now that I had not a penny to my name, what did they need me for?

There was no trust or warmth in my relationship with my daughters. In fact, my wife had used me as a rod of punishment when they were growing up. Without bothering to find out what was really going on, I had yelled at the girls or pulled their braids any time my wife had instructed me to mete out disciplinary measures to them.

I had not accompanied them to Israel, and they had been left alone during an exceedingly difficult acclimation period. It had taken me nine months to decide to join them, and during that time there had not been any semblance of family relations between us. If my daughters had abandoned me, whom could I blame but myself? Were we still a family?

They say that when a person leaves this world, he sees a replay of his life and is deeply pained by the mistakes that he can no longer rectify. In my prison cell, I experienced something similar.

My First Shabbos in Israel

The Fourth Day

Shabbos arrived, my first Shabbos in the Holy Land. The door to my lonely cell opened, and a tall, handsome man of about 30 entered, wearing a knitted *kippah* on his head and sporting a short red beard. He was an American prisoner, and he was accompanied by a police officer. He smiled warmly, nodded to me as though I was an old acquaintance, and said to me in English, "Come to the synagogue."

I do not understand English, but I recognized the word "synagogue." For some reason, the prison officers had decided that I was religious; perhaps it was because I did not remove my hat or because I had not shaved in several days. I did not argue. I preferred to go to the synagogue rather than to be tortured by my thoughts in solitary confinement. And so I was led, with police escort, to the synagogue.

The large room that served as the prison's synagogue held a few dozen prisoners. There were all types of *kippot* there — black, white, knitted. I was given a black cloth prison *kippah* and a *siddur*. The American who had invited me to the services was the *chazzan*, and he had a strong, pleasant voice. He sang some of the prayers in such a heartwarming tune that for a moment I forgot where I was.

I held the *siddur* in my hands for appearance's sake only. I had never learned from Bubbe Faiga how to read Hebrew, so the *siddur* was useless to me. To my surprise, however, as I listened to the services I began to recall the words of certain prayers that she had forced me to learn by heart, such as *Shema Yisrael*.

At the conclusion of the prayers, we were taken to a dining room to eat the Shabbos meal. Each of us received a tray containing our portion. Knowing what type of food was provided in Soviet prisons, I was pleasantly surprised to see good food on my tray: a small, fresh challah; fish; a quarter of a chicken; rice; and vegetables.

The American seated me at his side, and opposite me sat an intelligent young man who spoke Russian. The American had made sure that I would have someone to talk to.

It was two days since I had swallowed a morsel of food, and the meal tasted heavenly — almost like Bubbe Faiga's food.

A Shabbos table, challah — for so many years, not only had I not eaten a Shabbos meal, I hadn't even remembered what a Shabbos meal was like! "*Shabbos auf der gantzen velt*," I remembered Papa singing. It was exceedingly difficult for me hold back my tears.

My companion across the table, a former resident of Moscow, was a "political prisoner," as the Russians would say. He was very friendly. (To this day, this man's name appears in the newspapers on occasion, when he is arrested for the umpteenth time for the same "political" reasons.)

This prisoner told me all about the American prisoner and his wife, who was held in the women's section of the same prison. This couple, the Mennings, had been falsely convicted in America of having killed someone, and had been sentenced in absentia to death by the electric chair. They were living in Kiryat Arba, in Israel, at the time, and were imprisoned by the Israeli authorities, but the America government was demanding their extradition.

"We have to pray that they manage to avoid being extradited," my companion said firmly. "Why, they are suffering for the sake of other Jews! Their only guilt is that they were members of the Jewish Defense League."

Until now, I had thought that my predicament was the worst in the entire world, and that my life was completely joyless. But what did I see here? A prisoner who was under threat of death, but was nevertheless able to sing and smile! What gave him this strength, I wondered? Was it his faith in Hashem?

The Shabbos meal and the people around me revived me for a time. But when I was returned to my cell, the bitter memories washed over me with greater intensity. I had no respite from my morbid thoughts, because in solitary confinement I was alone with myself.

Shabbos morning, the kind American prisoner came again to fetch me. The joy I felt upon seeing him was like the joy of seeing a relative. Accompanied again by a police officer, we walked the now-familiar way down the long corridor to the synagogue. In a room full of worshipers, the American opened the *sefer Torah*, and began to read it and sing. And I, in the simplest way possible, asked Hashem to have mercy on him and his wife.

I don't know what happened to the American and his wife. When we parted, he jotted down his name for me on a paper. About a month later, I came to the prison to give him some cigarettes. I showed the prison guard the paper with the American's name, but he would not take the cigarettes from me, and no one could tell me anything about the prisoner I was seeking. All I could do was hope and pray that this couple had not been extradited to America for certain death.[16]

The Rav Who Spoke Russian

The Fifth Day

Shabbos came to an end. Seeing no other way to attract attention to myself, I began a hunger strike. When food was brought to me in the morning, I did not touch it. A prison worker

16. Reuven (Robert) and Rachel Menning were arrested in March 1991. In January of 1993, Reuven was extradited to the United States, where he was sentenced to life imprisonment. His wife Rachel died in prison several days before her extradition to the United States.

who spoke Russian came to me and tried to convince me to eat.

"I will not eat until a rabbi who speaks Russian comes to see me!" I declared, much to my own surprise. I don't know how or why these words emerged from my mouth. I had intended to ask for a Russian ambassador to help me return to Russia, but instead I had asked to see a rabbi!

I could easily have summoned a Russian consul, for the Russians would have taken me back with open arms. They would have rolled out the red carpet for me, while publicizing in the newspapers how difficult it was to live in Israel. But somewhere deep inside my heart was a spark from my parents' house that made me ask to see a rabbi.

My request was honored, and several hours later the door to my cell opened and a visitor entered. The visitor was not very tall; he had a white beard, and was wearing a black suit and a hat. He told me his name, which I did not catch, and he sat down next to me. He took my hands into his warmly, asked me all sorts of questions, and listened to me attentively. It seemed that every word of mine was important to him.

I felt completely comfortable talking to him. He understood even when I was silent or when I was too embarrassed to explain something, and he did not release my hands from his. I told him everything, as though he was a close friend, and eventually I could not hold back my tears: "Worst of all is that I am now left alone," I concluded miserably.

In response, he told me words that sounded very strange. "You'll see," he said, "everything will work out, and you will yet find relatives of yours!"

What relatives was he talking about? The only relatives I had in Israel were not acting like relatives at all.[17]

The rabbi continued to hold my hand, as he told me a bit about his life. He had been born in the Russian city of Kazan, and had

17. Author's note: This is why Shepsel became so excited when he came to our house for the first time.

suffered greatly in Russia. Like me, he had also been a prisoner. With a smile on his lips, as though he himself was still amazed by his ordeals, he told me how Hashem had helped him on many occasions, through the most difficult of times.

"The main thing is not to become disheartened!" he concluded, as he gazed at me with his young, beaming eyes.

His stories lifted some of the weight from my heart. He then asked that I stop my hunger strike, saying with a smile, "Don't take offense at food."

This aphorism melted my heart, for it was a common refrain of Bubbe Faiga's. I wanted to listen to the rabbi more and more, but the time of his visit came to an end. When he parted from me, he did not promise anything grand; he merely said that he would look into my file.

I'm sure he'll forget about me, I thought sadly.

Only later did I discover what this man meant when he said he would "look into my file."

The "Veteran" Prisoner

The Sixth Day

A short time after the rabbi left, the prison warden ordered me to take my blanket, pillow, and towel, and he led me down the hall to a different cell. He closed the door of this new cell behind me, and I stood face-to-face with the cell's inhabitants.

There were about a dozen men there, and all of their gazes were trained on me. From their faces, I could tell that I had been placed together with convicted criminals. One of them lay on the floor under a bunk. Apparently, he ranked the lowest in the group, due to his past, and was so reviled that the other prisoners would not allow him to lie on the bunks like the rest of them.

I thought that I knew how the criminal world operated, since I had heard many stories from acquaintances who had connections to that world. They had claimed that in prison, from the beginning, it was very important to give the impression of being a veteran prisoner, in order to avoid the degradations that new inmates in Soviet prisons were subjected to.

The first thing I did after crossing the threshold of the cell, therefore, was to throw my clean towel at my feet, wipe my shoes on it thoroughly, and stride into the cell. In the etiquette of Russian jails, this indicated that I had more respect for the cell and its inhabitants than for the world outside. I lifted the towel, then stood and waited for the "boss" to react.

[F.A. Kochubievsky, a former Prisoner of Zion, relates: "The narrator had heard something about new prisoners wiping their feet on a towel, but he confused the matter. The actual practice of veteran prisoners is as follows: When they enter a prison cell, they spot a towel on the floor, but they do not ask to whom it belongs, nor do they lift it up. Instead, they wipe their feet on it, and in doing so they display their independence and their unwillingness to serve the other prisoners."]

The cell's inhabitants looked at me with disinterest. Perhaps Israeli criminals use different sign language, I wondered? In truth, it made no difference to me, for I did not understand Hebrew anyway, and they did not understand me.

In the middle of the cell, on the bottom bunk, sat a large, dark-skinned man with a gloomy face. I quickly realized that he was the boss, since he wordlessly pointed to the third-tier bunk under the window, near the entrance to the bathroom. The toilet and shower were separated from the rest of the cell by a curtain.

By the prisoners' standards, the bunk I was assigned was a bad one; the only spot in the cell that was worse was that of the lowly prisoner who lay on the floor. I went up to my bunk without an argument, however.

The bunk was filthy, and I cleaned it thoroughly. Then I spread out the mattress, removed a clean handkerchief from my pocket, and used it to clean the mattress. I worked slowly and deliberately, knowing that several pairs of eyes were watching my every move.

I lay on the mattress for some time and surveyed the cell from my third-tier perch. The floor was dirty, with cigarette stubs strewn around. I descended from my bunk, took a broom from the bathroom, gathered all the dirt, and threw it into the garbage. Then, I took a few empty cigarette boxes and approached the cabinet belonging to the "boss." From my bunk, I had noticed some scotch tape there. Without asking permission, I took the roll of tape and used it to affix the empty cigarette box to his bed. I took a few other boxes and affixed them to other bunks in the cell. The prisoners watched me with idle curiosity. Through hand motions, I indicated to them that the cigarette stubs were to be thrown into the boxes from now on. Then I returned to my bunk.

What was I trying to achieve? I wanted to start an argument, to take my anger out on someone.

The boss finished smoking, and threw his cigarette stub on the floor. That was exactly the type of provocation I was waiting for. I climbed down from my bunk, pointed to the stub, and ordered the boss to pick it up.

He started saying something to me in Hebrew, and I opened my mouth and shouted back at him, cursing with the colorful prison language that I had learned from some old acquaintances: "Have you ever swallowed a pole? Go swallow one! I'll teach you what it means!" I went on to utter a long string of threats whose meaning was lost on both them and me. The main thing was my tone of voice.

It was clear to everyone that I had started up with the boss and was trying to provoke him into a fight. I had nothing to lose — my heart was so bitter that I was even willing to be killed in such a fight.

Apparently, however, the boss saw the desperation in my eyes, and realized that this could end in disaster. Without budging from his place, he shouted to the inmate lying on the floor: "Chaim!"

Chaim, who appeared to be around 40, stood up immediately, danced around me, gestured with his hands, and said something. "Pick it up!" the boss ordered him, pointing to the cigarette stub.

Chaim ran to pick it up, but I stopped him. "Get away!"

He jumped to the side.

This boss, it should be noted, was patient. I became annoyed and started shouting at him, but he did not react. He gazed at me calmly, as a doctor looks at a patient, and allowed me to rage. Then he said, "Come here, have a seat," banging his hand next to him on the bunk. This demonstrated that he accepted my authority. I no longer had anything to argue about, and the fight I was trying to pick didn't happen.

I had no choice but to approach the boss and sit next to him on the bunk. He patted my shoulder and began telling me something in Hebrew. Out of everything he said, I managed to understand only one word: "Siberia, Siberia."

As he spoke, he pointed alternately to himself, to me, or to the entire cell, as though indicating that I was one of them, someone who was looking for trouble.

After all these "speeches," he turned to the prisoner sitting on the bunk opposite him and ordered, "Go up there!" He meant that the other prisoner should go onto the bunk that had been assigned to me.

To me, he said, "You'll come down here."

He was giving me the place of honor on the lower bunk.

I declined, however. "I'll stay there," I said, motioning with my hands and making blowing motions with my mouth to indicate that up there, near the window, there was a breeze of fresh air. Then I went back up to my bunk.

At night, the prison officials returned me to solitary confinement. Apparently, they were afraid to leave a new arrival among the prisoners overnight. In the morning, they returned me to the same cell, where I was greeted as an old friend.

When we came to the dining room, the boss seated me next

to him, and placed tomatoes and cucumbers onto my plate with his own hands, evidently out of respect for the "comrade from Siberia."

As long as I was in their cell, order reigned. Chaim cleaned the cell and washed the floor every day.

In the course of my work in Russia, I had had to opportunity to visit a few prisons. The prison I was in now was like a hotel compared to what I had seen in Russia. I don't know if all Israeli prisons are like this one; perhaps it was because this prison is located in Jerusalem, the capital city, where everything is on public display.

When we were brought to the dining room, my eyes bulged from their sockets at the sight of the food that was being served. I could not believe that even during the week, the food was respectable, not merely some thin soup. In the corridors were public telephones. When the prisoners knocked on the door of the cell, it was opened, and prison officials came to see what was happening. The solitary confinement cell, where I had spent the night, was right next to the prison office. I had not slept all night, and I had seen how the prisoners who were brought in were treated respectfully. The police officers who had taken me from my house had behaved roughly and violently, but the other officials were remarkably civil.

Who Needs Me?

The Seventh and Eighth Days

Two days later, I was taken to a courthouse situated across the road from the prison. That same blue-eyed rabbi who had come to visit me in prison arrived for the hearing. There, I learned that his name was Rabbi Yitzchak Zilber. I do not know what he said there to the police, but I was immediately released. Later, I learned that he had posted bail for me.

Before being freed by the court, I had to sign that I would not come within 500 meters of the building where my family lived. Or, more accurately, where my *former* family lived.

Rabbi Zilber ushered me into a taxi and brought me to the Torah Ve'Emunah Yeshivah in the Geulah neighborhood. There, I received a meal in the dining room, and Rabbi Zilber arranged for me to sleep in the yeshivah dormitory. I told him that I was worried that my wife would take my daughters to the United States, far away from me, as she had threatened. Rabbi Zilber advised me to go to the police station and sign a declaration stating that I was opposed to my younger daughter — who was still a minor — leaving the country. He seated me in another taxi, and accompanied me to the police station. I was not particularly useful there, for I did not understand a thing; all I could do was sign in the places I was required to.

All these arrangements took quite a while. The rabbi sent me back to the yeshivah, and stayed in the police station himself to arrange my affairs.

I took his concern for granted, not realizing that this *tzaddik* took personal responsibility for anyone who needed it. And there were thousands of people like that.

The Ninth Day

Rabbi Zilber asked one of his students, N.K., to look after me, and in the evening this student brought me to his house. The following day, Rabbi Zilber sent his son, Rav Benzion, to me.

"How can I help you?" Rav Benzion inquired.

"Help me to reconcile with my family!" I begged. "I'm not allowed to go anywhere near the house. And please bring me a few things that I need from my house."

Rav Benzion and N.K. went over to my apartment. About an hour later, they returned with my two suitcases, and with something else that pained me greatly to see: the guitar that I had brought as a gift for my younger daughter.

I was furious. "Why did you bring me my belongings?" I shouted.

"I didn't ask you for that! Take them back! I want to make peace with my family!"

They tried to explain that my belongings had been brought out to the hall to them, but I was not interested in listening to their explanations. I somehow thought that as long as my things were *there*, I could still go back. In response to my shouting, Rav Benzion answered me softly, "It is true, I am at fault for having taken your belongings."

Rav Benzion saw my despair and took pity on me. He understood that no explanations would help; I had to see for myself what had happened. He and N.K. took me into a taxi and brought me to my family's apartment to show me where the suitcases had been thrown.

Knowing very well what the outcome of such a trip might be, they were careful not to leave me for a second, to ensure that I would not end up in prison again. And they were right for doing so.

I knocked on the door of my apartment, I yelled and I cried, but no one opened for me. After a few minutes the police came. Because I was not alone this time, however, the police did not arrest me. Instead, they sufficed with a verbal order to leave the premises, and allowed Rav Benzion and N.K. to take me away.

I could not sleep at all that night.

In the morning, N.K. took me to shul. I stood along with the rest of the congregation for the entire prayer service, thinking to myself that Papa's prayers had been more heartfelt. After the prayers, N.K. took me to the yeshivah. The students there were mostly young Russian *baalei teshuvah*, but there were some older students as well. They all sat and learned diligently.

What was I supposed to do in their company? I did not know any Hebrew, and all day I paced back and forth from corner to corner like a caged lion. The only thing I understood was the *shiur* of Rabbi Zilber.

N.K. looked after me the entire day. He understood the kind of state I was in and tried to comfort me. "Why are you so despondent?" he asked. Pointing to a man who was older than me, he said,

"You see that person? He is a professor, and he also went through a family breakup. But he's still alive and well."

No, I thought to myself. *This is not for me. I cannot be dependent on others.*

Not wanting to accept handouts, I helped clean the tables after the meals. No one asked me to do this, but I felt that if I would not do it, the food would stick in my throat.

In the meantime, a plan began to form in my head. Never before had I entertained thoughts of taking my life, but now this seemed to be my only recourse. *No one knows me, and no one needs me,* I thought. *I'll find myself a quiet corner and put an end to my misery.*

My Angel

The Tenth Day, Which Was Almost My Last

When darkness fell, I left the yeshivah and walked along the narrow streets of the Geulah neighborhood, to wherever my legs carried me. A light rain was falling. I was still wearing the same short-sleeved checked shirt and jeans that I had been wearing on the day of my arrest. I had not changed my clothing even once since then. All of my belongings, including my clothing, money, and documents, were in those ill-fated suitcases that Rav Benzion had brought me the day before. To me, it seemed as though my family had thrown me away together with the suitcases. So not only did I not open the suitcases, I didn't even want to touch them.

Now, I had nothing: no money, no documents, no family, no friends. All I had was my life. And who needed a life like that?

My eyes fell upon a clothesline strung between two pillars. I did not have a pocketknife, but I was in no hurry. Very patiently, I untied the knots holding the clothesline in place and rolled it up neatly. The clothesline was about five meters long.

I continued to walk along the street until I saw a bench under a tall tree. That was exactly the type of spot I needed. I located a suitable branch and sat down on the bench beneath it. I tied a loop in the rope and waited for the last passersby to disappear from the street. I was so tired, however, that while I was waiting I fell asleep, the noose in my hand.

I awoke when someone shook my shoulder forcefully. It was a man wearing a hat and a long kapote. He said something to me in Hebrew, and in response I cursed him in Russian. He did not understand me, however, and he would not leave me alone. Instead, he continued to speak to me in Hebrew. Finally, I turned to him and said in Yiddish, "*Vus vilst di mit mir* [what do you want from me]?"

"Yiddish!" the man exclaimed in delight, and seated himself beside me on the wet bench.

Attempting to get rid of him, I said, "Don't you have anything to do? Why are you bothering me?"

He paid no attention to my words, and began interrogating me. His Yiddish was so *heimish* and close to my heart that I found myself pouring out my heart to this stranger, who was the first person I had encountered along my way. I cried freely as I talked, without even feeling embarrassed; it was a rainy evening, and you couldn't see a thing. Besides, tears were streaming down his face too.

He sat with me for a long time on the cold, wet bench, and said something to me, although I don't remember a word. Afterward, he took me to his house, and said something to his wife in Hebrew. She served us supper and spread linens for me on the sofa in the living room. In the morning, my host took me to shul, and after the prayers he hurried somewhere. When he returned, he told me that he had found me a place where I could live and work.

He brought me to a cheder, where his friend Leizer was in charge of maintenance. He told Leizer my story, and asked him to arrange work for me.

"What do you know how to do?" Leizer asked me.

"I'm a doctor. A surgeon."

"I don't have work here for a doctor. Do you know how to put in a screw?"

"If the screw belongs to this wall, I can do it," I said. "If not, I can't."

Leizer chuckled. "Good, we'll live and learn."

Leizer was a chassidic Jew, about my age, and his outward appearance was similar to mine. His sixth sense intuited immediately that the hardest thing for me was to be dependent on the kindness of others. His first step was therefore to arrange a place for me to live. He removed a lock from the door to a small storage room under the stairs, where buckets and other cleaning supplies were kept, and said, "This is where you'll sleep."

Leizer then took me to a different storage room, from which we removed an old folding sofa. The room I was given to live in was so small and crowded that the sofa could not even be opened into a bed in it. Nevertheless, I was happy to have a corner of my own.

"Tomorrow morning you'll start working," Leizer said. "If you want to *daven*, the shul is on the second floor. Come, I'll show you. Did you eat yet?"

Embarrassed, I began to grasp at excuses. But I had a surprisingly easy time with Leizer, for he seemed to know what I needed better than I did. That's how it was with Leizer then, and it has remained that way ever since.

Leizer took me to his house, where his wife set the table and served us food. That night, I slept in his house, and for the first night since my arrival in Israel I had a good night's sleep.

That was how I met Leizer. With time, Leizer became closer to me than anyone else in the world, and his family embraced me as one of their own flesh.

I must have been in a state of shock during those days, for I completely forgot how I met Leizer. I was sure that Leizer was the one who extricated me from the noose I had made in the clothesline, and I did not remember that someone else had sat with me that night and brought me to him. Years later, when Leizer and I were reminiscing about how we had met, he told me what had happened. I became very confused when I learned that someone else had saved me, although that fact did not detract in the least from Leizer's greatness in my eyes. Saving me that one time would not have been enough, because in order to ensure that a person does not tie a noose around his neck a second time, you have to help him want to live. Leizer did that for me through his concern and friendship.

"Who *was* the one who saved me that night?" I asked in bewilderment.

Surprised, Leizer responded, "Don't you remember? His surname is Malachi [Hebrew for 'my angel']!"

Tefillin

The next morning, I went with Leizer to the Belzer shul. He *davened*, while I stood next to him and watched. I didn't pretend to be religious, I simply felt a desire to be like Leizer, who radiated integrity. If he believed and he prayed, I wanted to be like him and do as he did.

Leizer spoke to the *gabbai* of the shul, and they brought me a *tallis* and tefillin. The *gabbai* made a very powerful impression on me. He was an old man with a majestic appearance and a long white beard, and his kindheartedness was evident. *This must be how Avraham Avinu looked*, I thought.

When the *gabbai* began to place the tefillin on me, I mentioned to him that my father used to tie them differently. He was delighted. "You remember? Show me how!"

I then laid the tefillin the way I remembered Papa doing it. "That's is how the Litvaks lay tefillin," he said. "For the rest of your life you'll lay tefillin this way, just as your father taught you."

At the end of the prayers, I went with Leizer to work in the cheder. He showed me what had to be done, although he did most of the work for me. Fixing things and working with screws were unfamiliar tasks to me. Apparently, all of the screws were from a "different wall."

In exchange for my lodgings, I washed the floors of a mikveh that was located next to my little storage room. During the day, I ate together with the cheder students, and I helped to clean the kitchen in exchange for the food I received. This helped me to feel as though I was not accepting alms.

About a month later, I was summoned to *beis din*, where I was told that my wife wanted a *get*. I began to cry, and I refused to do so. "Not a *get*," I said in my halting Hebrew. I was still hoping that I could be reunited with my family.

Rabbi Yitzchak Zilber, who had arranged for my release from prison, was present at the *beis din* proceedings. He tried to persuade me to give the *get*, explaining why it was necessary, but I behaved in a deranged manner and even took offense at his words.

I returned from the *beis din* completely broken. When I told Leizer what had happened, he took me to his house, and called for the help of his wife Rina, who was a wise, goodhearted woman. Together, they tried to convince me to give a *get*.

I listened to them, and I went to *beis din* to give the *get*.

I went to pray in the Belzer shul every morning, and each day I was given a different pair of tefillin. After a week, however, the *gabbai* gave me as a gift the tefillin I had worn on the first day.

That *gabbai*, who looked to me like Avraham Avinu, had suffered many hardships in his life. He had survived Auschwitz, where he had lost his wife and children. But despite his own suffering, he did not become callous — on the contrary, he dedicated his time to helping the needy, and a warm smile illuminated his face. When I was near him, I was too embarrassed to complain about my bitter lot or to wallow in self-pity.

A year passed. One day, I was walking home via Davidka Square, when I saw a car hit a child who was crossing the street not far from where I was standing. The driver stopped and jumped out of his car, and we both dashed at the same time toward the child, who was lying unconscious on the road. I saw that the child was not breathing, and I immediately began to perform mouth-to-mouth resuscitation and CPR. A short while later, an ambulance arrived and whisked the child to the hospital.

I had not done anything unusual, but the child's mother — who had emigrated with her son from the Soviet Union — thought that I had saved his life. After he recovered, she searched for me in order to thank me.

From that time on, I took an interest in the child and followed his development. When the mother complained that the boy was not learning well, and that he was being taunted and hit in school, I had some advice for her. "If you want help making a *mentsch* out of him, transfer him to a religious school," I told her. She followed my advice, and had no regrets.

When the boy turned 13, he celebrated his bar mitzvah in school. I wanted to give him tefillin as a bar mitzvah present, so I approached the *gabbai* of the Belzer shul, from whom I had received my first tefillin, and told him, "Rabbi, take me to a place where I can buy nice tefillin."

"Why do you need tefillin?" he asked me. "You already have a pair!"

I told him about the boy. "I'm not pressed for money right now," I explained, "and I can afford to buy myself tefillin. But I don't want to part with the tefillin that you gave me as a present — I want to buy new tefillin for the boy."

The *gabbai* smiled. "That's how it is with us Jews," he said. "Everything we have, we give; we don't leave anything for ourselves." Then he brought me to a place where I could buy tefillin.

A few years later, this *gabbai* passed away one morning in shul. He finished his prayers, removed his tefillin, and returned his soul to his Maker. The world lost a *tzaddik*, and I lost a close friend.

An Unfulfilled Dream

I had made *aliyah* hoping that I would yet have the opportunity to preside over the operating table and do what I knew to do best. This hope dissipated completely during the first days after my arrival in Israel, however, when I became embroiled in domestic issues and was left alone, without a home and without knowing the language. I never did work officially as a surgeon, but I did find myself in the operating room again at some point.

At the same time that I made *aliyah*, a friend of mine named Dr. Yaakov R., who was a pediatrician, arrived in Israel along with his family. He was in a great hurry to make *aliyah*, since his young son was in urgent need of an operation, and he wanted the surgery to be performed in Israel. While we were still on the plane, he asked me to accompany him to the hospital in order to help him communicate with the doctors.

He knew that the operation his son required was the type that I had specialized in, and patients who needed this particular surgery used to come to me from afar. In professional circles, the operation was named "Hirschprung with Gutman's Modification"; "Gutman" referred to me.

A short time after I arrived in Israel, Dr. Yaakov located me and we traveled together to the hospital. There, the child was examined by Professor K., a pediatric surgeon, and I explained that this was a case of Hirschprung's disease. Dr. Yaakov introduced me to the doctors, and Professor K. asked, "Are you the same Gutman who introduced the modification?"[18]

"Yes, indeed," I answered. I felt as though a rush of fresh air was entering my lungs. Professor K. then invited me to assist him during the surgery, and I agreed without hesitation.

I arrived at the hospital at the appointed time. My hands were washed, and I was dressed in a surgical robe, mask, and sterile gloves. When I stood beside the operating table, everything seemed so familiar, so normal; my hands knew by themselves what to do. But something was different: For the first time in my life, I was unable to hold up until the end of the operation, and I had to leave the operating room for some fresh air. I felt weak and worn out.

Professor K. watched me during the operation, and apparently he was convinced that I was indeed the person I claimed to be, for he invited me to join him in the operating room again. During the second surgery I attended, Professor K. allowed me to perform a portion of the operation myself. This time, *he* assisted *me*, watching every movement of my hand attentively. For my part, I was astounded by the many technological innovations I saw here that I had never dreamed of in Russia.

The operation was successful, and I allowed myself to expect a recommendation from the professor. I had more than enough medical experience to begin working in Israel without having to be tested, and it seemed to me that my dream was about to be realized.

Apparently, however, professional expertise is not enough to make someone qualified to work as a surgeon; you also need a great deal of emotional strength. I had been sapped of this strength during my stay in prison and over the course of the ordeals I was going through at that time with my family. In addition, I no longer possessed the physical stamina to stand for many hours during a surgery. Nevertheless, I still dreamed of returning to the field of medicine.

18. There are a number of approaches to the surgery that treats Hirschprung's disease. Gutman's modification was an improvement to one of the approaches.

My Israeli Relatives

From My Mother's Side

A short time after I arrived in Israel and began living in the storage room under the steps, I became friendly with a Tolna *chassid* and his family. Tolna was the village where my mother was born, and I told the *chassid* that my grandfather Hershel had been married to Yides, the daughter of the Tolna Rebbe. In my family, we had always joked that we had "illustrious lineage" from my mother's side, although in my generation, no one cared at all about things like *yichus*.

The chassid told me that he had once heard a chassidic story about a woman named Yides who had managed to made "*a gitte Yid*" out of "Hershel *der katzev*."

A short while later, this *chassid* told me that in honor of his son's bar mitzvah, the Tolna Rebbe himself would visit his home. "You should come, too," he invited me, "and I'll introduce you to the Rebbe."

I arrived at his house on the day of the *simchah*, but I could not make my way inside because the house was full to capacity with *chassidim* who were struggling to get as close to their rebbe as possible. The *chassid* came to my rescue, steering me through the crowd, and told the Rebbe that I was a grandson of Yides.

"Whose son are you?" the Rebbe inquired with interest. "Leika's?" The Rebbe spoke a bit of Russian.

"No, I'm the son of her younger sister Zissel," I responded.

"Where is Zissel?" he asked in Yiddish.

"Zissel passed away in 1989," I answered, also in Yiddish.

"And Leah?"

"She passed away as well."

A shadow passed over his round face, a face that reminded me so much of my own mother's. "And how does the Rebbe know my mother?" I asked.

"We grew up together, as children," he responded.

I longed to hear more about my family, but the many *chassidim* gathered around us were clamoring for their turn to receive the Rebbe's blessing.

The Rebbe blessed me and invited me to come visit him. But I was living under the stairs at that time, and this was a source of great embarrassment to me. What would I answer the Rebbe when he asked me where I lived?

Much to my chagrin, the elderly Rebbe passed away a while later, before I managed to visit him.

From My Father's Side

I knew that distant relatives from my father's side were living in Israel. These were children of the cousin to whom my father had given his green card. That cousin had passed away in America some time earlier, and I did not expect his children to know who I was. So lonely was I, however, that I worked up the courage to call them. *What do I have to lose?* I reasoned.

To my great surprise, when I called and said that I was Moshe Gutman's son, the people at the other end of the line expressed a desire to see me immediately. I went to visit them without delay.

When I arrived at the address I had been given, I was very surprised to see that they lived in a large villa. It turned out that these relatives were very wealthy — they owned a well-known cosmetics company — and they employed a large staff of servants who were responsible for the upkeep of their home. One of these staff members opened the door for me and led me to a magnificent living room. The first thing that caught my eye there was a framed picture of my father hanging on the wall!

"How do you have this picture?" I wondered.

The woman of the house explained that their father, who had prospered greatly in America, had never forgotten that Moshe Gutman had saved his family by giving him his green card, and he had instructed his children to honor the memory of their rescuer.

My relatives were very friendly, and were ready to help me. But my abject poverty, combined with my self-pride, aroused in me a fierce desire to flee their house as quickly as possible. This desire persisted even after a maid approached me and inquired what type of bath to prepare for me. "Would you prefer Dead Sea salts, mineral water, or pinewood aroma?" she asked solicitously.

Claiming that I had urgent matters to take care of, I hurried to take leave of them and escape from their house. *Who needs a destitute relative like me?* I thought as I quickly descended the broad steps of the villa. I was probably wrong on that count, for my relatives were goodhearted people who were genuinely interested in showing me kindness. But I lived with the feeling that "a pauper is as good as dead," for neither the dead man nor the pauper can give to others. How could I accept favors from my relatives if I was unable to give back to them?

Our Arab "Cousins"

The Enemies

Engrossed in the problems of my daily life, I paid no attention to what was going on around me. In the meantime, the Arab intifada was gathering momentum, and the Jews were either shyly apologizing or fearfully giving in. I knew very little Hebrew, for my *ulpan* education had lasted all of three days, and the news of the uprisings did not reach my ears at all.

One evening after work, I went to the Kosel to pray. I went to the Kosel often: I would lean my head on the stones of the Wall and pour out the bitterness in my heart before my Creator. This gave me the strength to continue living.

That day, the bus left the Meah Shearim neighborhood as usual and turned onto the road that connects West and East Jerusalem. I heard some commotion, but I did not immediately grasp why the passengers on the bus were hurrying to close the windows, or why the driver was speeding up as he passed through the area.

I looked into the street and saw three insolent Arab youths hurling large rocks at the windows of our bus. My blood began to boil. *What's going on? Three miserable Arabs are degrading Jews in our own home, in Jerusalem, and we're allowing them to continue doing this without protesting?"*

"Open the door!" I shouted to the driver, and jumped out of the bus.

Both the passengers on the bus and the Arab youths were surprised. They had not expected any reaction, and they fled in all directions when they saw me approaching. I chased after one of them — the skinniest of the lot — and tripped him. When he landed on the ground, I kicked him in a way that assured that he would never again have any desire to start up with Jews.

In the meantime, the two other rock-throwing youths who had fled realized that no one but me had descended from the bus, and they gathered a crowd of older people and started running toward me. In order to protect myself from being stabbed from behind, I stood with my back to the wall.

The people on the bus had been asleep all this time. The driver had called the police, and within moments, a police vehicle approached my direction, lights flashing and sirens blaring. *Faster, dear police, faster!* I never loved the police as much as I did at that moment.

The Arab youths realized that they had to save their own skins, and they disappeared from the site, leaving the police to take care of me and the rock-thrower who was lying on the ground. And the police did indeed take care of us. They put us both in chains and brought us unceremoniously to the police station.

I seemed to have strange luck in Israel: For the third time, I had been found guilty and arrested even though I had done nothing wrong! Even this time, when there was a bus full of witnesses — albeit silent witnesses — I had turned into the aggressor and the Arab youth into the victim! The way the situation was presented to the police, it sounded as though the youth was but a child who had been playing innocently with his friends in the street, and I had jumped off the bus and beaten him for no reason; I had even broken his tooth in the process. And for that I would have to stand judgment.

The police opened a file — another file! — for me, and held me in prison until the morning. They then released me, promising to send me a court summons. Guilelessly, I gave them the address of the yeshivah where I slept under the stairs, since I had no other address to give. I should note that this time, the police officers treated me respectfully, unlike during my previous arrest. Apparently, they were also glad to see the Arab youth receive his comeuppance.

In any event, I never received a summons.

The Friends

My old classmate, Tarik the Arab (the youth whom Papa had considered a Jew), located me through mutual acquaintances, and he came to visit me together with his Russian wife Svetlana, who had since converted to Islam. By that time, I had already left my lodgings under the stairs and was living in my own apartment.

We sat together that entire evening, and reminisced about our mutual friends and about our shared years of study. Tarik could not forget how Papa had helped him, and now, he convinced me to come visit his father. Curious to see how Arabs live, I accepted his invitation.

Tarik's father, a former lawyer, lived in a large house in Atarot, an Arab village just outside Jerusalem. When I arrived at the house, Tarik said something to his father, and the old man embraced me forcefully, then seated me in a seat of honor at his side and began conversing with me in Arabic. I did not understand a word, but I nodded my head politely.

About a year later, Tarik invited me to his daughter's wedding in Ramallah. I agreed to come, even though by that time I understood that this could be a dangerous adventure. When Tarik came to get me, I was wearing my Shabbos clothing: suit, hat, and *tzitzis*.

He looked at me as though I were insane. "What are you thinking?" he asked in disbelief.

"Either I come like this, or I don't come at all," I answered.

"Fine," Tarik said. "Just don't move away from me for a minute."

He brought me to Ramallah and seated me at a table where distinguished-looking guests were sitting. Some where wearing striped cloths on their heads, while others wore red hats. Tarik brought me French fries in a closed package and a bottle of Coca-Cola. I didn't touch anything else at that party.

The air in the hall was suffocating, and I decided to go out to the street to smoke, completely forgetting where I was. When I was outside, Arab children began to run around me noisily, until they surrounded me in a tight circle. Suddenly, Tarik leaped outside toward me, his face pale. "Get back into the hall right away!" he hissed. "I can't protect you here!" He grabbed my hand and pulled me back inside.

Another time, I traveled to visit a different friend in the Gaza Strip. This friend, accompanied by Tarik, came to pick me up. For that trip, I had to obtain a special permit from the police, who asked me what missing item of mine I intended to find in Arab territory. I told him about my Arab classmates and about my father's claim that there are no Arabs in Israel, only Jews. The police officers who interrogated me burst out laughing. Clearly, it wasn't every day that such hearty laughter was heard within the walls of the police station.

The Meeting

In the days when I was taking my first hesitant steps in Eretz Yisrael, I crossed paths with a person with whom I had never sought to develop friendly ties. In the past he had caused me only trouble, and apparently Heaven was sending him to me again as a *nisayon* (test).

I had become acquainted with this person about a decade earlier in the city of Zhitomir. I was sitting in my office one day in the hospital, when the secretary entered and announced: "Semyon Moysevich, there is someone here from the city of Tashkent with a letter from your mother-in-law."

You don't start up with your mother-in-law, especially when she lives far away and does not often trouble you with requests. "Let him in," I instructed.

A handsome, dark-skinned young man named Boris entered and handed me a letter. In the letter, my mother-in-law had written to request that I find this young man work as a dentist, since this young specialist had had a hard time finding work in Tashkent.

I arranged work for Boris in a village hospital not far from Zhitomir. The arrangement was that he would begin working in the village in order to demonstrate his level of proficiency. After a short while, the news spread that an Uzbek dentist with golden hands was working in the village.

I traveled to the village myself and tested Boris personally by allowing him to give me dental treatment. Seeing that he was an excellent dentist, I offered him a position as a mouth and jaw surgeon in our regional hospital. He told me that he had always dreamed of specializing in that field, but he had yet to study it.

"That's already my department," I told him, and sent him to a half-year course in Kiev. Boris was delighted. Upon completing the course, he returned to Zhitomir to work in my hospital.

A short time later, I was shocked to see Boris in my office presenting me with a written request: "I am hereby requesting that you fire me due to my pending *aliyah* to Israel."

"What's your connection to Israel?" I asked in astonishment. "You're an Uzbek!"

"I'm Jewish," Boris replied, hanging his head.

"You're Jewish?" I nearly fell off my chair. I had been certain that he was an Uzbek!

As was customary during those years, the hospital arranged a general staff meeting in which we disparaged the "traitor who was traveling to Zionist land of Israel." I denigrated him more than anyone else did, but I was nevertheless reprimanded for having hired him and even sending him to a course for specialists. I didn't bother telling them that I had mistaken him for an Uzbek, because they would not have believed me anyway.

During the gathering, a doctor by the name of Kozhakov stood up and requested the floor. He was an intelligent person, a true expert in his field, but he was always a bit tipsy, and for that reason he had been banished from Riga (the capital of Latvia) to our far-flung region. When he stood up to speak, he surprised everyone by saying the truth, instead of disparaging Boris. "If people wish to emigrate, that's their right!" he said. "Let them leave!"

What ridicule he was subjected to for his words! People called him a drunkard, and claimed that he was speaking irresponsibly because he was drunk.

After the gathering, Kozhakov approached me in the corridor and told me in a voice that was perfectly sober: "If you don't want to emigrate, don't, but why are you poking your nose into someone else's business?"

Now I understood how unsympathetic I appeared in the eyes of the gentiles when I denigrated my fellow Jews. From then on, I no longer attempted to prove my loyalty to the Soviet Union by putting down other Jews.

Half a year later, the hospital received a letter from America. It was written by Boris, and addressed to me. Boris wrote that he was working temporarily as a taxi driver. I don't know why he sent the letter to the hospital's address; he should have known that this would only make my life more difficult. Now, the entire hospital staff knew that I had received a letter from a "traitor," and this caused me a great deal of trouble.

In order to defend myself, I showed the letter to the director of the hospital.

"Look what a liar he is," I said. "He fooled all of us! He said that he was traveling to Israel, and now he's in America. And he even has the audacity to send me a letter from there!" I made a dramatic show of throwing the letter into the garbage.

Who would have thought then that I would yet meet up with Boris one day? This is the story of my surprising reunion with Boris:

In January of 1992 (5752), heavy snow fell in Jerusalem, piling up in the streets.

When I had the opportunity, I would make my way in the evenings to the Chabad yeshivah, where there were *shiurim* in Russian. One evening, during a break, I went out of the yeshivah to smoke. Near the entrance, I saw a man who looked like Boris. "Boris!" I called out.

The man turned around to detect where the voice was coming from. After looking all around, he threw me an indifferent look and turned away again. I had aged by this time, and he did not recognize me.

I called out to him again by name.

He approached me and asked, "How do you know me?"

I identified myself, and he looked at me in disbelief. He had known me as a secular Soviet doctor, and now I looked like a bearded religious Jew. I had to show him my identification papers, where my old picture appeared, in order for him to recognize me. He embraced me and kissed me, clearly on the verge of tears.

"If you are here," he sobbed, "then no evil will befall me!"

"What are you talking about?" I asked him. "I myself am barely surviving!"

He did not listen, but instead reiterated, "Now everything will be okay."

He told me that he was living with his parents. I did not cross-examine him; the last thing I needed was to add him to my list of problems.

Boris went on his way, and I stayed to help the cook clean up after supper. When I finished, one of the yeshivah *bachurim* approached me and asked, "That man you were just talking to — do you know where he sleeps?"

"He told me that he sleeps in his parents' home."

"His parents?" the *bachur* asked incredulously. "He sleeps in a metal shack that belongs to the shoemaker in Geulah. He works there during the day and sleeps there at night."

It was raining and snowing outside. "Take me to him," I told the *bachur*.

We set out for the tin shack. When we arrived, I knocked on the iron door and said, "Open up!"

A frightened Boris opened the door, thinking that the police were coming for him. We peered inside. Boris slept on a worktable, and next to him was an electric heater with no grounding wires. I shouted at him, "Have you gone mad? You're going to die here of electrocution! Come with me."

I brought him to my little room under the stairs. To ensure that no one would know that he was sleeping there, I awoke him at five in the morning, before anyone else arrived. I went with him to the mikveh, and then to shul. (Over the years, Boris, too, became a *baal teshuvah*.)

For six months, Boris and I slept opposite each other on the same sofa. I told my friend Leizer that Boris was sleeping with me under the stairs, but my conscience continued to gnaw at me, for the little storage room had been given to me as a *chessed* — and here I was, bringing someone else in?

I later learned that the evening when I had met Boris in the Chabad yeshivah, he had entered purely by coincidence.

That winter, I heard a story from one of the students of Rabbi Yitzchak Zilber, a story that helped me start thinking more about others. This is the story the student told:

I was accompanying R' Yitzchak through the narrow streets of Geulah, where the snow on the ground had melted and turned into mud. R' Yitzchak was hurrying, as he always did. Suddenly, an overgrown brute appeared in front of us, clearly the type of person who paid no heed to passersby, and certainly would never think of yielding to allow someone else to pass. Rudely, he collided with the rav, knocked him to the ground, into the mud, and continued on his way without even turning his head.

Infuriated at this behavior, my first impulse was to run after the brute, but I restrained myself and hurried to lift R' Yitzchak from the ground. But R' Yitzchak had already managed to pull himself up. He was covered with mud, and his hat was askew, but he didn't care. He raised his hands heavenward and called out, "He didn't do anything to me! I fell by myself, by myself! He didn't do anything to me!"

"Kim!"

More than three months passed from the time I began working with Leizer. He silently put up with me for that long, and then he told me, "You're not the right kind of worker for me."

I understood myself that I was not really any help to Leizer; he had to do everything for me. "Leizer, did I ever claim that I knew how to do anything?" I responded.

Now, I had to look for different work. I remembered that my father had once taught me to bind *sefarim*, and I mentioned that to Leizer.

"Good," he replied. "Give it a try."

I found myself a place in a workshop where *sefarim* were bound, and I began to work there. I continued to sleep under the stairs, and in return for my accommodations I cleaned the mikveh.

Two weeks passed. Leizer visited my workshop and asked, "How much are they paying you?"

"Six shekels an hour [approximately $1.50]," I replied.

"That's not appropriate for you," he said. "*Kim* [come]!"

Leizer had said, "*Kim!*" so I left everything and followed him. He brought me to an old age home, where I was hired as a nurse.

This new job revitalized me. True, I was working only as a nurse — but I was working with people, and I was able to put my medical knowledge to some use.

I saved practically every shekel I earned, spending almost nothing on myself. I constantly cried to Leizer that I wanted to buy my own place, even if it was just a basement.

A year passed from the time Leizer "adopted" me. In October, he came to me and uttered his famous one-word directive: "*Kim!*"

I followed Leizer without asking any questions. As we walked, Leizer told me that he had found me an apartment in Geulah. It was a two-room on the ground floor of an old house. This apartment had belonged to R' Aryeh Levin, the *tzaddik* of Jerusalem who had passed away over 20 years earlier. No one had lived in his apartment after his death.

Leizer led me through the winding alleyways of Geulah until we reached a small courtyard and entered through the gate. It was a two-story house that had been built over 90 years earlier for the purpose of "*hekdesh*" (free housing for the needy), and served as a refuge for poor Jews. The second floor of the house was inhabited by the daughter of R' Aryeh Levin and her family.

The place that Leizer had termed an "apartment" was actually more like a disaster zone. It was partly destroyed, and did not even have doors. Peering into the dim, dank interior, I spotted large rats running all around the apartment.

Leizer and I did not dare cross the threshold of the house; we just stood at the entrance peering into the darkness. I was baffled: What could I do with this dump? This was obviously not a place where anyone could live.

Suddenly, my mother's image appeared inside the apartment, in the doorway between the rooms. I saw her very clearly — she was saying, "My son, I taught you that the eyes fear, but the hands do!"

"Leizer," I called out, pointing into the darkness, "there's my mother!"

"Are you crazy?" he asked, agape. "Your mother?" He rotated his finger around his temple, indicating that he thought I had gone insane.

"Mama!" I called again, but her image faded into the distance until it disappeared completely. I realized then that only I had seen and heard her.

After my mother appeared to me in the apartment, I was no longer afraid to live there.

When Mama was gone, I said to Leizer, "I like this apartment. How much is it?"

"Twenty thousand dollars," Leizer replied.

"Where will I get that money?"

"Don't worry. Do you have some of it?"

"I have $5,000."

The following evening, I was sitting in my room under the stairs when Leizer appeared. "*Kim!*" he said. Leizer took me to the director of the nursing home where I worked and spoke to him in Hebrew. The director withdrew a checkbook, wrote out a check for $17,000, and handed it to me.

"I can't take this check," I demurred.

"Why not?"

"First of all, I don't know if I'll be able to repay it," I said. "Second, I don't want you to keep me on as a worker just because I owe you money."

The director smiled and said something to Leizer about my oversensitivity. Leizer did not try to persuade me; he knew how to handle me better than that. He took the check and asked the director, "How much do I owe you?"

"Seventy thousand," the director replied.

I hadn't known that Leizer also owed him money. *Wow*, I thought to myself. *Look what kind of debt my friend has!*

"Add this check to my account," Leizer requested. "Shepsel, you'll start to repay your loan to me."

In that simple way, Leizer arranged the financing of my new apartment. The apartment was registered under my name, with the stipulation that it was considered a "sheltered lodging," meaning that I was not allowed to sell it to anyone else. In this way, I ceased to be homeless, although my new apartment was still in desperate need of renovation.

The Reason for the Fire

L eizer had golden hands.
"Don't worry," he told me. "We'll renovate the apartment ourselves."

We had to invest quite some time into this project. Other people besides Leizer helped me, including Boris. When the renovations were completed, I invited Boris to join me in the apartment. From my own experience, I understood how important it was for a person to have his own place, and I wanted to help Boris find his own place as well. We began to search for suitable lodgings for Boris in my neighborhood, where I was already acquainted with many good people.

After a short time, these good people helped Boris to find a suitable place, and he bought himself a one-room apartment. Not only did he live in that apartment, he also managed to transform it into a dental clinic, which was the realization of an old dream for him. He did not actually have a license to perform dentistry in Israel, but because he was a true expert in his field he had no dearth of patients.

The *gabbai* of a nearby shul helped Boris a great deal in purchasing and setting up his apartment. Despite his advanced age, this saintly *gabbai* was always busy helping others. A month after Boris moved into his new apartment, he had an argument with this *gabbai*. In his rage, Boris slapped the old man across the face!

Thing like this don't happen in Geulah every day, and when

Leizer heard about Boris's deplorable behavior, he was furious. I had never seen him so angry before.

"*That man* should not dare to cross the threshold of your house!" Leizer thundered to me. He didn't even want to utter Boris's name.

Boris's punishment was not long in coming. Several days later, he left his apartment and forgot to turn off an electrical appliance. His dental clinic went up in flames, and everything was burnt to ashes. Again, Boris was left with nothing.

Leizer was insistent that I no longer have anything to do with *that man*, but I took pity on the hapless Boris and allowed him to sleep in my apartment. He begged me to accompany him to visit influential people and enlist their assistance in rebuilding his clinic, and I could not refuse.

He did manage to rebuild his clinic, but patients stopped coming to him. Boris was forced to leave Jerusalem, and I no longer had to defy the instructions of my master and teacher, Leizer, who had commanded me not to allow Boris into my house.

Maaser

I called Leizer "my master and teacher," for I can truthfully say that thanks to Leizer I was reborn and became a *baal teshuvah*. Whatever I have in this world, both spiritually and physically, I owe to him.

Leizer was the oldest of a large family of Hungarian descent. His father was a rebbi. Leizer was orphaned at the age of 13, and from that time he began working at various trades — as the saying goes, "What the eyes see, the hands do."

Relatives adopted the orphaned children of Leizer's family. Those who were adopted by chassidic families became *chassidim*, and those who were adopted by Litvish families became Litvaks. Leizer took on the customs of his wife's family, who were Belzer *chassidim* of Romanian origin. When they married, she was 17 and he was 20.

Many people referred to Leizer as a *tzaddik*. Before meeting him, I had thought that a *tzaddik* is someone who is very calm and patient, and never argues with anyone. Leizer, in contrast, did whatever he thought was right, and when he deemed it necessary to intervene in an altercation, he did.

Leizer was always helping people. He would help an old lady to fix her clogged pipes, or replace a window pane for someone in need. He spoke little, but did a lot. He simply *lived* kindness, and drew others — including myself — after him to do *chessed*. Watching Leizer live life was to me the best possible *mussar* lesson.

When Leizer and his wife Rina celebrated their fortieth wedding anniversary, all their children and grandchildren gathered to celebrate the occasion. At that time, I gave Leizer a gift of a soup tureen — which was to me the symbol of wealth and happiness.

The first time I presented Leizer with my paycheck as payment for my debt, I told him, "Out of these 1,800 shekels, I need 120: 100 for a monthly bus pass, and 20 for cigarettes."

"And what about food?"

"That's none of your business."

I then told him that I wished to give *maaser* from my salary. He told me that I was not obligated to give *maaser* because this was not my money; it was money that I owed.

I was no expert in the halachic intricacies of this issue, but I insisted on giving *maaser* anyway. "Why not?" I retorted. "I want to give *maaser* to the cheder, since they saved me from death."

"If you want, you can give *maaser*," he relented.

And so I began to separate *maaser* from all my earnings and donate the money to the cheder.

Hearing one of R' Yitzchak Zilber's *shiurim* had aroused in me a desire to fulfill the mitzvah of giving *maaser*, although I had heard about giving *maaser* earlier as well. During that period, I paid frequent visits to the yeshivah where R' Yitzchak taught, and one day, R' Yitzchak quoted the following story from the Gemara:

A person complained to R' Pinchas ben Yair that his city was suffering from an onslaught of mice, which were eating everything. "Do you separate *maaser*?" R' Pinchas ben Yair inquired.

"No," the person admitted.

"Do you give to the poor, to the Levites, and to the *Kohanim*?"

Again, the answer was no.

"If you wish to get rid of the mice," R' Pinchas ben Yair advised them, "you should begin to separate *maaser*."

As soon as the people of the city began to give *maaser*, the mice disappeared.

"I'll give an example of my own," R' Yitzchak Zilber added. "Once, I was hospitalized for a heart problem in Hadassah Hospital's intensive care unit. A Jewish doctor of about 60 performed an EKG on me, and we conversed about various things. He told me that he still remembers the great *tzaddik* R' Aryeh Levin, and he related a story that he had personally witnessed."

This is the story the doctor told R' Yitzchak Zilber:

I was once walking with R' Aryeh in the street when a young Jew approached him and lamented that store he had recently opened was not earning a penny. "I have only losses to show," he complained. R' Aryeh called him to the side, conversed with him quietly, and the two parted ways.

Later, I discovered what that private conversation had been about. R' Aryeh had asked the young man, "Tell me the truth — was the money that you invested into opening the business money that you earned honestly?"

The young man admitted that he had concealed a portion of his revenues from his partner and had used that money to open the store.

The tzaddik instructed him to return the money to his partner. A short while later, the young man met R' Aryeh and told him that he had fulfilled his instructions, and from that time his business had begun to flourish.

This story touched my heart. It was, after all, about R' Aryeh Levin, the *tzaddik* whose home I had the merit of inhabiting.

A short time later, I learned a lesson of my own regarding giving *maaser*.

I had earned 10 dollars, and had been paid with a 10-dollar bill. I was too tired to go change the bill for 10 single bills so that I could give one dollar to *maaser*, and it was such a small sum that I decided to postpone giving *maaser* until a larger sum would accumulate.

I came home and removed my coat. That day, people came to my apartment to take away books and other objects that had been stored in the apartment when no one had lived in it. A short while earlier I had asked them to come to remove these objects.

The door to the outside was open during this time. As I was helping the people pack up the objects in the apartment, a stranger appeared in the second room.

"Did this man come with you?" I asked the people.

"No," they replied.

"Then he must be a thief!" I declared. I dashed after him, and he began to run away, darting into the street. But he limped, and I caught up with him easily. He was a thin man, and I grabbed him, shook him, and gave him a kick. Then I let him go.

What can he possibly take from me, I thought to myself. *My tzaros?*

When I returned home, I saw that my wallet was missing! The thief had managed to remove my wallet from my coat pocket, along with my money and documents and the 10 dollar bill that I had not yet separated *maaser* from.

I took this as a sign from heaven. Since then, I separate *maaser* immediately from any income I receive.

Let Their Names Be Called in Yisrael ...

One day, I told Leizer that from then on I wished to repay 100 shekels less of my debt to him every month.

"Why?" he asked.

"I want to open a bank account and start saving money for the wedding of your son Moshe."

At the time that Leizer had brought me into his family, his son Moshe had been 15 years old. Instead of playing outside with his friends, Moshe had taken care of me: He had taught me how to pray from a *siddur*, and had told me stories from the Torah in Yiddish. Thanks to his efforts, I managed to remember some of what Bubbe Faiga had taught me.

Leizer laughed when he heard my plan. "Isn't it a bit early to start saving money for his wedding?"

But he consented nevertheless.

A few years later, when Moshe married a girl from Canada, it turned out that I had assessed the situation correctly. Leizer invited me to come to the wedding in Canada, and he wished to buy me a plane ticket. "What do you mean?" I said proudly. "I've already saved enough money for a ticket *and* for a gift."

When Moshe's first daughter was born, he came to me and said, "Shepsel, our family has already given all the names we had to give, and we'd like to name our daughter after your grandmother Faiga. Do you mind?"

He was asking if I minded!

"I'll be deeply grateful to you if you do that," I said, deeply moved.

The baby was named Faiga Liba.

When Moshe's second daughter was born, he told me that they wanted to name her after my mother. She was called Zissel Malka.

As we sat around the table and celebrated the birth of Zissel Malka, Moshe mentioned regretfully that if he would have a baby boy, he would not be able to name him after my father, who was named Moshe as well. Leizer's brother-in-law was sitting with us at the time, and when he heard this, he said, "My wife is expecting. If she has a boy, I'll name him Moshe."

The baby was a boy. The parents wanted to give the name "Baruch" as well, since that had been the name of Leizer's father, so they went to ask the Belzer Rebbe what to do. He advised them to name the baby "Baruch Moshe" — the first name after Leizer's father and the second name after my father — and that's what they did. But to this day everyone calls the boy "Moshe Baruch."

"Alte Zachen"

In 1994 (5754), a cousin of mine visited Israel and brought me some items from my parents' house. I opened the package, and saw Bubbe Faiga's worn, tattered *sefarim*.

Bubbe Faiga's words echoed in my head: *"Zissel, kim, ich hub gefunnen eppes nayes* [Zissel, come, I've found a *chiddush*]!"

The package also contained Papa's tefillin — which had previously belonged to my grandfather — sans the straps. And to think that my daughters had used those straps to tie skates to their feet ....

The package also contained my parents' *Sefer Torah* — the very same *Sefer Torah* that I had hidden away after my father' arrest.

I showed the *Sefer Torah* to people in the know, and they said that it was damaged beyond repair and required *genizah*. I didn't understand then the importance of putting a *Sefer Torah* in *genizah*, and I decided that if it could not be used, I might as well sell it. I brought the *Sefer Torah* to a Judaica store in the Meah Shearim area, and the owner offered me 600 shekels for it. I sold the *Sefer Torah*, and after splitting the 600 shekels with my cousin, I forgot about the matter completely.

But when I passed by the store at a later point, I pictured my *Sefer Torah* lying on the other side of the opaque glass along with other dusty items. My heart contorted at the thought, and I felt as though I had betrayed a loved one. I resolved then that the moment I would have enough money, I would redeem the *Sefer Torah*.

A year later, I went into the store, prepared to pay whatever the storeowner would demand. But he told me that the *Sefer Torah* had long disappeared from his store.

I decided then to have Papa's old tefillin checked. Perhaps those were still usable?

I brought the tefillin to a well-known *sofer* in Geulah. He opened the worn *battim*, removed the yellowing *parashiyos* inside, and examined them carefully. Then, he turned his gaze to me and asked, "Where did you get these tefillin?"

"They were an inheritance from my grandfather," I replied.

He asked me to wait, and called someone on the telephone. A few minutes later, an elderly Jew wearing a long coat and a round hat burst into the room, out of breath. The *sofer* handed him my tefillin, and he did not even pause to catch his breath before examining them.

"I'd like to buy your tefillin," the elderly Jew then told me. "I'll give you $1,000 for them. They were written by my great-grandfather, who was the famous sofer, K. I am also a *sofer*, and these tefillin are very dear to my heart."

It was painful for me to disappoint him, but by now, I understood the significance of the tefillin myself, and I was not willing to part with tefillin that had been worn by my father and grandfather. I answered him in Yiddish with one of Bubbe Faiga's aphorisms: "We're not rich enough to wear cheap clothing." I then added, "I am going to wear these tefillin myself — they are dear to me as well."

After I explained why the tefillin were precious to me, he understood and did not try to persuade me further.

Incredibly, the tefillin were not damaged at all. The *sofer* made one tiny repair to them, affixed new straps, and returned them to me. I have worn those tefillin ever since.

Continuing the Tradition

I decided that since I had the merit of living in the house of R' Aryeh Levin and restoring it to livable condition, it was incumbent upon me to uphold the legacy of this house and its former owner. I knew that R' Aryeh's house had served as a refuge for the needy, including those who were persecuted during the British Mandate.

Having personally experienced what it means to be without a roof over your head, I was particularly sensitive to the plight of the homeless. I therefore invited many a homeless person into my apartment. Some of my "guests" took advantage of my kindness and betrayed me. But others, like the two I am about to discuss, were gifts from heaven.

These two "guests" stayed with me in different years, but I met both of them in the winter, around Chanukah, when the weather in Jerusalem is cold and rainy.

The First Meeting

Once, I was walking in the street on a rainy, stormy day in December when I saw a barefoot young man in a thin shirt sitting on a bench at a bus stop with two suitcases next to him.

I began talking to him, and he was happy to hear that I spoke Russian. He told me that his name was Misha, that he was religious, and that he come from a community of Caucasian Jews. He had recently made *aliyah*, and had rented an apartment together with two other young men. But they had just now quarreled with him over the rent, and had thrown him into the street together with his belongings.

I brought Misha to my house.

Misha, it turned out, was a gifted silversmith. In Russia, his works were displayed in the Hermitage. Misha showed me an album containing photos of his collection, and I could see that his work was outstanding.

Just then, Leizer came to visit me. I showed him the album and said, "Look — these works are his. We have to help this fellow find a job!"

"*Kim!*" Leizer said, and without any further ado he drove us to a jewelry factory in the Talpiyot neighborhood. Leizer knew a master craftsman who worked at that factory, and the craftsman gave Misha a gold thread and said, "Make something out of this."

Misha requested some tools, and within a few minutes he managed to create a beautiful earring in the shape of a rose.

"Make another one," the craftsman requested. Misha obliged, and the craftsman took the earrings and gave him a job on the spot.

Several months passed, and Misha became engaged. His bride was also from the Caucasus, and her parents made the new couple a beautiful wedding, observing all of the customs of their community. Misha set out for his wedding from my house, and I represented the groom's side at the wedding.

A short time later, Misha opened his own chain of factories, and these factories did very well. Later, he built himself a house on the sea, and he invited me to visit. When I came to his house, he showed me to a comfortable room with a private entrance. "This room is yours," he said. "You can use it whenever you want."

I slept there a few times, just to make Misha feel good.

The Second Meeting

The second meeting took place one rainy Chanukah evening, a number of years after I met Misha. Again, I saw a young man sitting at a bus stop, his suitcases beside him and an expression of hopelessness on his face. He looked to me like an immigrant from the Soviet Union, and he was clearly in no hurry to go anywhere.

I approached him and asked, "Do you have a place to sleep?"

"No," he admitted quietly.

"Come to me, then."

He rose and followed me. We were both silent all the way to my apartment. When we arrived, I told him, "One room is for you and the other is for me. This is your bed — make yourself comfortable." I then gave him to eat.

I knew nothing about him, other than the fact that his name was Elisha, but I did not ask him any questions. Why pry into a person's soul? *When he wants to, he'll speak up,* I told myself.

We lived that way for a while, each of us in his room, and Elisha's story remained a mystery to me. I noticed, however, that he ran every day to the Interior Ministry, just as a person would run to work, and one day I asked him about this.

"I don't have a *teudat zehut* [Israeli identification card]," he explained. "My father is Jewish, and my mother is Russian. In Russia, I underwent a Reform conversion and *bris milah*. But now, the Interior Ministry refuses to recognize me as a Jew."

Then, Elisha went on to relate his story.

"Two weeks ago, I made *aliyah* from Russia and went directly to Bnei Brak, to a relative from my father's side named Rabbi M."

Elisha gave the name of one of the *gedolei hador*. Upon hearing his name, I unwittingly let out an exclamation of surprise. Thousands of people considered it a great merit just to visit that house! Clearly, Elisha had no inkling of whose house he had stayed in. I did not interrupt the flow of his words, however, for I did not want to alarm him.

"Rabbi M. welcomed me warmly," he continued, "and I stayed at his house for a week. Then, suddenly, he told me, 'It's time for you to go learn, so that you can become a Jew.'

"'But I already underwent a Reform conversion!' I protested.

"'Better to remain a gentile than to be a Reform Jew,' he replied resolutely.

"I didn't understand what he meant, and I left Bnei Brak in a huff.

I decided to travel to Jerusalem, but since I didn't know anyone and I had nowhere to go, I simply sat down at the bus stop. That was when you came and took me in."

I explained that Reform conversion does not make a person Jewish. Then I turned to him and added purposefully, "Elisha, why do you need to be a Jew? Even with your current status, you enjoy the Right of Return, and you can live here in Israel. Why don't you just remain a gentile?"

Elisha did not sleep at all that night; I heard him tossing and turning in his bed.

In the morning, he said to me, "Reb Shepsel, take me to a place where I can learn to be a Jew!"

I was delighted. But it turned out that my joy was premature, for no one was interested in accepting Elisha as a student. I took him to one place, and another, until we gave up and returned to my apartment dejectedly.

Just then, we met Rabbi R., a distinguished person who often came by to visit his relatives, who lived on the second floor of my house.

"Honored rabbi," I said to him, "this young man wants to become a Jew, but no one will accept him. What should we do?"

Rabbi R. advised us to go to particular yeshivah for new immigrants. "Tell them I recommended you," he said.

We followed his advice, and Elisha was accepted to that yeshivah. There was no room for him in the dormitory, however, so he continued to stay at my apartment. In the mornings he learned in the yeshivah, and in the evenings he worked in a printing house.

Some time later, I went to the yeshivah myself, and the people at the yeshivah asked me, "Where did you find this Rabbi Akiva?"

"Which Rabbi Akiva?" I asked, puzzled at the question.

"The young man that you brought us," they explained. "He never budges from his *sefer!*"

"He's like that at home, too," I told them. "He's always learning!"

Elisha studied diligently, and after a few months his teachers at the yeshivah decided that he was ready to undergo halachic conversion. Elisha then asked me to accompany him to the Rabbinate to open a conversion file.

We went to the Rabbinate and opened a file. Some time later, Elisha was summoned to the Rabbinate, and he asked me excitedly to accompany him.

I accompanied him to the Rabbinate, but the reception we received was strange and insulting. They did not ask Elisha anything; they simply sent him home. Elisha left the Rabbinate in distress, and he began to cry. It is difficult to watch a grown man cry, and I cried along with him, not knowing how to comfort him.

Hoping to shock him out of his misery, I said, "Why do you need to bother being a Jew? I told you already — you have the right to live in Israel regardless. Let's go have a drink and forget about the whole thing."

As I had hoped, Elisha stopped crying immediately. "What are you talking about, Reb Shepsel?" he thundered. "How can I not become a Jew?"

I looked at him and pondered the irony of Elisha's situation compared to mine. For most of my life, Judaism had been an unbearably heavy burden for me, and I had never bothered to inquire what it demanded of me. Elisha, on the other hand, was eager to accept the yoke of Judaism upon himself and was prepared to keep the entire Torah — but try as he might, he could not be granted entry into the Jewish people!

The Rabbinate sent Elisha away several times, and each time he cried. When I accompanied him on his fourth visit to the Rabbinate's offices, the clerk informed us that his file had been lost. I stood with him in the lobby, not knowing what to do. Finally, we made our way to the elevator, and that's where we met our redeeming angel: R' Yitzchak Zilber. As he walked toward us, he recognized me and asked, "What are you doing here?"

"Rabbi Zilber," I responded furiously, "I want to ask you where I am — in a *Yenta Devoireh* or in a *beis din*?"

"What do you mean by '*Yenta Devoireh*'?" he wondered.

"When my grandmother wanted to say that someone was sloppy," I explained, "she used to say, '*Yenta Devoirah veist nisht vi ba ir a shich vi ba ir a zok*' [Yenta Devoirah doesn't know where her shoe is and where her sock is]. They claim that they've lost the file."

As if on cue, just at that moment the clerk who had told us that the file was lost passed through the corridor. I pointed to him and said, "Here you are, he's the one who says the file is lost."

R' Zilber told us to sit down and wait. He said something to the clerk and they walked away together.

We waited about 20 minutes. Elisha looked piteous, and he was shaking from nervousness and excitement. Finally, the clerk emerged and summoned Elisha into his office. Although I was not invited, I did not want to leave Elisha alone, and I accompanied him inside.

In the office, behind the desk, sat two people: R' Zilber and another rav. They spoke to Elisha and asked him questions. Apparently, they were satisfied with the answers they received, since they immediately sent him for a *bris milah*. I took a day off from work that day to be at Elisha's side during his *bris*, and I served as his *sandek*.

After the *bris*, we returned home, set the table, and made a *seudas mitzvah*. Elisha was ecstatic, and I shared in his joy.

Elisha was asked to return to the *beis din* a week later to immerse in a mikveh. When we arrived at the *beis din*, we were accompanied to the mikveh by a representative of the *beis din* and one of the *roshei yeshivah* of the yeshivah where Elisha learned. To make Elisha feel more confident, I asked permission to immerse along with him.

Time passed, and at some point Elisha informed me that he was planning to marry. He introduced me to his *kallah*: a serious girl, just like him, who had studied in a Bais Yaakov seminary.

"She's right for you!" I pronounced, giving the couple my blessing.

Upon Elisha's request, I traveled with him to Ashdod to meet the *kallah's* parents. Her background was similar to Elisha's: Her father was Jewish, her mother was not, and she herself had converted. I negotiated with the parents over the amount of money they were willing to give the young couple, and I promised that I, too, would give something.

Elisha insisted that the wedding be held in Bnei Brak, near Rabbi M., his relative. I told him, "You have to go to Rabbi M. and invite him to the wedding."

Elisha adamantly refused.

"If so," I threatened, "I won't come to the wedding either, and I won't give any money."

"Reb Shepsel," he begged, "come with me and we'll go to Rabbi M. together. I'm embarrassed to go by myself."

I traveled with him to Bnei Brak, and we visited Rabbi M. Elisha looked just right, wearing a hat and a long suit and sporting a beard. He handed the rav an invitation, and at first the rav did not understand what was going on. But then he recognized Elisha, and he was delighted.

I could not help but boast, "Rabbi, *ich hub oisgechapt ba dir a mitzvah* [I grabbed a mitzvah from you]!"

"*A groisse dank dir* [thank you very much]," the rav replied. "You brought a lost branch of my family back to *Yiddishkeit!*"

Rabbi M. attended the wedding, accompanied by his students, and gave the new couple a beautiful table and chairs as a gift, as well as money. Rav Benzion Zilber, the son of R' Yitzchak, was the *mesader kiddushin*. Many people were present at the wedding, including all the students of Elisha's yeshivah. What a joyous wedding it was! I danced and celebrated as though it were the wedding of my own son.

The young couple rented an apartment in Jerusalem, not far from where I live. A short while later, Elisha studied *milah* and *shechitah*, and he and his wife then traveled on *shelichus* to Russia. A daughter was born to them, and then a son. Their son's *bris* was held in Ashdod, and Elisha himself was the *mohel*.

Rabbi M. expressed a desire to attend the *bris*, but no one thought that he would be able to come, since he had recently suffered a stroke and had just been discharged from the hospital. But he managed to come, even though he was confined to a wheelchair.

When Elisha asked Rabbi M. to be the *sandek*, Rabbi M. turned to me and said, "You were the father's *sandek* — now you'll be the son's *sandek*."

Rabbi M. passed the baby to me. I held him on my lap and squeezed my eyes shut, for I did not wish to see Elisha performing the *bris*. This was me, an old surgeon! For the first time, I experienced the feeling of being a grandfather.

The baby was named "Yisrael."

Cast Your Bread

I allowed many people to live in my house, although I myself was rarely there. During the day I worked; in the evening I studied whatever Torah I could; and at night I worked as a private nurse for patients.

I cautioned my guests to behave in a way that suited the atmosphere of a building inhabited by observant Jews, but at times, they would behave inappropriately despite my exhortations. When the neighbors would complain, I would banish my ungrateful guests.

I had to pay a price for my undiscriminating open-door policy. One of the neighbors accused me personally of violating the building's code of conduct, and he registered a complaint with the *beis din* in an attempt to expel me from my home.

People in the know advised me to either seek different lodgings or retain the services of an expensive lawyer. "Otherwise," they warned me, "you are bound to lose the court case. You have no connections, and you will not manage to prove anything."

I did not have money to pay a lawyer, however. I had given all the money I had earned in the previous years to my daughter, to enable her to buy herself an apartment. (Over time, I had managed to re-build a relationship with my daughters, much to my satisfaction.) I had also used my money to help the *chassanim* who had been married from my house.

As usual, Leizer came to my rescue. He accompanied me to the *beis din* and proved that the accusations were baseless. Thanks to his testimony, the *beis din* postponed its final verdict in my case for a number of weeks.

Even so, however, it was clear that I would not manage to win the case without the help of a professional lawyer. At the end, I found a very competent lawyer — but that is a story in itself.

Six years before the court case, I was waiting for a bus in the Jerusalem Central Bus Station, and an elderly man approached me and began staring at me. *He's either crazy or very rude,* I thought to myself. Not wanting to have anything to do with him, I moved over to the side. But he followed me and continued staring. Finally, I had enough, and I decided to confront him.

"What do you want from me?" I asked him.

"Doctor Gutman?" he queried, clearly overjoyed to hear my voice.

"Yes," I replied. How did this man know me?

"Semyon Moysevich?"

"Indeed."

"Igor, come here!" he shouted joyfully, motioning with his hands to a young man in the crowd.

The young man approached us. "Igor, look," the old man said excitedly. "This is the doctor who saved your life when you were born!" The old man was very excited, and he kept trying to hug me.

"Who are you?" I asked, trying to free myself from his embrace.

"Do you remember that 30 years ago I came to Zhitomir from Minsk with my week-old baby?"

Now I remembered him and his son. It was a typical story: They had flown to Leningrad, and they had been referred to me from there. Not wanting to travel to a far-flung city like Zhitomir, they had opted to travel to Moscow instead. From there, they were once again referred to me. When they finally arrived in Zhitomir, the hourglass was almost empty, but the operation had succeeded. After the baby recovered somewhat, the family had moved to Israel. That was in 1971 (5731).

I asked Igor, who was a stocky young man, all sorts of questions about his health. He told me that he was perfectly healthy, and had suffered no complications due to his medical crisis in infancy. He was already a father of two, working as a lawyer in Jerusalem.

"If you ever need anything, you can always turn to Igor," the father promised. "He'll help you free of charge — after all, he owes you his life!"

"I'm sure you expressed your appreciation to me for the surgery at the time," I objected.

"No," the father replied, "I could not. I was warned against bringing you money; they told me that you would refuse it and chase me out. They advised me to approach your wife and give the money to her instead, but at that time she had just then traveled away on vacation. I came to your house to give the money to you, but when I saw a police officer standing near the entrance to the building I became frightened and left. So I still owe you!"

We exchanged telephone numbers, and parted ways. Some time later, the father and son came to pick me up and bring them to their house, where I visited them and became acquainted with their whole family.

Six years passed.

Two weeks before my day in *beis din*, on Yom Haatzmaut, a national holiday and a day off from work, I got a call from Igor's father inviting me to his house. I was very dispirited at that moment. For many nights I had been unable to sleep, distraught over the false accusations leveled against me and frightened that I would be left without a home. I explained to the old man that I was in no mood to visit, and I told him about my upcoming court case.

"Why didn't you tell us about this earlier?" he exclaimed. "I'm coming to see you right away with my son."

Half an hour later, the two were at my door.

I showed the young lawyer all the paperwork. He sat himself in a corner, leafing through all the papers and scrutinizing the information. Then, he invited me to come the next day to the legal office where he worked.

I was amazed at the way events had unfolded. After six years, they had suddenly remembered me and called me just at the moment when I needed their help!

I arrived at the lawyer's office the next day. Igor seemed befuddled — apparently, his employer had not authorized him to represent me pro bono. I told him that I would pay him happily, since I trusted him and did not want to turn to any other lawyers, who would undoubtedly be much more expensive, in any case.

I borrowed money from Leizer, and paid the 5,000 shekels that Igor's boss requested.

Igor represented me faithfully, and the *beis din* ruled that there was insufficient evidence to support the accusations. The file was closed, and the apartment remained mine. I thanked the young lawyer wholeheartedly and shook his hand as we parted.

That was in the afternoon. In the evening, when I returned home from work, I noticed an envelope in my suit pocket containing all the money I had paid the lawyer. It was accompanied by a note stating, "Thank you for my life!"

The following day I ran to Igor's office, accompanied by Leizer. When we arrived, Igor adamantly refused to accept the money he had returned to me.

At this point, Igor's boss, the owner of the firm, entered and said, "Igor told me the whole story, and I'm the one who instructed him to return your money. If you had saved my life, I would have bought you an entire house!"

This man looked older than he actually was, and it turned out that he suffered from a rare, incurable disease affecting the muscles of his abdomen. He asked me to examine him, and I did so on the spot. I gave him some advice for easing his condition, but I could not help him in any significant way. I tried again to convince him to accept my payment, but he refused.

At some point during this argument, Leizer became fed up, and he interceded. "You," he said to me, "where did you get the money to pay the lawer? You borrowed it from me. The money is mine, and I'm taking it."

An Unintended Consequence

The nursing home where I worked provided me with more than just *parnassah*; it gave me fulfillment and satisfaction as well. I was able to put my medical knowledge to some use there, and that was deeply meaningful to me.

When I saw patients who were suffering unnecessarily, I would try to intervene and alleviate their pain. I could not care indifferently for my elderly patients, simply feeding them, changing their diapers, and giving them their medication. Instead, I worked on rehabilitating my patients and helping them to live out their remaining time on this world in the most pleasant way possible.

The department I worked in admitted a patient in his nineties who was confined to a wheelchair and in need of oxygen round the clock. He was a wealthy man, the owner of a prosperous business. His children had arranged a private room for him, and in addition to the standard services provided by the nursing home, the family hired me to watch him at night to ensure that their dying father would not be left alone. Had they only known what would happen as a result ....

Observing this old man, I sensed that he possessed far more vitality than his family surmised. Any person, even a healthy person, who remains motionless for an extended period will become weak and forget how to move. He was also large and heavy, which made mobility even more of a challenge. How could I help him to awaken his weakened body?

The old man indicated that he wished to relieve himself, and I decided to take a chance. I wheeled him to the door of the bathroom and suggested that he stand up and enter alone.

"By myself?" he asked in horror. He had not been allowed to walk or stand for so long that he was afraid even to try. But he needed to use the bathroom. With my help, he managed to rise to his feet and stand. He took one step, and then another — he was walking! I took away his wheelchair, and told him in Yiddish (the language I used with my elderly patients), "Let's start to learn to walk! I will yet walk with you to the *brissin* and bar mitzvahs of your great-grandchildren."

His eyes lit up, and I saw that my words had hit their target. This old man had been dismissed as an invalid far too soon.

With time, I earned his trust, and he took me into his confidence.

He was born at the turn of the twentieth century in the city of Zhitomir (what a coincidence!), and he still remembered the city's horse-drawn train — a long-forgotten mode of transport. He had come to Israel prior to the founding of the State.

His mind was lucid, and his memory was excellent, probably owing a great deal to the fact that all his life he had studied Torah whenever he wasn't working. On Shabbos, he refused to take any medication. To avoid incurring the doctors' wrath, he would hide the pills where they could not see them. "Shabbos itself is the best healer," he would say.

As I worked on helping the old man to regain his mobility, I also began to work on weaning him off oxygen and enabling him to breathe on his own. At first he objected to this, but I came up with a strategy to enlist his cooperation in my rehabilitation plan for him. He was always fretting that he could not go down to his office and check what was happening there. "Do you want to go to the office?" I offered.

"How can I?" he lamented. "I'm in a wheelchair, and there are stairs there."

"We'll learn to go up and down steps," I informed him.

Despite his advanced age, this man was still the primary decision-maker in his business, and his children would bring him business reports to review every week. He would arrange the invoices on his bed, remembering every tiny detail, and he would scold them for one thing or another. It was amusing to watch how the old man's sons and sons-in-law — who were no youngsters themselves — hung their heads guiltily and attempted to defend themselves like little children.

Now, I managed to reawaken his desire to go down to his office and put things in order. His spirits lifted, and he stopped resisting my attempts to rehabilitate him. Each day, we exercised determinedly: At first, we went up three stairs, and then a full flight of stairs. After a while, his condition improved to the extent that he was able to manage without any help, and he no longer required my supervision at night.

Finally, the long-awaited day arrived: The "dying" man appeared in person at his office, to the shock of his employees. Panic ensued. The old man demanded to see paperwork, and he checked the books and sent everyone scurrying to do his bidding. This was his victory. Once again, he felt that he was capable of managing his business, which yielded a respectable living for his many descendants.

I was very happy for him, for only he and I knew how much effort he had invested in order to reach this milestone.

The next day, the old man's children came to the director of the nursing home to complain: Why had I brought the old man to the office? I was taken to task and given to understand that it was not a good idea for me to exert myself too much to rehabilitate the old man.

I was duly chastised, but inside my heart swelled with joy. I was happy that a man whose family had considered him over and done with could live out the rest of his time on this world with the best quality of life possible.

As I had predicted, I traveled with him to several *brissin* and bar mitzvahs of his great-grandchildren and great-great-grandchildren.

Typically, a person who was admitted to the nursing home remained there until his dying day. Like many patients, Rabbi B. was admitted in a wheelchair, and I stayed with him at night. I began to perform exercises with him, and these exercises were so successful that after a short while he returned home from the nursing home on his own two feet, leaning on only a cane.

Unfortunately, however, happy occasions like that were rare.

Bubbe Mayses

I did not have an easy time communicating with all of my elderly patients. What saved me on many occasions were the *bubbe mayses* I recounted. I told my patients stories about my mother and grandmother, and this relaxed them and lifted their spirits. They were curious why I did not talk about my father, however.

"Papa would leave the house in the morning, when I was still sleeping, and return at night when I was already asleep," I explained. "I, too, am pained by the fact that I don't know much about my father."

There was one distinguished elderly gentleman whom I escorted each morning to the first minyan, where we *davened* together. When he would eat breakfast, bits of food would fall onto his clothing, for he refused to wear an apron and he became angry any time the idea was suggested. He thought that wearing an apron was degrading.

"You are behaving like Hershele Ostropolier," I told him. Then I told him the story of Hershele, who arrived at a wedding in rags and was seated in a far corner of the hall. At the wedding celebration the next day, he arrived in expensive clothing, and was seated right next to the groom. When the food was served, Hershele began throwing it onto his clothing.

"What are you doing?" the people shouted at him.

"I am feeding my coat," he replied. "After all, it wasn't me you invited — it was my coat! So I'm giving my coat to eat!"

The old man burst out laughing, and from then he agreed to wear an apron.

Pirkei Avos

When I began working in the nursing home, I was broken and lonely, with no relatives and no friends. In the past, I had had everything — and it had all disappeared in a flash. After losing everything, I had no interest in continuing to live.

To my surprise, the people I treated in the nursing home were in a far worse physical state than I was, but their helpless condition did not seem to bother them. They had a value system and they had *middos*, which gave them resources of strength that were out of proportion to their frail bodies. It was as though they had a secret that gave meaning to every moment of their lives. When I saw people in their nineties sitting and learning Torah until their last breath, I was embarrassed at my own weakness.

One of my patients was a 99-year-old artist. He was childless, and had no surviving family members. He could barely hold a pencil in his hand, yet his drawings were joyous and full of light. To this day, they hang on the walls of the nursing home, adding a delightful dimension to the atmosphere. The last picture he drew before he passed away was of *chassidim* dancing.

Among my patients were famous *rabbanim, dayanim,* and *roshei yeshivah.* These people had hundreds of students, who clamored to see them all day. But at night, when sleep eluded them, I was their only companion. Their sole objective in life was to learn and to teach, and each one of them studied his particular area of Torah with me. I listened, and even though I did not always understand, I was happy to be in their company.

Dayan N., aged 98, was confined to bed due his illness. He usually reacted swiftly to anything that happened around him, and intervened if he thought someone had been slighted. Once, however, he whispered to me weakly, "I am tired, I don't have strength to live anymore."

"You still have another 21 years and eight months to live — until 120!" I responded, trying to distract him from the depressing thoughts that were going through his mind.

He lifted himself up, and said with a smile, "Living many years is still not living a long life, you know."

"How is that?" I asked.

"Every day of a person's life, he is either climbing to a lofty goal or, *chas v'shalom*, falling short of that goal. The days when he acts improperly are subtracted from the sum total of his days, and his soul will be punished for this misused time if he does not do *teshuvah*. It can happen, therefore, that a person lives many years in this world, and yet his lifetime is still short."

For a few months, I spent the night shift beside the bed of Rabbi A., a famous rav and rosh yeshivah who had written many *sefarim*. During this time, I was his nightly conversation partner.

One sleepless night, the rav told me, "This world is the place in which our souls are rectified. Our main task is to learn to give and not to take, and in that way to cleave to the *middos* of Hashem. The entire Torah revolves around this concept alone! A person should always ask himself: 'What does Hashem want from me now?'"

One Friday afternoon, I was sitting near the bed of this rav as Shabbos was approaching. His daughter was supposed to take my place, but she was delayed.

"Go home," the rav urged me. "Don't worry, I'll wait for her by myself. Otherwise, you'll be late for Shabbos."

I did not listen to him, however, and I waited instead until his daughter arrived. The moment I left his room, the rav closed his eyes and his soul departed.

I developed strong ties to each of these wonderful people I cared for, and I took their inevitable deaths as a personal loss. This time, I could not forgive myself. "Why do they always pass away when it's not my shift?" I tortured myself. "Why did I leave the room? Maybe I would have managed to hold onto him for another day?"

"Why are you so distraught?" the young doctor on duty asked in an exasperated tone when he heard my self-flagellations. "You're not working in a kindergarten, you know."

I saw no use in trying to explain it to him; he would never have understood.

With each distinguished patient who passed on, I lost a cherished friend and teacher. I helped their frail bodies, and they helped my parched soul. In their presence, my heart softened and became refined. I always had the sense that I was not the one treating them — they were treating me, and they loved me. Each one of them, in his own unique way, made me understand that a person has to grow spiritually all the time and aspire to transcend the barriers of this world and change his self-centered nature. I marveled at the way these people continued to grow spiritually every minute, until their last moments in this world.

"The Torah tells of the ladder in Yaakov's dream," Rabbi A. once told me. "One end of that ladder leans on the earth, while the other end reaches the heavens. Each rung of the ladder represents the struggle to rise above our natural characteristics and draw nearer to the Source of our souls."

From their vantage point on the frontier between life and death, my patients had a special connection to Hashem. I had the feeling that they were trying to pull me to their level, so that through them I could grab onto this special connection as well.

In Lieu of an Epilogue

Aprominent Jew who heard my life story posed a question to me. "You were a celebrated surgeon with a dazzling reputation, and when you made *aliyah* you became nothing more than a nurse in an old age home. Do you not regret leaving everything behind and coming to Israel?"

My answer was wholehearted and unequivocal: "I have fulfilled what my father prayed for his whole life — *L'shanah habaah b'Yerushalayim*. I came home! I learn in kollel, and even though my Torah cannot compare to the Torah of those who have learned from a young age, the crumbs that I manage to gather give me life, and are more precious to me than gold."

This year, on Purim, I brought my seven-year-old granddaughter with me to shul to hear the reading of *Megillas Esther.* We are good friends, my granddaughter and I. She was born in Israel, but she speaks fluent Russian.

"Saba," she said to me reproachfully, "are you Jewish?"

"Yes, I'm Jewish," I replied.

"So why do you read *Megillas Esther* in Russian?" she wanted to know. "You should read it in Hebrew!"

"You are right, my dear," I told her. "I'll try to do that next year — as we say, *l'shanah habaah* …."

When I stand and pray at the Kosel, I do not ask for health or *parnassah.* I ask for only one thing, uttering the same words that my beloved Bubbe Faiga uttered when she lit the Shabbos candles: "*Guttenyu, Tattenyu meine tayere, fir meine kinder tzu Torah deine* [Hashem, my dear Father, lead my children to Your Torah]!"